Communications
in Computer and Information Science   1898

Rationale

The CCIS series is devoted to the publication of proceedings of computer science conferences. Its aim is to efficiently disseminate original research results in informatics in printed and electronic form. While the focus is on publication of peer-reviewed full papers presenting mature work, inclusion of reviewed short papers reporting on work in progress is welcome, too. Besides globally relevant meetings with internationally representative program committees guaranteeing a strict peer-reviewing and paper selection process, conferences run by societies or of high regional or national relevance are also considered for publication.

Topics

The topical scope of CCIS spans the entire spectrum of informatics ranging from foundational topics in the theory of computing to information and communications science and technology and a broad variety of interdisciplinary application fields.

Information for Volume Editors and Authors

Publication in CCIS is free of charge. No royalties are paid, however, we offer registered conference participants temporary free access to the online version of the conference proceedings on SpringerLink (http://link.springer.com) by means of an http referrer from the conference website and/or a number of complimentary printed copies, as specified in the official acceptance email of the event.

CCIS proceedings can be published in time for distribution at conferences or as post-proceedings, and delivered in the form of printed books and/or electronically as USBs and/or e-content licenses for accessing proceedings at SpringerLink. Furthermore, CCIS proceedings are included in the CCIS electronic book series hosted in the SpringerLink digital library at http://link.springer.com/bookseries/7899. Conferences publishing in CCIS are allowed to use Online Conference Service (OCS) for managing the whole proceedings lifecycle (from submission and reviewing to preparing for publication) free of charge.

Publication process

The language of publication is exclusively English. Authors publishing in CCIS have to sign the Springer CCIS copyright transfer form, however, they are free to use their material published in CCIS for substantially changed, more elaborate subsequent publications elsewhere. For the preparation of the camera-ready papers/files, authors have to strictly adhere to the Springer CCIS Authors' Instructions and are strongly encouraged to use the CCIS LaTeX style files or templates.

Abstracting/Indexing

CCIS is abstracted/indexed in DBLP, Google Scholar, EI-Compendex, Mathematical Reviews, SCImago, Scopus. CCIS volumes are also submitted for the inclusion in ISI Proceedings.

How to start

To start the evaluation of your proposal for inclusion in the CCIS series, please send an e-mail to ccis@springer.com.

Sven Casteleyn · Tommi Mikkonen ·
Alberto García Simón · In-Young Ko ·
Giuseppe Loseto
Editors

Current Trends in Web Engineering

ICWE 2023 International Workshops:
BECS, SWEET, WALS, Alicante, Spain, June 6–9, 2023
Revised Selected Papers

 Springer

Editors
Sven Casteleyn 🆔
Universidad Jaime I
Castellón de la Plana, Spain

Tommi Mikkonen 🆔
University of Jyväskylä
Jyväskylä, Finland

Alberto García Simón 🆔
Universitat Politècnica de València
Valencia, Spain

In-Young Ko 🆔
Korea Advanced Institute of Science
and Technology
Daejeon, Korea (Republic of)

Giuseppe Loseto 🆔
LUM "Giuseppe Degennaro" University
Casamassima, Italy

ISSN 1865-0929   ISSN 1865-0937 (electronic)
Communications in Computer and Information Science
ISBN 978-3-031-50384-9   ISBN 978-3-031-50385-6 (eBook)
https://doi.org/10.1007/978-3-031-50385-6

This Springer imprint is published by the registered company Springer Nature Switzerland AG
The registered company address is: Gewerbestrasse 11, 6330 Cham, Switzerland

Paper in this product is recyclable.

Preface

This volume collects the papers presented at the workshops co-located with the 23rd International Conference on Web Engineering (ICWE 2023), which was held from June 6th until June 9th, 2023 in Alicante, Spain. The conference brought together researchers and practitioners from both academia and industry, representing various disciplines, to address and discuss the emerging challenges in the engineering of Web applications and associated technologies. In addition, an important theme was assessing the impact of these technologies on society, media, and culture.

Similarly to previous years, the main conference program was complemented by a number of co-located workshops. The goal of these workshops was to act as a forum for participants to discuss novel and cutting-edge topics, both within the Web engineering community and at the crossroads with other communities. This year, we accepted three workshops, whose revised papers are included in this volume. As a part of the process, all articles underwent a rigorous single-blind peer review process, with at least 2 reviews per submitted article. A total of 23 papers were received, of which 10 were accepted as full papers and 2 as short papers. Accepted papers were presented during the workshops on June 6, 2023. In addition, after the workshop, the authors got the opportunity to update their paper and produce a final version, taking into account the comments received during the workshop. The three workshops were:

- Third International Workshop on Big Data Driven Edge Cloud Services (BECS2023), a venue to discuss ongoing work on providing value-added Web services for users by utilizing big data in edge cloud environments.
- Second International Workshop on the Semantic WEb of Everything (SWEET 2023), a forum where ongoing work in the field of Artificial Intelligence in the Web of Everything and pervasive computing scenarios is discussed.
- Second International Workshop on Web Applications for Life Sciences (WALS 2023), a venue that considers Web Engineering as a means for facing the challenges that emerge when designing and developing applications for life sciences, focused on several branches such as healthcare, precision medicine, molecular biology, genomics, and virology.

We wish to express our sincere gratitude to all those who contributed to the success of the ICWE 2023 Workshops. To begin with, we thank the workshop organizers for their excellent work in identifying and proposing cutting-edge, cross-disciplinary topics in the rapidly moving field of Web engineering, as well as organizing inspiring workshops around them. Secondly, we wish to thank all the reviewers who provided thorough and thoughtful evaluations of the papers, including suggestions for improvement, and contributed to the promotion of the workshops. Thirdly, we thank the conference organizers and hosts for their hospitality and support. Finally, we wish to thank all the authors who submitted and presented papers at the workshops for having shared their work with the community and for contributing to the success of these events, as well as the whole ICWE community for its dedication to Web Engineering-related research.

September 2023   Sven Casteleyn
                                                                                 Tommi Mikkonen

Organization

ICWE 2023 Workshop Co-chairs

Sven Casteleyn	Universidad Jaime I, Spain
Tommi Mikkonen	University of Jyväskylä, Finland

BECS 2023 Workshop Co-chairs

In-Young Ko	Korea Advanced Institute of Science and Technology, South Korea
Michael Mrissa	InnoRenew CoE & University of Primorska, Slovenia
Juan Manuel Murillo	University of Extremadura & COMPUTAEX Foundation, Spain
Abhishek Srivastava	Indian Institute of Technology Indore, India

SWEET 2023 Workshop Co-chairs

Giuseppe Loseto	LUM "Giuseppe Degennaro" University, Italy
Hasan Ali Khatthak	National University of Sciences and Technology, Islamabad, Pakistan
Agnese Pinto	Polytechnic University of Bari, Italy
Michele Ruta	Polytechnic University of Bari, Italy
Floriano Scioscia	Polytechnic University of Bari, Italy

WALS 2023 Workshop Co-chairs

Anna Bernasconi	Politecnico di Milano, Italy
Alberto García S.	Universitat Politècnica de València, Spain
Pietro Pinoli	Politecnico di Milano, Italy

Technical Program Committee

BECS 2023

Jongmoon Baik	Korea Advanced Institute of Science and Technology, South Korea
Hamza Baniata	University of Szeged, Hungary
Zhipeng Cai	Georgia State University, USA
Ben Njima Cheyma	MARS Lab, Tunisia
Eunkyoung Jee	Korea Advanced Institute of Science and Technology, South Korea
Minsu Jeon	Korea Advanced Institute of Science and Technology, South Korea
Minsoo Kim	Korea Advanced Institute of Science and Technology, South Korea
Taewoo Kim	Korea Advanced Institute of Science and Technology, South Korea
Faïza Loukil	Université Polytechnique Hauts-de-France, France
Simon Mayer	University of St.Gallen, Switzerland
Ayan Mondal	Indian Institute of Technology Indore, India
Martin Musicante	UFRN, Brazil
Munam Ali Shah	COMSATS University Islamabad, Pakistan
Placido Souza Neto	IFRN, Brazil
Victoria Torres	Polytechnic University of Valencia, Spain
Javier Troya	University of Málaga, Spain
Chan-Hyun Youn	Korea Advanced Institute of Science and Technology, South Korea
Seongwook Youn	Korea National University of Transportation, South Korea

SWEET 2023

Carmelo Ardito	LUM "Giuseppe Degennaro" University, Italy
Fernando Bobillo	University of Zaragoza, Spain
Eugenio Di Sciascio	Polytechnic University of Bari, Italy
Francesco M. Donini	University of Tuscia, Italy
Giancarlo Fortino	University of Calabria, Italy
Alessandro Massaro	LUM "Giuseppe Degennaro" University & LUM Enterprise, Italy

Andrea Omicini   University of Bologna Alma Mater Studiorum,
                          Italy
Evan Patton   Massachusetts Institute of Technology, USA
Luigi Ranieri   LUM "Giuseppe Degennaro" University, Italy
William Van Woensel   University of Ottawa, Canada

WALS 2023

Giuseppe Agapito   Università Magna Graecia Catanzaro, Italy
José Alberto Benítez-Andrades   University of León, Spain
Stefano Ceri   Polytechnic University of Milan, Italy
Pietro Cinaglia   University Magna Graecia of Catanzaro, Italy
Tommaso Dolci   Politecnico di Milano, Italy
Jose Luis Garrido   University of Granada, Spain
Giancarlo Guizzardi   University of Twente, The Netherlands
Ana León Palacio   Universitat Politècnica de València, Spain
Sergio Lifschitz   Pontifical Catholic University of Rio de Janeiro,
                                    Brazil
Giovanni Meroni   Technical University of Denmark, Denmark
Ignacio Panach   University of Valencia, Spain
Oscar Pastor   Universitat Politècnica de València, Spain
Rosario Michael Piro   Polytechnic University of Milan, Italy
José Fabián Reyes Román   Universitat Politècnica de València, Spain

Contents

Third International Workshop on Big Data Driven Edge Cloud Services (BECS 2023)

3rd International Workshop on Big Data driven Edge Cloud Services (BECS 2023) – Preface

In-Young Ko[1] , Michael Mrissa[2] , Juan Manuel Murillo[3] ,
and Abhishek Srivastava[4]

[1] School of Computing, Korea Advanced Institute of Science and Technology,
Korea
iko@kaist.ac.kr
[2] InnoRenew CoE, and Faculty of Mathematics, Natural Sciences and
Information Technologies, University of Primorska, Slovenia
michael.mrissa@innorenew.eu
[3] COMPUTAEX Foundation, and Advanced Software Engineering Techniques,
University of Extremadura, Spain
juanmamu@unex.es
[4] Department of Computer Science and Engineering, Indian Institute of
Technology Indore, India
asrivastava@iiti.ac.in

Abstract. To harness the full potential of edge-cloud environments, it becomes imperative to establish novel paradigms and methodologies within the realm of web engineering. These advances aim to enhance the efficiency and dependability of data-driven, edge-cloud AI applications. The third edition of the international workshop on Big data-driven Edge Cloud Services (BECS 2023) served as a platform for scholars and practitioners to exchange insights and showcase their ongoing efforts in delivering efficient and scalable web services. These services cater to users' needs by leveraging extensive datasets in edge cloud environments.

Keywords: Edge cloud, Big data, Machine learning, AI applications.

1 Introduction

Due to the rapid proliferation of Web of Things (WoT) devices connecting to the cloud, we have witnessed an increase in latency and a reduction in the efficiency of gathering extensive data from these devices and delivering services through data analysis. To address this challenge, edge clouds have emerged as a novel computing infrastructure aimed at enhancing efficiency, scalability, and data privacy in delivering data-centric services.

An edge cloud comprises multiple tiers, including edges, fogs, and clouds, which facilitates the collection and processing of large-scale data in a localized fashion. This is made possible through the use of low-latency and dependable communication technologies such as 5G and beyond. To fully capitalize on the advantages offered by these edge-cloud environments, it is imperative to dynamically deploy and provide required services while ensuring optimal utilization of distributed computing resources across the edge-cloud layers.

The third edition of the international workshop on Big data-driven Edge Cloud Services (BECS 2023) was organized to serve as a platform for scholars and practitioners to exchange insights and showcase their ongoing research on providing data-driven WoT services in edge cloud environments. The workshop was held in conjunction with the 23rd International Conference on Web Engineering (ICWE 2023), which was held in Alicante, Spain on June 6-9, 2023.

The topic area of the third BECS workshop includes the following: Web services in edge clouds; Web of Things in edge clouds; AI in edge computing (Edge AI); dependable and highly usable big data platforms; distributed data collection, analysis, and prediction; stream data processing in edge clouds; big knowledge graphs for distributed edge cloud environments; modeling and mashup of edge cloud services; micro-service architecture for edge cloud environments; and edge-cloud interaction and collaboration.

2   Keynote

During the BECS 2023 workshop, there was a keynote talk titled "Service governance on the edge, challenges ahead," delivered by Prof. Pablo Fernández from the University of Sevilla, Spain.

In his enlightening keynote, Prof. Fernández emphasized the significance of edge clouds as a pivotal environment capable of consolidating multiple domains. He underscored that the primary advantage of edge clouds lies in their capacity to foster a new generation of service chains, which can thrive and adapt in a continuous environment offering distinctive integration and customization prospects. Additionally, he delved into the challenges that emerge as service chains become more intricate, including issues related to elasticity, privacy, and capacity management. Prof. Fernández examined critical facets that must be tackled to harness these opportunities and effectively govern the development and operation of services within edge clouds.

3   Paper Presentations

At the BECS 2023 workshop, five full papers and two short papers were selected for presentation.

The first full paper, titled "A Novel Priority-based Scheduler for Asymmetric Multi-core Edge Computing" authored by Rupendra Hada, Abhishek Srivastava, addresses the scheduling challenge within the Linux operating system. The paper introduces a novel approach designed to function efficiently in both symmetric and asymmetric multi-core edge systems. The authors demonstrate that this proposed method can enhance task processing speeds by up to 16% for high-priority tasks.

In the second full paper presented at the workshop, authors Taewoo Kim, Minsu Jeon, Changha Lee, SeongHwan Kim, Fawaz Al-Hazemi, and Chan-Hyun Youn introduce an approach titled "SLO-aware DL Job Scheduling for Efficient FPGA-GPU

Edge Cloud Computing." This approach considers the diverse service-level objectives associated with deep learning tasks and periodically adjusts the accelerator configuration for deep learning processing while minimizing computational costs. They conducted experiments using a heterogeneous field-programmable gate array (FPGA)-GPU cluster to assess the performance of their proposed scheduler.

In the third full paper, titled "DESA: Decentralized Self-Adaptive Horizontal Autoscaling for Bursts of Load in Fog Computing," the authors, EunChan Park, Kyeong-Deok Baek, Eunho Cho, and In-Young Ko, address a crucial challenge in microservices orchestration: ensuring service elasticity when faced with unpredictable load bursts. They propose DESA, in which each microservice instance autonomously makes scaling decisions by either cloning or terminating itself through continuous self-monitoring. Experimental results demonstrate that DESA significantly reduces scaling reaction times in large-scale fog computing systems compared to the centralized approach.

In the fourth full paper, titled "TiME: Time-sensitive Multihop Data Transmission in Software-Defined Edge Networks for IoT," authored by Simran Gurung and Ayan Mondal, a software-defined edge architecture is proposed. Additionally, a game theoretic model is designed to optimize multi-hop data transmission. The authors employ a dynamic coalition game to determine the most efficient data transmission paths within edge networks for IoT. Furthermore, they evaluate and compare the performance of this proposed scheme with existing literature.

The fifth full paper presented at the workshop, authored by Changha Lee, Kyungchae Lee, Gyusang Cho, and Chan-Hyun Youn, introduces "DELCAS: Deep Reinforcement Learning based GPU CaaS Packet Scheduling for Enhancing QoE in 5G Multi-Access Edge Computing." DELCAS addresses a resource scheduling challenge arising from resource limitations that prevent offloading all users' packets to the edge server. To tackle this issue, the authors propose a deep reinforcement learning-based approach for GPU container as a service (CaaS) packet scheduling, aiming to enhance the quality of the AI experience.

Following the full paper presentations, two short papers were presented at the workshop. In the first short paper titled "Towards Integrating Digital Avatars in Urban Digital Twins on the Cloud-to-Thing Continuum," authors Lorenzo Toro-Gálvez, Rafael García-Luque, Javier Troya, Carlos Canal, and Ernesto Pimentel propose the integration of citizens through their digital avatars (DAs) into urban digital twins (UDTs). DAs allow for the exploitation of citizens' information, behavioral habits, and personal preferences while giving them full control over their data. The authors present an envisioned architecture that leverages the cloud-to-thing continuum to optimize available processing resources.

In the second short paper, titled "Exploring the Feasibility of ChatGPT for Enhancing the Quality of Ansible Scripts in Edge-Cloud Infrastructures through Code Recommendations," authors Sunjae Kwon, Sungu Lee, Taehyoun Kim, Duksan Ryu, and Jongmoon Baik investigate the feasibility of utilizing ChatGPT to improve the quality of Ansible scripts used for infrastructure as code (IaC). Through an evaluation of ChatGPT's code recommendation capability on various code revision cases from different Ansible project repositories, the authors confirm that ChatGPT can reasonably recognize and understand Ansible scripts. They also discuss the importance of effective prompt engineering to achieve consistent code recommendation results.

4 Poster Presentations

Three posters were selected for showcasing at the BCD 2023 workshop. Here are the titles and authors of these posters:

- "An Analysis about Federated Learning in Low-Powerful Devices" presented by Daniel Flores-Martin, Francisco Díaz-Barrancas, Javier Berrocal, and Juan Manuel Murillo Rodríguez
- "IoT-NGIN ML as a Service (MLaaS), MLOPs for IoT" presented by Jorge Mira, Iván Moreno, Hervé Bardisbanian, and Jesús Gorroñogoitia
- "An Adaptive Spatial-Temporal GPU Scheduling in Edge Cloud Computing Environment" presented by Taewoo Kim, Tuan Manh Tao, Khac Tuyen Dinh, Minsu Jeon, Changha Lee, and Chan-Hyun Youn.

Acknowledgment. We extend our gratitude to all the program committee members and reviewers for their dedicated efforts in delivering high-quality reviews and valuable feedback. The BECS 2023 workshop was supported by the Ministry of Science and ICT (MSIT), Korea, under the Information Technology Research Center (ITRC) support program (IITP-2023-2020-0-01795) supervised by the Institute of Information & Communications Technology Planning Evaluation (IITP). We would like to thank their support. Last but certainly not least, we extend our thanks to the authors who submitted and presented their research work at the workshop, as well as to all the participants whose contributions played a pivotal role in the workshop's success.

A Novel Priority Based Scheduler for Asymmetric Multi-core Edge Computing

Rupendra Pratap Singh Hada$^{(\boxtimes)}$ (ID) and Abhishek Srivastava (ID)

Indin Institute of Technology Indore, Indore 452020, India
{phd2101101004,asrivastava}@iiti.ac.in

Abstract. Asymmetric multi-core processors require careful assignment
of tasks to the appropriate cores. Most of the edge computing devices are
operated on Linux. However, the current Linux scheduler assigns tasks to
cores without considering their capabilities. This can lead to high-priority
tasks being assigned to energy-efficient cores while low-priority tasks are
assigned to high-performance cores. This results in a decrease in the overall system performance. A new algorithm has been proposed to address
this issue that considers the core's capabilities and the task's priority.
This algorithm requires prior knowledge of the core's speed due to the
asymmetric nature of the cores. The priorities of the tasks are fetched,
and then tasks are divided into high, medium, and low classes. High-
priority tasks are scheduled on high-performance cores, while medium
and low-priority tasks are scheduled on energy-efficient cores. The proposed algorithm performs better than the existing Linux task scheduling
algorithm for high-priority tasks, improving task scheduling time by up
to 16%.

Keywords: Asymmetric Multi-core Processors · Completely Fair
Scheduler · Edge Computing · Scheduling

1 Introduction

As the number of applications generated daily increases in the personal computer
era, end-users demand faster and more capable systems to run them. There are
two types of computer architecture: single-core and multi-core. In single-core
architecture, the speedup is achieved by increasing the clock speed, which is limited due to heat. In contrast, multi-core architecture adds multiple processing
cores to a single chip, allowing for the execution of multiple instructions at a
time, thus increasing the program's execution speed [2]. However, adding multiple cores to a single-chip processor presents challenges related to memory, cache
coherence, power consumption, and load imbalance among cores [3]. Due to its
high performance and energy efficiency, asymmetric multi-core architecture has
become increasingly popular in computing devices, such as personal computers, cell phones, and General Purpose computing on Graphics Processing Units
(GPGPU) [5].

S. Casteleyn et al. (Eds.): ICWE 2023 Workshops, CCIS 1898, pp. 7–18, 2024.
https://doi.org/10.1007/978-3-031-50385-6_1

To meet the user's requirements, computing devices need to operate efficiently. Among the challenges posed by multi-core architecture, the assignment of tasks to the appropriate core is also a significant challenge because the assignment of tasks or task scheduling is an NP problem [6]. The present Linux (Completely fair scheduler) scheduler is designed with a symmetric multi-core processor keeping in mind that the tasks are scheduled without knowing the capability of the core, which degrades the overall performance of the Asymmetric multi-core systems.

The proposed method can work effectively with both symmetric and asymmetric multi-core systems. Initially, the method extracts the capability of the core to determine whether it is high-performance or energy-efficient. Subsequently, the method determines the priority of the tasks and divides them into three classes or batches based on priority. Finally, the method schedules the tasks according to their priorities, with high-priority tasks assigned to high-performance cores and medium and low-priority tasks assigned to energy-efficient cores. The proposed method has shown an improvement in speed of up to 16% for high-priority tasks.

The remainder of the paper is organised as follows: Sect. 2 discusses existing techniques for priority based scheduling in Linux and Windows; Sect. 3 includes the details of the proposed approach; Sect. 4 includes experimental results that help validate the efficacy of the proposed approach; and finally, Sect. 5 concludes the paper with pointers to future work.

2   Previous Works

A considerable amount of literature is available on scheduling techniques for the Linux scheduler, all of which aim to improve its scheduling ability. This section will cover some of these efforts.

In **Task Snatching Technique** the high-performance core snatches the tasks from energy-efficient cores; some times high-performance core may snatch a task with less execution time from an energy-efficient core while another slow core has a task with more execution time and results in poor execution time [1]. **CAMP:** In CAMP scheduling, two tasks, utility factor and scheduling algorithm, are performed. A metric utility factor produces a single value as CAMP to evaluate the application's work. The rhythmic design helps the scheduler choose the best threads to run on fast cores. The scheduler must recognise the most eligible contenders to run on fast cores [19]. Calculations of the applications are done after utility factors are computed. Depending on the individual utility factors, CAMP recognises the threads that could be placed on different types of cores [26]. As we discussed above, CAMP is a thread-level scheduler because tasks in the same task-based programs can often achieve similar speedup ratios on fast cores; it does not facilitate the performance of a single parallel program. Therefore, CAMP did not consider the scheduling problem in parallel applications [14].

Bias Scheduling: This scheduling dynamically monitors the thread bias to match them with the suitable cores, eventually amplifying the system throughput. Each application gives a bias that supplements its resource needs appropriately in this work [15]. Though bias scheduling can be easily implemented and requires fewer changes in actual code, the problem with this approach is that it requires a bias scheduling matrix. If the information of any task is absent in this matrix, it performs similarly to regular scheduling, resulting in degradation of performance [7].

The task scheduling techniques like task snatching [1] snatch tasks from the slow-core with less remaining execution time and increases the overall execution time of the system. CAMP [12] works based on individual utility factor tasks, and then the task is scheduled according to utility factor, but it only works with threads. Therefore, in the proposed work, the task scheduling problem is addressed via CPU affinity (in which any task can be scheduled explicitly on a particular core). The proposed task scheduling algorithm determines the priority of individual tasks and schedules the task based on priority on an appropriate core as per its capability [11].

The [4, 10, 16, 20], and [17] also shows some great work in the field of Linux scheduling, but they doesn't consider the priority of the tasks for scheduling.

2.1 Windows Scheduler

In Windows, scheduling is performed by threads, and it is determined by their priority level, which ranges from 0 to 31. The allocation of time slices to the threads follows a round-robin approach. Initially, the threads with the highest priority are assigned time slices, followed by lower priority threads, based on their runtime. To ensure a responsive experience, the priority of low preference threads is dynamically adjusted. However, Windows differs from other SMP (Symmetric Multi-Processor) systems in that it also takes into account the thread's affinity for the processor. Nonetheless, the scheduling mechanism remains the same for other SMP systems. In an ideal scenario, the processor with the highest cache availability for a particular thread is considered the optimal processor [13].

2.2 Solaris Scheduler

The processes in this context are classified as either kernel or user mode threads, depending on the environment they operate in. Whenever a user thread is created, a lightweight process is also initiated, establishing a connection between the user thread and the kernel thread. Solaris 10 has introduced several scheduling classes, which can coexist on a single system. These scheduling classes offer different approaches to scheduling, accommodating various types of applications. An adaptive model has been proposed by these scheduling classes to cater to the specific needs of different applications [18].

2.3 Linux Scheduler

Prior to version 2.6.23, the Linux scheduler utilized priority arrays and per-CPU run-queues, resulting in a complex scheduling mechanism. To address the drawbacks of the old scheduler, a Complexity Fair Scheduler (CFS) was introduced. The CFS accurately determines whether applications are CPU-intensive or interactive, eliminating the differentiation between processes. To align tasks according to their specific requirements, a red-black tree data structure was implemented. This data structure is capable of accommodating all types of processes. However, the adoption of the red-black tree has increased the overall scheduling complexity.

Consequently, the new scheduler completely disregards the concept of different process types and treats all processes equally. The red-black tree data structure is employed to organize tasks based on their entitlement to utilize processor resources within a predefined interval until a context-switch occurs. The process positioned at the leftmost node of the tree has the highest priority in accessing processor resources during its corresponding position in the tree. The position of a process in the tree is solely determined by its wait-time in the run-queue (including the time it spends waiting for events) and its priority. This concept is relatively straightforward but effectively handles all types of processes, particularly interactive ones, as they receive a boost by accounting for their I/O-waiting time [25].

3 Proposed Work

The remainder of the section is organised as follows: Sect. 3.1 discusses the problem of scheduling in Linux operating system; Sect. 3.2 includes the system architecture; and Sect. 3.3 represents the proposed solution.

3.1 Detailed Problem Statement

We have an Asymmetric Multi-core Processor (AMP) having one fast core and three slow cores C_0, C_1, C_2, C_3, respectively. We have four tasks T_0, T_1, T_2, T_3 with priority low, medium, high and low, respectively, to schedule on these cores. Suppose tasks T_0, T_1, T_2, T_3 takes S_0, S_1, S_2, S_3 times on slow cores and F_0, F_1, F_2, F_3 times on fast core respectively. We can reasonably deduce that $F_0 < S_0$, $F_1 < S_1$, $F_2 < S_3$, $F_3 < S_3$ [8]. Figure 1 visualizes the overall scheduling in AMP.

If the tasks are allocated according to optimal priority scheduling means allocating the tasks such as high-performance core get high priority tasks, then overall completion time T_{opt} (make-span) can be expressed as,

$$T_{opt} = \mathbf{max}(F_0, S_1, S_2, S_3) = F_0$$

Because $F_0 < S_0$, we can say that $T_{opt} < S_0$.

In another traditional allocation technique, task T_0 is scheduled on slow core C_3, and task T_3 is scheduled on fast core C_0. The make-span for traditional allocation time T_{opt} can be expressed as,

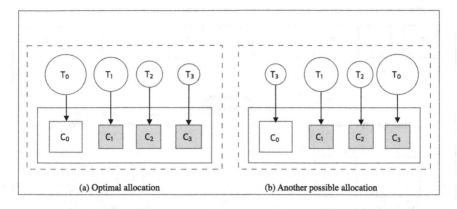

(a) Optimal allocation   (b) Another possible allocation

Fig. 1. Scheduling In AMP.

$$T_{trad} = \mathbf{max}(S_0, F_1, S_2, S_3) \geq S_0 > F_0.$$

Obviously, allocating a high-priority task to a slowcore would often degrade the overall performance of high-priority tasks. Allocation of the process to a particular core in such a way that the tasks having high priority will schedule on cores with high performance and tasks having medium and low priority will schedule on low-performance cores [15]. Allocation of a task in an optimal way is the NP-hard problem, and due to changes in run time behaviour, we can't allocate the task to the appropriate core, but we can schedule them in a near-optimal way [9].

3.2 System Architecture of Task Scheduling

The priority-based task scheduling in AMP, in which we have multiple tasks (T_1, T_2, ..., T_{n-1}, T_n) in the ready queue and having n cores (C_0 to C_n), such that C_0 to C_k are high-performance cores and C_{k+1} to C_n are energy-efficient cores. We have to map functions in such a way that the task having high priority will be scheduled on high-performance cores and tasks having medium and low priority will be scheduled on low-performance cores. The map function works in such a manner that it generates three priority classes low, medium and high. It maps tasks in these three priority classes and, according to their priority, the task is allocated to that core.

Figure 2 shows the task scheduling process in AMP, in which we have tasks from T_1 to T_n and cores from C_0 to C_3, where cores C_0 and C_1 are high-performance cores and C_2 and C_3 are energy-efficient cores. The map function schedules the task on the basis of priority, such as the task with high priority will schedule on high-performance cores and the tasks with medium and low priority will schedule on energy-efficient cores.

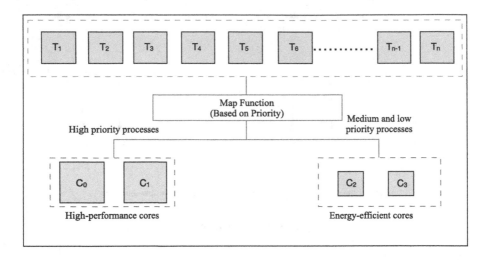

Fig. 2. Proposed task scheduling process.

3.3   Proposed Algorithm

3.3.1   CPU Rank Assignment
In Asymmetric Multi-core Architecture, at least two different cores are present. One core is performance-efficient (big cores), and another is energy-efficient (LITTLE cores). The big cores or performance-efficient cores are designed for efficient performance, and the LITTLE cores are designed for efficient energy [22].

3.3.2   Parallel Priority Class-Based Scheduling Algorithm
In Multi-core Architecture, OpenMP (Open Multi-Processing) is used to create task or thread-level parallelism in Operating Systems to run concurrently on different cores. With the help of this, the overall execution of the task becomes fast. In OpenMP, the task can run on the same or different cores. In this, tasks are scheduled on different cores according to their priority. Suppose we have four cores C_0, C_1, C_2, C_3 where $(C_0$ and $C_1) > (C_2$ and $C_3)$, so the task having high priority will schedule on core C_0 or C_1, medium and low on core C_2 or C_3. In the proposed work, CPU Affinity is used to bind the task with a particular core and the set of CPUs on which a thread can be eligible to run is determined by the thread's CPU affinity mask [24]. On a multi-core processor system, the performance benefits can be obtained with the help of CPU affinity mask. By dedicating one CPU to a particular thread (i.e. setting the affinity mask of that thread to specify a single CPU and setting the affinity mask of all other threads to exclude that CPU), [23] it is possible to ensure maximum execution speed for that thread. Restricting a thread to run on a single CPU also avoids the performance cost caused by the cache invalidation that occurs when a thread

ceases to execute on one CPU and then recommences execution on a different CPU.

Algorithm 1. Algorithm for Parallel Priority Class

Input: Different Tasks, CPU Ranks
Output: Execution Time of Task according to their Priority
Process:

1. Initiate all the cores according to CPU Ranks
   i.e. $(C_0, C_1) > (C_2, C_3)$ and so on.
2. Get the priority of the tasks.
3. Divide the tasks in to classes according to priority
   (in low, medium and high class).
4. Bind the tasks to particular core according to class
   (medium & low class tasks on energy-efficient cores and high class tasks on high-performance cores).
5. Calculate Execution Time of each high priority tasks.
6. Calculate Speedup of the task execution.

---

4 Evaluation

This section provides the performance evaluation of the proposed model. Therefore the computed performance parameters are reported in this section.

4.1 System Requirements

The experiments are performed on Dell G15, AMD Ryzen processor, with 6.8 GHz frequency, 8 cores and 20 MB cache size. The proposed method is deployed on Ubuntu, Linux kernel 4.20.

4.2 Implementation Requirement

These are the packages and source code required for the implementation of the proposed algorithm.

– **Packages Required:**
   • **libomp-dev:** LLVM OpenMP runtime - dev package The runtime is the part of the OpenMP implementation that manages the multiple threads in an OpenMP program while it is executing (Fig. 3).
   • **gcc-multilib:** allows the user to run and build 32-bit applications on 64-bit installations of Arch Linux.

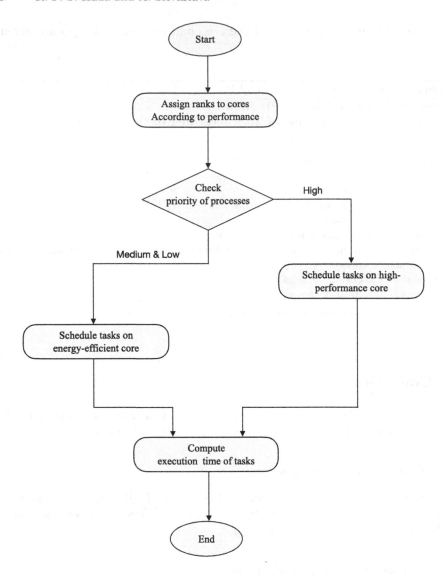

Fig. 3. Flow chart of proposed task scheduling process.

- **Source Code and Documentation Required:**
    - **Kernel-doc:** These are documentation files from the kernel source. Various portions of the Linux kernel and the device drivers shipped with it are documented in these files.

– **Compiler and Version Control Software Required:**
  - **GCC:** GNU Compiler Collection, GCC is a collection of programming compilers including C, C++, Objective-C, Fortran, Java, and Ada. GCC is used to compile the modified kernel.

4.3   Comparison

The experiments are performed on multiple tasks with a proper mixture of high, medium and low priorities. The tasks are first scheduled on a normal scheduler Completely Fair Scheduler (CFS), then the same tasks are scheduled with our proposed approach. The overall execution time of high prioritised tasks are calculated, that can be shown in Table 1.

Table 1. Comparison of proposed algorithm and linux scheduling algorithm.

Batch	Number of Tasks	Average Priority	Time in Linux	Time in Porposed
Batch_1	990	99	6.13975	5.54364
Batch_2	910	99	6.12872	5.52790
Batch_3	1000	79	6.12692	5.39783
Batch_4	870	81	6.12898	5.41726
Batch_5	980	91	6.28981	5.23411
Batch_6	880	85	6.23981	5.24321
Batch_7	780	93	9.76146	7.98019
Total			46.8155	40.3441

Figure 4, compares the execution time of high priority tasks (which are scheduled in form of different batches) of our class based algorithm (in red line) with existing Linux based task scheduling(in blue line). It shows that our proposed algorithm take less execution time as compared to existing Linux scheduling for high priority tasks.

4.4   Performance Measure

To measure the performance of our proposed algorithm, we have used *speedup*, which can be calculated as,

$$Speedup = \frac{\text{Total time in linux}}{\text{Total time in new algorithm}} = \frac{46.81545}{40.34414} = 1.1604 \tag{1}$$

The proposed algorithm shows the speedup of 1.1604 or up to 16 %.

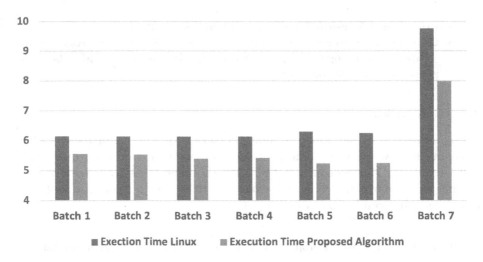

Fig. 4. Execution time - Linux vs Priority class based scheduling

5   Conclusion

In this work, the existing Linux scheduling technique modified with priority class-based scheduling. In AMP, the performance of cores are different (in terms of the execution time of tasks), and without knowing tasks priority, tasks are scheduled on any core. Parallel priority class-based scheduling is implemented using the OpenMP Technique and CPU affinity. Proposed algorithm is based on parallel mechanism, therefore tasks can be scheduled on different cores. It is very effective for high priority processes and results in reducing execution time. The proposed algorithm tested on a proper mix of high, medium and low priority processes. It shows up to 16 % improvement in the execution time of high priority tasks compared with the existing Linux scheduling algorithm. However, the performance of the proposed algorithm is reduced when more high priority tasks are scheduled.

The proposed parallel priority class-based scheduling strategy assigns high priority tasks to high-performance cores. In contrast, low and medium-class tasks to low-performance cores occasionally lead to low performance for medium and low priority class tasks. Future work in this direction may approach this issue. The proposed method can also be combined with load balancing to migrate low and medium-class tasks to the high-performance core in case it is idle to improve overall performance [21].

References

1. Bender, M.A., Rabin, M.O.: Scheduling cilk multithreaded parallel programs on processors of different speeds. In: Proceedings of the Twelfth Annual ACM Symposium on Parallel Algorithms and Architectures, pp. 13–21 (2000)

2. Bhadauria, M., McKee, S.A.: An approach to resource-aware co-scheduling for CMPS. In: Proceedings of the 24th ACM International Conference on Supercomputing, pp. 189–199 (2010)

3. Bienia, C., Kumar, S., Singh, J.P., Li, K.: The PARSEC benchmark suite: characterization and architectural implications. In: Proceedings of the 17th International Conference on Parallel Architectures and Compilation Techniques, pp. 72–81 (2008)

4. Bilbao, C., Saez, J.C., Prieto-Matias, M.: Rapid development of OS support with PMCSched for scheduling on asymmetric multicore systems. In: Singer, J., Elkhatib, Y., Blanco Heras, D., Diehl, P., Brown, N., Ilic, A. (eds.) Euro-Par 2022. LNCS, vol. 13835, pp. 184–196. Springer, Cham (2022). https://doi.org/10.1007/978-3-031-31209-0_14

5. Cao, K., Liu, Y., Meng, G., Sun, Q.: An overview on edge computing research. IEEE Access **8**, 85714–85728 (2020)

6. Chen, Q., Guo, M., Deng, Q., Zheng, L., Guo, S., Shen, Y.: HAT: history-based auto-tuning MapReduce in heterogeneous environments. J. Supercomput. **64**, 1038–1054 (2013)

7. Chronaki, K., et al.: Task scheduling techniques for asymmetric multi-core systems. IEEE Trans. Parallel Distrib. Syst. **28**(7), 2074–2087 (2016)

8. De Vuyst, M., Kumar, R., Tullsen, D.M.: Exploiting unbalanced thread scheduling for energy and performance on a CMP of SMT processors. In: Proceedings 20th IEEE International Parallel & Distributed Processing Symposium, pp. 10-p. IEEE (2006)

9. Fahringer, T.: Optimisation: operating system scheduling on multi-core architectures. In: seminar Parallel Computing (2008)

10. Goel, S., Mikek, B., Aly, J., Arun, V., Saeed, A., Akella, A.: Quantitative verification of scheduling heuristics. arXiv preprint arXiv:2301.04205 (2023)

11. Guo, Y., Barik, R., Raman, R., Sarkar, V.: Work-first and help-first scheduling policies for ASYNC-finish task parallelism. In: 2009 IEEE International Symposium on Parallel & Distributed Processing, pp. 1–12. IEEE (2009)

12. Hofmeyr, S., Iancu, C., Blagojević, F.: Load balancing on speed. ACM Sigplan Not. **45**(5), 147–158 (2010)

13. Janiak, A., Janiak, W.A., Krysiak, T., Kwiatkowski, T.: A survey on scheduling problems with due windows. Eur. J. Oper. Res. **242**(2), 347–357 (2015)

14. Keckler, S.W., Hofstee, H.P., Olukotun, K.: Multicore Processors and Systems. Springer, New York (2009). https://doi.org/10.1007/978-1-4419-0263-4

15. Koufaty, D., Reddy, D., Hahn, S.: Bias scheduling in heterogeneous multi-core architectures. In: Proceedings of the 5th European Conference on Computer Systems, pp. 125–138 (2010)

16. Kuhn, D.: Investigation of the relation between the Linux operating system scheduler and scheduling decisions at thread and process level (2022)

17. Lee, H., Jung, S., Jo, H.: STUN: reinforcement-learning-based optimization of kernel scheduler parameters for static workload performance. Appl. Sci. **12**(14), 7072 (2022)

18. McDougall, R., Mauro, J.: Solaris Internals: Solaris 10 and OpenSolaris Kernel Architecture (Paperback). Pearson Education (2006)

19. Saez, J.C., Prieto, M., Fedorova, A., Blagodurov, S.: A comprehensive scheduler for asymmetric multicore systems. In: Proceedings of the 5th European Conference on Computer Systems, pp. 139–152 (2010)

20. Salami, B., Noori, H., Naghibzadeh, M.: Online energy-efficient fair scheduling for heterogeneous multi-cores considering shared resource contention. J. Supercomput. 1–20 (2022)
21. Tam, D., Azimi, R., Stumm, M.: Thread clustering: sharing-aware scheduling on SMP-CMP-SMT multiprocessors. ACM SIGOPS Oper. Syst. Rev. **41**(3), 47–58 (2007)
22. Torvalds, L.: Kernel code (2021). https://www.kernel.com
23. Torvalds, L.: Kernel documentation (2021). https://www.kernel.org/doc/readme/
24. Windows: Windows specification (2021). https://msdn.microsoft.com/en-us/library/windows/
25. Wong, C.S., Tan, I., Kumari, R.D., Wey, F.: Towards achieving fairness in the Linux scheduler. ACM SIGOPS Oper. Syst. Rev. **42**(5), 34–43 (2008)
26. Xu, C., Lau, F.C.: Load Balancing in Parallel Computers: Theory and Practice, vol. 381. Springer, New York (1996). https://doi.org/10.1007/b102252

SLO-Aware DL Job Scheduling for Efficient FPGA-GPU Edge Cloud Computing

Taewoo Kim[1]([⊠]) [iD], Minsu Jeon[1] [iD], Changha Lee[1] [iD], SeongHwan Kim[1] [iD],
Fawaz AL-Hazemi[2] [iD], and Chan-Hyun Youn[1] [iD]

[1] Korea Advanced Institute of Science and Technology, Daejeon 34141, South Korea
{taewoo_kim,msjeon,changha.lee,s.h_kim,chyoun}@kaist.ac.kr
[2] University of Jeddah, Jeddah 21959, Saudi Arabia
fmalhazemi@uj.edu.sa

Abstract. Deep learning applications have become increasingly popular in recent years, leading to the development of specialized hardware accelerators such as FPGAs and GPUs. These accelerators provide significant performance gains over traditional CPUs, but their efficient utilization requires careful scheduling configuration for given DL requests. In this paper, we propose a SLO-aware DL job scheduling model for efficient FPGA-GPU edge cloud computing. The proposed model takes into account variant service-level objectives of the DL job and periodically updates the accelerator configuration of DL processing while minimizing computation costs accordingly. We first analyze the impact of various DL-related parameters on the performance of FPGA-GPU computing. We then propose a novel scheduling algorithm that considers the time-variant latency SLO constraints and periodically updates the scheduling configuration. We evaluated our scheduler using several DL workloads on a FPGA-GPU cluster. Our results demonstrated that our scheduler achieves improvements in terms of both energy consumption and SLO compliance compared to the traditional DL scheduling approach.

Keywords: DL Scheduling · FPGA-GPU Computing · Edge Computing for DL Serving

1 Introduction

Deep learning (DL) has gained immense significance across various domains due to its general characteristics and capabilities. DL's ability to learn from large volumes of data and automatically extract complex patterns and features makes it a powerful tool in solving diverse problems. They have proven promising solutions in transforming industries by enabling automation, improving accuracy, and driving innovation. Its capacity to handle unstructured and high-dimensional data, coupled with its scalability, enables practical solutions in various fields such

S. Casteleyn et al. (Eds.): ICWE 2023 Workshops, CCIS 1898, pp. 19–29, 2024.
https://doi.org/10.1007/978-3-031-50385-6_2

as medical data analysis [12,20,22,24], autonomous vehicles [2,5,7,21,26], natural language processing [13,14], and smart manufacturing [3,25]. With its extensive influence and innovative potential, DL is improving the decision-making process and leading the development of technology. Complex data analysis requirements further complicate the architecture of deep learning models, from convolutional neural networks (CNN) [16,18] and short- and long-term memory (LSTM) [15] to increasingly complex architectures such as transformers [4,9,11]. As a result, from the perspective of computing resource providers for DL services, efficiently managing user requests regarding computation-intensive DL models on HW accelerators has become an important issue. Especially in delay-sensitive applications such as VR or autonomous driving, it is imperative to adhere to service-level objectives (SLO), normally defined in response time, to satisfy user experience.

In edge cloud computing, where resource limitations and power consumption are crucial concerns, optimizing resource utilization is vital for delivering high-performance deep learning (DL) services. Graphics processing units (GPUs) and field-programmable gate arrays (FPGAs) are commonly used hardware accelerators that enable parallel processing of large-scale matrix operations. With advancements in hardware technology, the heterogeneity of AI accelerators in edge environments has increased. Thus, a key challenge in DL job scheduling for FPGAs and GPUs is to efficiently allocate resources while meeting the service level objective (SLO) requirements of different applications. To handle this challenge, various approaches have been proposed [8,19,23,27]. These include adjusting batch sizes and employing spatial-temporal scheduling schemes to maximize resource throughput, primarily focusing on homogeneous GPU clusters. However, effectively scheduling DL jobs on heterogeneous FPGA-GPU clusters remains a difficult problem due to the varying processing performance characteristics in terms of throughput and energy consumption.

In this paper, we present a novel scheduling approach that focuses on optimizing the use of heterogeneous accelerators while ensuring latency SLO of DL applications in FPGA-GPU edge cloud computing. Our proposed method considers various scheduling primitives depending on the type of accelerator and adjusts the scheduling configuration according to the time-varying latency SLO and DL requests. We conducted experiments on a heterogeneous FPGA-GPU cluster to evaluate the performance of our proposed scheduler.

2 Related Work and Problem Description

In this section, we discuss various approaches to handling GPU scheduling for DL jobs and some approaches addressing heterogeneous FPGA-GPU scheduling. The conventional GPU schedulers like Nexus [23] and Clippers [8] exploit a one-at-a-time scheduling mechanism, where the entire GPU resources including parallel cores and memory are occupied by a single DL job. In this situation, they fix a batch size as the maximum value which can be accepted in the GPU memory while satisfying the latency SLO to get a high throughput (requests per second).

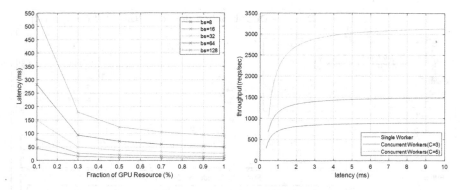

Fig. 1. The effect of processing performance with concurrent workers running on the same GPU resource; Latency according to the fraction of GPU resource (i.e. parallel cores) and batch size *bs* (left). Latency-throughput relationship according to the number of concurrent workers *C* (right).

One limitation of this mechanism is that it can result in significant idle time for GPUs when serving DL jobs with low request rates, which can decrease overall resource utilization in edge cloud computing. To address the limitation, NVIDIA developed multi-process service (MPS) [1] to support the concurrent execution of DL jobs over multiple workers. Dynamic spatial-temporal scheduling scheme [17] has also been shown to improve the performance of DL processing. Other GPU scheduling approaches, such as GSLICE [10] and Salus [27], use fine-grained partitioning of parallel cores and spatial-temporal scheduling to maximize capacity and reduce memory occupancy for deploying given DL models.

On the other hand, [19] uses layer-level management scheme on FPGA-GPU clusters to derive optimal data distribution and batch size while minimizing energy costs for heterogeneous FPGA-GPU clusters. Nevertheless, there is still potential for enhancing the effectiveness of resource utilization in the context of FPGA-GPU scheduling. This is because the scheduling primitive is different depending on HW architecture. Existing studies focus solely on managing a common scheduling variable (batch size for assigned tasks) without considering hardware-specific characteristics. The utilization of concurrent workers within a single hardware setup plays a crucial role in managing the runtime performance of DL clusters. In order to assess the impact of concurrent workers on DL processing, we conducted an experiment by executing the ResNet architecture [18] on an NVIDIA RTX 3080 GPU, while varying the number of workers running concurrently. We focused on measuring batch latency and throughput when multiple workers shared the internal resources of GPU, as depicted in Fig. 1. To enable this, we used the Volta NVIDIA-MPS tool [1], which allows each worker to utilize only a fraction of the available parallel cores (i.e. the streaming multiprocessors). The result implies that there is a saturation point where the latency is rarely reduced even if more parallel cores are used. Furthermore, as shown in the right side of Fig. 1, we observed that by running multiple workers on a

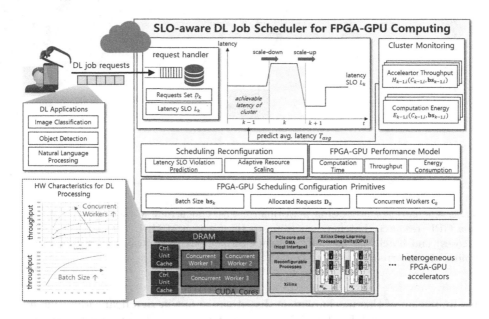

Fig. 2. The proposed architecture of SLO-aware DL job scheduling for FPGA-GPU edge cloud computing.

single hardware, it is possible to achieve higher throughput at the same level of latency constraint. As a result, elaborate control of the current workers in the DL scheduler can be an important factor in an edge computing environment with limited resources. Unfortunately, the common DL libraries for FPGA do not support the mechanism of concurrent worker execution. In this paper, we propose a novel scheduling approach that takes into account the distinctive scheduling primitives of GPUs and FPGAs, as well as variations in latency service level objectives (SLOs). By doing so, we aim to enhance resource efficiency in edge cloud computing for DL services.

3   A Proposed SLO-Aware DL Job Scheduling Model

In this section, we describe our proposed approach for SLO-aware DL job scheduling in FPGA-GPU computing, as illustrated in Fig. 2. The system receives DL inference jobs, each with a request set (i.e. a bunch of input data) and latency SLO. The latency SLO represents the required time for processing a given request set. The scheduler continuously monitors the feasibility of satisfying the SLO with the current scheduling configuration in the cluster. If it is determined that the current configuration cannot meet the required latency SLO, the scheduler updates the configuration based on FPGA-GPU performance predictions. Otherwise, it can adaptively reduce resources for computation costs in edge cloud computing when the current scheduling configuration is sufficient for serving requests.

In terms of edge cloud computing resources, we describe a computing environment in k-th time slot. We refer $\mathbf{S}_k^{GPU}$ and $\mathbf{S}_k^{FPGA}$ as a set of N_k^{GPU} GPUs and N_k^{FPGA} FPGAs available in an edge cloud environment, respectively. The total number of FPGA-GPU accelerators is $N_k = N_k^{GPU} + N_k^{FPGA}$. We assume that the available accelerators are limited for each particular time slot. The latency consumed for processing DL inference can vary depending on the state of the scheduling configuration. The latency SLO L_k and service requests $\mathcal{D}_k$ can also be time-variant but we assume that it is fixed in the same time slot. In terms of components for processing DL inference, especially in accelerators, they consist of the pre-processing time conducted in host platforms such as CPU, memory, and storage, feed-forward computation time executed in an accelerator, and return time notifying inference result to a service user. Our scheduling algorithm only considers the computation time of an accelerator since the other components are consistent regardless of accelerator type.

3.1   Performance Model for FPGA-GPU Computing

In edge cloud computing with heterogeneous FPGA-GPU accelerators, we conduct the performance modeling when processing DL inference. To reduce processing costs and maximize the availability of user requests, especially in GPU, we utilize a concurrent execution mechanism [6,10,17,27] that executes multiple workers on an accelerator. In particular, it is possible to increase the overall utilization of GPU by sharing simultaneous streaming multiprocessor and global memory.

As the controllable factors for computation time in an accelerator, we consider two factors; batch size and concurrency (i.e. the number of concurrent workers). We derive the computation time $T_{k,i}^j$ for processing a single batch in j-th worker of i-th accelerator as follows:

$$T_{k,i}^j(C_{k,i}, bs_{k,i}^j) = (\alpha_i \cdot bs_{k,i}^j + \beta_i) \cdot Q_{k,i}(C_{k,i}), \tag{1}$$

where $Q_{k,i}(C_{k,i}) \in \mathbb{R}$ is slowdown ratio due to concurrent workers (i.e. $Q_{k,i}(1) = 1$), and α_i, β_i are coefficients determined by an accelerator and a DL model. In FPGA, we fix a single worker (i.e. $C_{k,i} = 1, \forall i \in \mathbf{S}_k^{FPGA}$). As described in $\alpha_i \cdot bs_{k,i}^j + \beta_i$, the computation time is a linear model by a batch size, and the time increases due to contention of shared resources by multiple workers. From the computation time modeling, we can derive the throughput and energy cost of an accelerator. From Eq. 1, the throughput (requests per second) of i-th accelerator $H_{k,i}$ can be derive as follows:

$$
\begin{aligned}
H_{k,i}(C_{k,i}, \mathbf{bs}_{k,i}) &= \sum_{j=1}^{C_{k,i}} \frac{bs_{k,i}^j}{T_{k,i}^j(C_{k,i}, bs_{k,i}^j)} \\
&= \sum_{j=1}^{C_{k,i}} \frac{bs_{k,i}^j}{(\alpha_i \cdot bs_{k,i}^j + \beta_i) \cdot Q_{k,i}(C_{k,i})},
\end{aligned} \tag{2}
$$

where we denote $\mathbf{bs}_{k,i} \in \mathbb{R}^{C_{k,i}}$ as a set of batch size in each worker. It can be presented as the sum of the throughput of all workers simultaneously executed in i-th accelerator. From Eq. 2, the energy cost consumed for processing a unit request in i-th accelerator can be given to:

$$
E_{k,i}(C_{k,i}, \mathbf{bs}_{k,i}) = \frac{P_{k,i}(C_{k,i})}{H_{k,i}(C_{k,i}, \mathbf{bs}_{k,i})}
$$
$$
= \sum_{j=1}^{C_{k,i}} \frac{(\alpha_i \cdot bs_{k,i}^j + \beta_i) \cdot Q_{k,i}(C_{k,i})}{bs_{k,i}^j} \cdot P_{k,i}(C_{k,i}), \qquad (3)
$$

where the active power of i-th accelerator with $C_{k,i}$ concurrent workers is denoted as $P_{k,i}(C_{k,i})$. It implies that the energy consumption of an accelerator is dependent on j-th concurrent worker having the slowest computation time.

3.2   Proposed Scheduling Scheme

Based on the performance model of FPGA-GPU accelerators, we describe the SLO-aware DL job scheduling in k-th time slot under the aforementioned environment. The variable for the number of concurrent workers allocated to each accelerator is denoted as $\mathbf{C}_k = \{C_{k,i} | \forall i \in \mathbf{S}_k^{FPGA} \cup \mathbf{S}_k^{GPU}\}$ and its batch size is represented as $\mathbf{bs}_k = \{bs_{k,i}^j | \forall i \in \mathbf{S}_k^{FPGA} \cup \mathbf{S}_k^{GPU}, \forall j \in [C_{k,i}]\}$. The number of requests (i.e. DL inputs) assigned to each accelerator is denoted as $\mathbf{D}_k = \{D_{k,i}^j | \forall i \in \mathbf{S}_k^{FPGA} \cup \mathbf{S}_k^{GPU}, \forall j \in [C_{k,i}]\}$. Let $|D_{k,i}| = \sum_j D_{k,i}^j$ be the total number of requests, and If $D_{k,i}^j = 0, \forall j \in [C_{k,i}]$, i-th accelerator is deactivated (i.e. there are no DL jobs allocated).

We now present the scheduling problem of edge cloud computing with heterogeneous FPGA-GPU accelerators. Given latency SLO L_k in k-th time slot, the objective is to maximize the overall throughput of FPGA-GPU accelerators while reducing the energy consumption in an edge cloud environment. We now formulate an optimization problem as follows:

$$
\underset{\mathbf{C}_k, \mathbf{bs}_k, \mathbf{D}_k}{\text{maximize}} \sum_{i=1}^{N_k} \frac{|D_{k,i}|}{|\mathcal{D}_k|} \cdot \frac{H_{k,i}(C_{k,i}, \mathbf{bs}_{k,i})}{E_{k,i}(C_{k,i}, \mathbf{bs}_{k,i})}, \qquad (4)
$$

$$
\text{subject to } T_{k,i}^j(C_{k,i}, bs_{k,i}^j) \cdot D_{k,i}^j \le L_k, \ \forall i \in [N_k], \forall j \in [C_{k,i}], \qquad (5)
$$

$$
\sum_{i=1}^{N_k} \sum_{j=1}^{C_{k,i}} D_{k,i}^j = |\mathcal{D}_k|, \qquad (6)
$$

where $|\mathcal{D}_k|$ is the total number of received requests. The objective function in Eq. 4 is to maximize the energy efficiency for DL processing, which is represented as achievable throughput per energy while multiplying the ratio of allocated requests as a weighting factor. This can achieve efficient resource usage in edge cloud computing with low power consumption. The constraints is follows; Eq. 5 describes the satisfaction of latency SLO, which we only consider computation

Algorithm 1. SLO-aware DL Job Scheduling for FPGA-GPU Computing.

Input: received requests $\mathcal{D}_k$, latency SLO L_k, $\mathbf{S}_k^{GPU}$ GPUs and $\mathbf{S}_k^{GPU}$ FPGAs, total number of accelerators N_k.

1: $k \leftarrow 1$
2: $\mathbf{I} \leftarrow Arr\,[0 : N_k]$.
3: **for all** $i \in \mathbf{S}_k^{GPU} \cup \mathbf{S}_k^{FPGA}$ **do** $\triangleright$ initialize
4:    Initiate $\mathbf{bs}_{k,i}^*, C_{k,i}^*$ maximizing Eq. 2
5:    $\mathbf{I}[i] \leftarrow 1$
6: **end for**
7: **while** true **do**
8:    $k \leftarrow k + 1$
9:    **if** $T_{avg} \geq L_k$ **then** $\triangleright$ tight workloads
10:       **while** $|\mathcal{D}_k| / \sum_i H_{k,i}(C_{k,i}, \mathbf{bs}_{k,i}) \leq L_k$ **do**
11:          $\mathbf{Z} \leftarrow \{i | \mathbf{I}[i] = 0\}$
12:          $z^* \leftarrow \arg_{z \in Z} \max H_{1,z}(C_{1,z}^*, \mathbf{bs}_{1,z}^*) / E_{1,z}(C_{1,z}^*, \mathbf{bs}_{1,z}^*)$
13:          $\mathbf{I}[z^*] \leftarrow 1$
14:          Update $\sum_i H_{k,i}(C_{k,i}, \mathbf{bs}_{k,i}), \forall \{i | \mathbf{I}[i] = 1\}$
15:       **end while**
16:    **else** $\triangleright$ loose workloads
17:       **while** $|\mathcal{D}_k| / \sum_i H_{k,i}(C_{k,i}, \mathbf{bs}_{k,i}) \leq L_k$ **do**
18:          $\mathbf{Z} \leftarrow \{i | \mathbf{I}[i] = 1\}$
19:          $z^* \leftarrow \arg_{z \in Z} \min H_{1,z}(C_{1,z}^*, \mathbf{bs}_{1,z}^*) / E_{1,z}(C_{1,z}^*, \mathbf{bs}_{1,z}^*)$
20:          $\mathbf{I}[z^*] \leftarrow 0$
21:          Update $\sum_i H_{k,i}(C_{k,i}, \mathbf{bs}_{k,i}), \forall \{i | \mathbf{I}[i] = 1\}$
22:       **end while**
23:    **end if**
24:    Assign $\mathcal{D}_k$ proportion to throughput of each accelerators
25: **end while**

time constraints for simplicity, and Eq. 6 implies that the received requests should be allocated to an accelerator.

Since the optimization problem is non-convex (multiplication of control variables), we propose a heuristic configuration method with updating scheduling parameters periodically. For this purpose, we introduce a simple way to verify computing loads in the starting of k-th time slot. Given the volume of requests $\mathcal{D}_k$ and its latency SLO L_k, the scheduler evaluates the feasibility of the average expected computation time with previous scheduling parameters. If the number of requests is $|\mathcal{D}_k|$ in k-th period, the average expected computing time is as follows:

$$T_{avg} = \frac{|\mathcal{D}_k|}{\sum_i H_{k-1,i}(C_{k-1,i}, \mathbf{bs}_{k-1,i})}. \tag{7}$$

Algorithm 1 shows the heuristics for the proposed scheduler. It utilizes Eq. 2 to determine the optimal batch size and concurrency for each accelerator that maximizes overall throughput. This configuration is set as a baseline in the initialization step, which serves as a benchmark for efficient resource utilization over time slots. Additionally, all accelerators are activated by the scheduler. This initial point guarantee that the total throughput of the cluster becomes maximum regardless of energy consumption and latency SLO. From this point with maximizing throughput, the heuristic reconfigures the scheduling variables on the basis of the latency SLO and energy consumption of FPGA-GPU.

At the beginning of $k \geq 2$ time slot, the proposed approach evaluates whether the latency SLO is met by the scheduling configuration at $k - 1$ by checking if the time required to complete the requests is within the latency SLO L_k. If the task can be completed within the SLO, the scheduler reduces the allocated accelerators one by one, starting with the least energy-efficient one. This is done to minimize power consumption by deactivating unnecessary accelerators. However, if the task cannot be completed within the required latency, the scheduler increases the allocated accelerators one by one, starting with the most energy-efficient one, until the latency SLO is met. Finally, it divides the requests $\mathcal{D}_k$ among the available accelerators in proportion to their respective throughput. This is to balance the elapse time of all FPGA-GPU accelerators.

Table 1. The heterogeneous FPGA-GPU clusters used in the experiment.

Cluster	Module	Specification
Server1	CPU	2xIntel(R) Xeon(R) Silver 4214R CPU @ 2.40 GHz
	Host Memory	8 xDDR4 32 GB ECC Register
	DL accelerators	NVIDIA RTX 3080 GPU * 4EA
Server2	CPU	2x Intel(R) Xeon(R) Silver 4214R CPU @ 2.40 GHz
	Host Memory	8 x DDR4 32 GB ECC Register
	DL accelerators	NVIDIA RTX 2080 GPU * 2EA Xilinx Alveo U200 FPGA * 2EA

4   Performance Evaluation and Discussion

In order to evaluate the performances of the proposed scheduling algorithm in an edge cloud environment, we constructed the heterogeneous FPGA-GPU computing environments. We prepared the two server nodes that consist of 4 NVIDIA RTX 3080 GPUs, 2 NVIDIA 2080 Super GPUs, and 2 Xilinx Alveo U200 FPGAs. Table 1 describes the FPGA-GPU cluster environment for the experiment. To evaluate the performance of the proposed scheduling method, we compared it to the scheduler in Nexus [23] as a baseline that allocates only the maximum batch size with a single worker to achieve the maximum throughput regardless of the power consumption. For performance metrics, we measured the

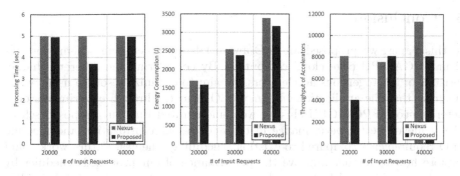

Fig. 3. Comparison of processing time (left), energy consumption (center), and throughput of accelerators (right) in FPGA-GPU cluster under relaxed latency SLO $L_k = 5$ sec.

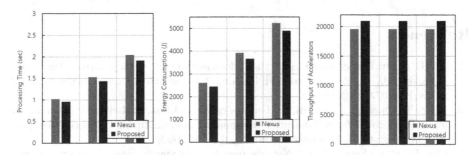

Fig. 4. Comparison of processing time (left), energy consumption (center), and throughput of accelerators (right) in FPGA-GPU cluster under tight latency SLO less $L_k = [1, 1.5, 2]$ s.

processing time delayed from all received requests, the total energy consumption to complete the inference, and the total throughput of the allocated accelerators.

Initially, we evaluated the performance of the proposed model by varying the input loads $\mathcal{D}_k$ under a relaxed latency SLO of $L_k = 5$ s. We measured the performance metrics for input loads $|\mathcal{D}_k| = [20000, 30000, 40000]$. Figure 3 depicts the comparison results, where the proposed model demonstrates lower energy consumption 6.6% than the baseline by finding a better configuration through the allocation of multiple workers in each accelerator. Moreover, the proposed model allocates fewer accelerators for $|\mathcal{D}_k| = 20000$ and 40000 but still satisfies the $L_k = 5$ s latency SLO.

Furthermore, we evaluated the model's performance under a narrower latency SLO of $L_k = 2$ s. As shown in Fig. 4, the proposed model searches for the optimal configuration to minimize the total processing time while meeting the latency SLO. Compared to the baseline, which slightly violates the given latency SLO, the proposed scheduler reduces the processing time by 7% and shows lower energy consumption 6.5%.

5   Conclusion

In this paper, we proposed an SLO-aware DL job scheduling scheme for efficient FPGA-GPU edge cloud computing. By considering the different characteristics of heterogeneous accelerators, we aim to optimize resource usage while ensuring that the application's latency SLO is met. Through experiments on a heterogeneous FPGA-GPU cluster, we demonstrated that our proposed scheduler achieved better performance in terms of resource utilization and meeting SLO requirements compared to existing scheduling schemes. Future work could explore how to further improve the performance of our proposed scheduler by considering additional factors such as power consumption, network bandwidth, and system heterogeneity.

Acknowledgements. This work is supported by Samsung Electronics Co., Ltd.

References

1. NVIDIA multi-process service. https://docs.nvidia.com/deploy/mps/index.html
2. Bojarski, M., et al.: End to end learning for self-driving cars. arXiv preprint arXiv:1604.07316 (2016)
3. Brito, T., Queiroz, J., Piardi, L., Fernandes, L.A., Lima, J., Leitão, P.: A machine learning approach for collaborative robot smart manufacturing inspection for quality control systems. Procedia Manuf. **51**, 11–18 (2020)
4. Cao, H., et al.: Swin-UNet: UNet-like pure transformer for medical image segmentation. In: Karlinsky, L., Michaeli, T., Nishino, K. (eds.) ECCV 2022. LNCS, vol. 13803, pp. 205–218. Springer, Cham (2022). https://doi.org/10.1007/978-3-031-25066-8_9
5. Chen, C., Seff, A., Kornhauser, A., Xiao, J.: DeepDriving: learning affordance for direct perception in autonomous driving. In Proceedings of the IEEE International Conference on Computer Vision, pp. 2722–2730 (2015)
6. Choi, S., Lee, S., Kim, Y., Park, J., Kwon, Y., and Huh, J.: Multi-model machine learning inference serving with GPU spatial partitioning. arXiv preprint arXiv:2109.01611 (2021)
7. Codevilla, F., Müller, M., López, A., Koltun, V., Dosovitskiy, A.: End-to-end driving via conditional imitation learning. In: 2018 IEEE International Conference on Robotics and Automation (ICRA), pp. 4693–4700. IEEE (2018)
8. Crankshaw, D., Wang, X., Zhou, G., Franklin, M.J., Gonzalez, J.E., Stoica, I.: Clipper: a {low-latency} online prediction serving system. In: 14th USENIX Symposium on Networked Systems Design and Implementation (NSDI 2017), pp. 613–627 (2017)
9. Devlin, J., Chang, M.-W., Lee, K., Toutanova, K.: BERT: pre-training of deep bidirectional transformers for language understanding. arXiv preprint arXiv:1810.04805 (2018)
10. Dhakal, A., Kulkarni, S.G., Ramakrishnan, K.: GSLICE: controlled spatial sharing of GPUs for a scalable inference platform. In: Proceedings of the 11th ACM Symposium on Cloud Computing, pp. 492–506 (2020)
11. Dosovitskiy, A., et al.: An image is worth 16×16 words: transformers for image recognition at scale. arXiv preprint arXiv:2010.11929 (2020)

12. Esteva, A., et al.: Dermatologist-level classification of skin cancer with deep neural networks. Nature **542**(7639), 115–118 (2017)
13. Galassi, A., Lippi, M., Torroni, P.: Attention in natural language processing. IEEE Trans. Neural Netw. Learn. Syst. **32**(10), 4291–4308 (2020)
14. Gu, Y., et al.: Domain-specific language model pretraining for biomedical natural language processing. ACM Trans. Comput. Healthc. (HEALTH) **3**(1), 1–23 (2021)
15. Hochreiter, S., Schmidhuber, J.: Long short-term memory. Neural Comput. **9**(8), 1735–1780 (1997)
16. Huang, G., Liu, Z., Van Der Maaten, L., Weinberger, K.Q.: Densely connected convolutional networks. In: Proceedings of the IEEE Conference on Computer Vision and Pattern Recognition, pp. 4700–4708 (2017)
17. Jain, P., et al.: Dynamic space-time scheduling for GPU inference. arXiv preprint arXiv:1901.00041 (2018)
18. He, K., Zhang, X., Ren, S., Sun, J.: Deep residual learning for image recognition. In: CVPR (2016)
19. Kim, W.-J., Youn, C.-H.: Cooperative scheduling schemes for explainable DNN acceleration in satellite image analysis and retraining. IEEE Trans. Parallel Distrib. Syst. **33**(7), 1605–1618 (2021)
20. Litjens, G., et al.: State-of-the-art deep learning in cardiovascular image analysis. JACC: Cardiovas. Imaging **12**(8 Part 1), 1549–1565 (2019)
21. Ouyang, Z., Niu, J., Liu, Y., Guizani, M.: Deep CNN-based real-time traffic light detector for self-driving vehicles. IEEE Trans. Mob. Comput. **19**(2), 300–313 (2019)
22. Ronneberger, O., Fischer, P., Brox, T.: U-net: convolutional networks for biomedical image segmentation. In: Navab, N., Hornegger, J., Wells, W.M., Frangi, A.F. (eds.) MICCAI 2015, Part III. LNCS, vol. 9351, pp. 234–241. Springer, Cham (2015). https://doi.org/10.1007/978-3-319-24574-4_28
23. Shen, H., et al.: Nexus: a GPU cluster engine for accelerating DNN-based video analysis. In: Proceedings of the 27th ACM Symposium on Operating Systems Principles, pp. 322–337 (2019)
24. Singh, A., Sengupta, S., Lakshminarayanan, V.: Explainable deep learning models in medical image analysis. J. Imaging **6**(6), 52 (2020)
25. Wen, L., Gao, L., Li, X.: A new deep transfer learning based on sparse auto-encoder for fault diagnosis. IEEE Trans. Syst. Man Cybern.: Syst. **49**(1), 136–144 (2017)
26. Xu, H., Gao, Y., Yu, F., Darrell, T.: End-to-end learning of driving models from large-scale video datasets. In: Proceedings of the IEEE Conference on Computer Vision and Pattern Recognition, pp. 2174–2182 (2017)
27. Yu, P., Chowdhury, M.: Salus: fine-grained GPU sharing primitives for deep learning applications. arXiv preprint arXiv:1902.04610 (2019)

DESA: Decentralized Self-adaptive Horizontal Autoscaling for Bursts of Load in Fog Computing

EunChan Park[✉][iD], KyeongDeok Baek[iD], Eunho Cho[iD], and In-Young Ko[iD]

School of Computing, Korea Advanced Institute of Science and Technology, Daejeon, Republic of Korea
{eunchan.park,kyeongdeok.baek,ehcho,iko}@kaist.ac.kr

Abstract. With the increase of Web of Things devices, fog computing has emerged as a promising solution to lower the communication overhead and congestion in the cloud. In fog computing systems, microservices are deployed as containers, which usually require an orchestration tool like Kubernetes for service discovery, placement, and recovery. One key challenge in the orchestration of microservices is establishing service elasticity in case of unpredictable bursts of load. Commonly, a centralized autoscaler in the cloud dynamically adjusts the number of microservice instances depending on the metric values monitored from distributed fog nodes. However, monitoring an increasing number of microservice instances can cause excessive network overhead and delay the scaling reaction. We propose DESA, a DEcentralized Self-adaptive Autoscaler through which each microservice instance makes its own scaling decision adaptively, cloning or terminating itself through a self-monitoring process. We evaluate DESA in a simulated fog computing environment with different numbers of fog nodes. The results show that DESA successfully reduces the scaling reaction time in large-scale fog computing systems compared to the centralized approach while resulting in a similar maximum number of instances and average CPU utilization during a burst of load.

Keywords: Web services in edge clouds · Self-adaptive microservice autoscaling · Service elasticity

1 Introduction

Recently, an unprecedented number of Web of Things (WoT) devices have been deployed in our everyday environment. WoT devices such as smart cameras and traffic sensors in smart cities constantly generate huge amounts of data that require processing and analysis to extract useful information. Since resource-constrained WoT devices alone cannot handle such heavy computational tasks, attempts have been made to transfer the data to a distant global cloud server or local fog computing nodes, mitigating the communication overhead by placing computational resources closer to the end devices as shown in Fig. 1. Even though the distributed fog nodes have less computing power than the cloud, they effectively mitigate the communication overhead and congestion in the cloud by placing computational resources closer to the end devices [1]. In this system, along with the increase of end devices, the number of fog nodes in between the cloud and the end devices may also increase.

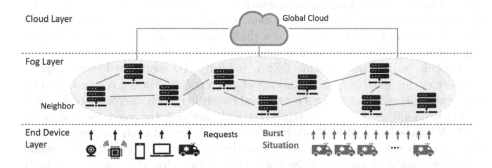

Fig. 1. A fog computing system during a burst of load

Meanwhile, in such fog computing systems, MicroService Architecture (MSA) has been increasingly adopted and utilized for operating web applications, As an evolution of the conventional service-oriented architecture style, MSA emphasizes dividing a system into small and lightweight services that each run its own process that collaborate with each other with different roles. These microservices are often deployed in lightweight and portable containers [4,5], which are monitored and managed through container orchestration tools such as Kubernetes.

A key challenge in the orchestration of microservices is service elasticity. Service elasticity indicates the ability of the microservices to be automatically scaled up or down corresponding to the computational demand [11]. For example, in a disaster situation, requests for emergency medical services may suddenly increase, leading to bursts of computational load at the related microservices, as shown in Fig. 1. To handle such bursts of load, the load should be distributed across enough instances of the microservices, which means that the number of instances across the fog nodes should be temporarily increased [7,10].

For the scaling of microservices, there mainly have been two approaches: proactive and reactive scaling. In proactive scaling, prediction models predict the bursts of load in advance and perform scaling actions prior to the actual burst. However, these prediction models require reliable historical data for training and cannot predict unprecedented situations. On the other hand, reactive scaling approaches maintain global controllers that monitor the active microservice instances to make scaling decisions according to predefined rules. Although reactive scaling may be less efficient than proactive scaling for predictable bursts of load [10], reactive scaling is inevitably used for unpredictable bursts of load [10,15].

However, reactively autoscaling in case of an unpredictable burst of load requires an expensive process of monitoring. Especially in fog computing, where a vast number of microservice instances are deployed over geographically distributed fog nodes, centralized monitoring-based autoscalers lack scalability as the number of fog nodes and microservices increases, due to the excessive networking cost of monitoring [13]. Furthermore, the scaling decisions may be delayed by the monitoring latency, which is aggravated as more fog nodes and microservices are deployed in the system. Therefore, rapidly reacting to unpredictable bursts of load has remained a challenge in realizing service elasticity in fog computing with a myriad of nodes.

In this work, we present DESA, a fully DEcentralized Self-adaptive Autoscaler, for handling bursts of load at microservices in fog computing environments. Instead of utilizing a centralized controller, each microservice instance regularly monitors its own metric value and analyzes the need for scaling by itself. When a burst of load occurs, the metric value of each instance exceeds the upper threshold, and instances clone themselves to the current or a neighboring fog node. Then, when the burst fades away, cloned instances gradually terminate themselves as the metric values fall below the lower threshold. We design DESA based on the Monitor-Analyze-Plan-Execute (MAPE) model [3] for self-adaptiveness, with the MAPE control loop running in each microservice instance.

We evaluate the performance of DESA through a widely adopted network simulator, iFogSim2 [8]. We compare DESA with Horizontal Pod Autoscaler (HPA) as the baseline, which is the default autoscaler provided by Kubernetes. The simulation results show that DESA successfully reduces the scaling reaction time compared to the baseline approach by eliminating the delay caused by centralized controllers. Moreover, even without a centralized controller, DESA achieves a performance of scaling similar to the baseline in terms of the maximum number of microservice instances created during burst and the average CPU utilization.

The main contributions of this work are summarized as follows:

- We extend the service elasticity problem to consider bursts of load in fog computing systems with increasing amounts of distributed fog nodes.
- We propose DESA, a fully decentralized self-adaptive autoscaler that reactively scales microservices across geographically distributed fog nodes in fog computing systems. DESA applies a fully decentralized MAPE loop for reactively scaling microservices.
- We evaluate the performance of DESA through iFogSim2, and experimental results show that our proposed autoscaler reacts faster to unpredictable bursts of load by reducing the overall network overhead. Also, DESA results in a similar performance of scaling to that of Kubernetes' HPA, the de facto standard reactive autoscaler.

The remainder of this paper is organized as follows. In Sect. 2, we discuss related works. In Sect. 3, we present our approach along with the problem definition. In Sect. 4, we show and discuss the results of our experimental evaluation. Finally, we present some concluding remarks in Sect. 5.

2   Related Works

Autoscaling and self-adaptive systems have been studied extensively by researchers of microservices. In this section, we discuss some existing proactive and reactive autoscaling approaches and introduce some works that utilize a decentralized self-adaptive system to handle autoscaling of microservices.

2.1   Proactive Autoscaling Approaches

Previous works propose proactive approaches in horizontally autoscaling microservices, predicting the load of microservices using machine-learning-based methods [6,9,15]. Ming et al. go further to create a hybrid of proactive and reactive approaches, handling the decision conflicts between the two approaches to optimizing the elastic expansion [15]. However, prediction models used in these works require reliable historical metric data for training. Moreover, proactive approaches heavily assume that bursts of load are predictable and can be handled prior to the burst, meaning that they can be domain-specific and not applicable to unexpected and unpredictable bursts of load.

2.2   Reactive Autoscaling Approaches

Kubernetes' HPA is the de facto standard for reactively autoscaling microservices [10]. For scaling purposes, a metric server collects resource metric data every 15 s, querying each node in the cluster. Then, a central controller fetches the metric data from the metric server and makes scaling decisions based on the threshold values that are manually set by the developer prior to deployment. While HPA is the most popular tool available on the market, the centralized metric server lacks scalability and suffers significant performance degradation as the number of fog nodes in the system increases.

Rossi et al. suggest a hierarchical autoscaling control model in which a centralized controller collects proactive or reactive scaling actions requested by decentralized microservice managers [12]. While this approach can successfully distribute the monitoring component of the autoscaling system, the centralized controller can still act as a bottleneck in fog computing systems, where instances of microservices are geographically distributed to multiple fog nodes.

2.3   Decentralized Self-adaptive Systems

Tangari et al. apply a self-adaptive decentralized framework for monitoring network resources for Software-Defined Networking (SDN) [14]. Through this decentralization of the monitoring module, resources are dynamically reallocated to the services in the system. The results show that the overall switch control bandwidth is reduced while maintaining similar or better performance compared to the existing methods. However, their approach requires a synchronization interface that may have significant overhead in fog computing environments. Moreover, since the work focuses on the specific domain of SDN, their method does not consider the characteristics of microservices that are required for scaling container-based microservices across fog nodes. Zhang et al. propose a multilevel self-adaptation model for microservice scaling, extending the Kubernetes infrastructure to demonstrate its ability [16]. However, their work is only partially decentralized and can lack scalability in fog computing systems as more fog nodes enter the system.

3   Decentralized Self-adaptive Horizontal Autoscaler

3.1   Problem Definition

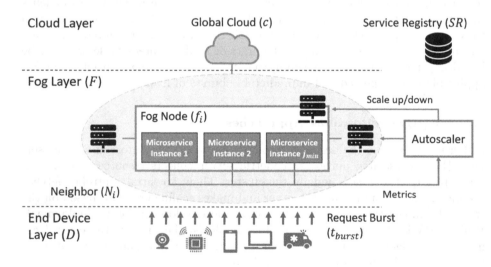

Fig. 2. Overview of the target environment

Figure 2 shows the overview of our target environment. Our target environment is a fog computing system in which geographically distributed fog nodes, $f_i \in F$, are connected to the central cloud, c, with various network latencies, l_i, depending on their geographical location. Fog nodes are connected to each other, and each fog node maintains a list of its neighboring fog nodes ($N_i \subseteq F$) that have short communication latencies due to geographical locality. Instances of the microservice, $\mu_j \in I$, are placed across fog nodes upon deployment. The developer of the microservice sets the minimum number of instances, $j_{min} > 0$, before deployment, and j_{min} instances are deployed initially by the system. We define the total number of instances at a given time t as $j(t)$, with $j(0) = j_{min}$.

Various end devices, D, send data-processing requests, r, to the instances, I, that are placed across the system. Following the service-oriented architecture, a device initially queries a global service registry to establish the connection with an available microservice instance. The service registry assigns end devices to microservice instances in a round-robin manner to equally distribute the requests to the instances. Note that there is no single-point load balancer that dynamically balances the requests. Once the assignment is established, the end device sends requests to the assigned microservice instance until the processing is done or the device is handed over to another instance. Also, when scaling occurs, the service registry is updated accordingly to add the newly generated instances or delete the terminated instances.

A burst of load happens at an unpredictable point in time, t_{burst}, and stops at t_{end}. During the burst, the active microservice instances suffer from heavy networking and computing loads. We use CPU utilization of an instance at a given time t, $CPU_j(t)$, as the performance metric of the instances, which is the most common performance metric of computation-intensive applications [2].

The goal of this problem is to stabilize the performance metric of the system during the burst by dynamically scaling the microservices shortly after a burst. The autoscaler in the system makes the scaling decisions by periodically monitoring the metric values of the microservice instances. During a burst, the autoscaler should notice the burst and increase the number of microservice instances as soon as possible. Then, after the burst ends, the autoscaler should decrease the number of instances to reduce the cost of maintaining an excessive number of instances.

There are two concerns for the autoscaler: (1) minimizing the scale-up reaction time after a burst occurs, RTU, and (2) maintaining average CPU utilization, CPU_{avg}, in an acceptable range during a burst. Firstly, we define the scale-up reaction time, RTU, as the time at which the burst of load has been successfully handled. RTU is measured as the first time after a burst at which the metric values of the entire microservice instances, I, fall below the upper threshold α, as follows:

$$RTU = \min(\{\, t \mid \forall \mu_j, CPU_j(t) \le \alpha \,\}), \qquad (1)$$

where $t_{burst} < t \le t_{end}$. Secondly, to measure the stabilization of the metric value resulting from scaling, we define the average CPU utilization of all microservice instances during burst, CPU_{avg}, as follows:

$$CPU_{avg} = \frac{1}{t_{end} - t_{burst}} \sum_{t=t_{burst}}^{t_{end}} \frac{1}{j(t)} \sum_{\mu_j} CPU_j(t). \qquad (2)$$

3.2 System Architecture and Algorithm

As a solution to the defined problem, we propose DESA, as shown in Fig. 3. Instead of placing a global and centralized controller over the microservices, we place a self-adaptive and decentralized controller for each microservice instance.

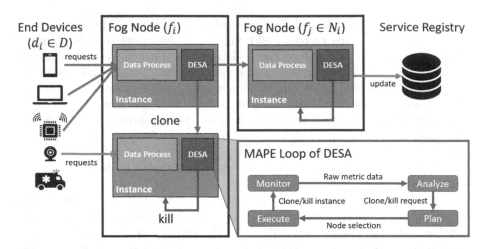

Fig. 3. Overview of DESA's architecture

Through this controller, each microservice instance individually decides whether to scale up (cloning) or scale down (cooling). To implement the self-adaptiveness of DESA, we design DESA based on the Monitor-Analyze-Plan-Execute (MAPE) model [3], with the MAPE control loop running in each microservice instance. Each step of the MAPE loop is represented as an independent component within an instance, with each component passing commands to the next component in a loop.

Monitor. In the monitor component, each microservice instance periodically collects the metric value (e.g. CPU utilization, memory utilization, workload) for every custom interval. The monitor component only fetches the metric value within the container holding the instance, which means that no network communication is involved in this monitoring process.

Analyze. The analyze component receives the metric value from the monitor component and makes cloning or cooling decisions using threshold-based policies. DESA clones the instance as a child instance when the metric value exceeds the upper threshold (Algorithm 1). Then, when the burst of load has been relieved and the metric values fall below the lower threshold, child instances terminate themselves (Algorithm 2). The metric data provided by monitor are analyzed through threshold-based policies, making decisions to clone the microservice instance when the metric value exceeds the upper threshold. DESA label all newly generated instances as children, and each child instance holds its parent container's ID.

Algorithm 1 shows the cloning algorithm of DESA. The cloning algorithm of DESA is as follows, For every custom interval, the metric value is fetched from the monitor (line 3), and a cloning decision is made if the metric value exceeds the upper threshold, α (line 4). For cloning, the number of new child instances to be cloned, $newChildNum$, is decided similarly to HPA, using the ratio of the current and desired metric values to estimate the number of instances that are needed to lower the metric value below α (line 6). Then, actual cloning commands are sent to the plan component (line 7–8). Note that without any buffers, microservices may repeatedly alternate between cloning and cooling in a short period of time if the metric value is on the border of the threshold. Therefore, a different *cooltime* is assigned to each child instance to make the cooling process gradual (line 9).

Algorithm 1: Cloning Algorithm

    Input   : α, monitoringInterval, monitor

1 **Procedure** *cloningAnalysis*
2   **for** *every* monitoringInterval **do**
3   metric $\leftarrow$ monitor.getMetricValue()
4   **if** metric $> \alpha$ **then**
5   cooltime $\leftarrow 0$
6   newChildNum $\leftarrow$ ceil(metric $\div \alpha$)
7   **for** *steps* $\leftarrow 1$ **to** newChildNum **by** 1 **do**
8   this.clone(cooltime)
9   cooltime $\leftarrow$ cooltime $+$ monitoringInterval
10   **end**
11   **end**
12   **end**
13 **end**

Algorithm 2 shows the details of the cooling algorithm. Note that this algorithm The cooling algorithm only runs in child instances and does not run in the initial j_{min} instances to guarantee that at least j_{min} instances of the microservice are always active. The cooling algorithm begins by waiting for the given cooltime (line 2). Then, as in the cloning algorithm, the metric value is fetched from the monitor every custom interval (line 4). If the metric value falls below the threshold, β, the instance terminates (line 5–6).

Plan. When the plan component receives a cloning command from the analyze component, the fog node for deploying the clone is selected. If the current node has enough computing resources to place the cloned instance, the current node is selected. If the resource is insufficient, then the cloning command is forwarded to a neighboring node in a round-robin manner. When a neighboring node receives this forwarded command, it restarts this node selection process. Once a node with enough resources is found, the loop proceeds to the execute component.

Execute. With the selected node received from the plan component, the execute component makes the actual cloning or terminating request to the selected node. In the case of cloning, as the child instances are placed, some of the end devices connected to the parent instance are directly handed over and distributed across

---

Algorithm 2: Cooling Algorithm

    Input   : β, cooltime, monitoringInterval, monitor
1 **Procedure** *coolingAnalysis*
2 | wait(cooltime)
3 | **for** *every* monitoringInterval **do**
4 | | metric ← monitor.getMetricValue()
5 | | **if** metric $< \beta$ **then**
6 | | | this.terminate()
7 | | **end**
8 | **end**
9 **end**

---

newly generated child instances without the end devices having to revisit the service registry. Finally, the service registry is updated with the network address of the newly generated instances.

4   Experimental Evaluation

We evaluate DESA by comparing the RTU and CPU_{avg} with the baseline in a simulated fog computing environment. For simulation, we use iFogSim2, which is the most commonly used simulator of fog computing environments [8,11].

4.1   Simulation Setting

We choose HPA as the baseline since it is the representative de facto standard of centralized monitoring-based reactive autoscalers [10]. HPA utilizes a metric server in the cloud that collects the metric values from each fog node's monitor component. The central controller, also located in the cloud server, fetches the metric value from the metric server and makes scaling decisions for the microservices.

Generally, we set the parameters of the simulations based on the default settings of HPA. We set the upper threshold, α, of the CPU utilization metric to 50%, following a common threshold value of HPA. We set the lower threshold, β, to 10% empirically since HPA does not use a lower threshold. We set the monitoring interval of the autoscalers to 15 s, the default setting of HPA. The initial and minimum number of microservice instances is set to 4. Finally, the network latencies, l_i, from node f_i to cloud c, are set between 50 to 900 ms, considering the distributed nature of fog nodes. We perform 50 independent simulations for the number of fog nodes from 100 to 5000 since the metric server used by HPA officially supports up to 5000 nodes. Note that the number of fog nodes in the system remains fixed for each simulation. Each simulation lasts for 15 min, and the simulations are repeated four times with different random seeds.

In the simulation, the number of requests to a microservice suddenly increases at t_{burst}, which is set as a random time within the first five minutes of the simulation. As a result, the CPU of the initial instances exceeds α, and the autoscalers eventually scale the microservice in order to lower the CPU below α. We assume that the fog nodes in our system, F, have enough computing resources to host the additional microservice instances generated by scaling.

4.2   Result and Analysis

Figure 4a shows the scale-up reaction time, RTU, of HPA and DESA as the number of fog nodes increases. Specifically, DESA has 16.6% faster RTU from N = 100 to 1000, 48.7% for 1100 to 2000, 87.3% for 2100 to 3000, 132.5% for 3100 to 4000, and 178.1% for 4100 to 5000. The result shows that DESA reacts faster to bursts of load overall, especially as the number of fog nodes increases (Table 1).

Table 1. Simulation parameters

Parameter	Value
Number of nodes	100–5000
Simulation time	15 min
Burst time (t_{burst})	Random within first 5 min
Burst duration ($t_{end} - t_{burst}$)	5 min
Min instances (j_{min})	4
Upper threshold (α)	50%
Lower threshold (β)	10%
Monitoring interval	15 s
Network latency (l_i)	50–900 ms

Figure 4b shows the maximum number of instances, $max(j(t))$, created during the burst of load as the number of fog nodes increases. The result shows that DESA produces similar $max(j(t))$ compared to the baseline, generating 4.0% more instances on average. There are four exceptional cases in which DESA generates less instances than HPA, with the largest difference of 1.3% when $N = 4400$. Regardless, the result overall shows that although DESA does not have a centralized controller, the maximum number of instances generated during the burst does not overly exceed that of the baseline.

Figure 4c shows the CPU_{avg} during the burst as the number of fog nodes increases. Specifically, CPU_{avg} of DESA is 2.4% lower than that of HPA on average, with the largest difference of 4.1% when $N = 600$. In terms of the maximum number of instances, $max(j(t))$, created during the burst, DESA generates 4.0% more instances on average. With these results, we can conclude that CPU_{avg} of DESA closely follows that of HPA during a burst.

In summary, by reducing the network overhead caused by a centralized controller, DESA reacts faster to bursts of load while resulting in a similar performance of scaling in terms of the maximum number of instances created and the average CPU utilization during a burst.

4.3 Threats to Validity

We use iFogSim2 [8,11] to establish the external validity of the simulations. Because there is no implementation of HPA in iFogSim2, we implement both DESA and HPA in iFogSim2 by ourselves, translating the components of DESA and HPA as application modules in iFogSim2. Our implementation includes all the components in HPA so that the scaling behavior closely follows the actual behavior of HPA.

DESA requires developers to choose appropriate parameter settings such as the upper (α) and lower (β) thresholds of the metric values, and the performance of DESA can be affected by such parameters. While we empirically choose reasonable values of these parameters for our simulations, we plan to perform in-depth experiments to analyze the influence of these parameters on DESA's performance in future work.

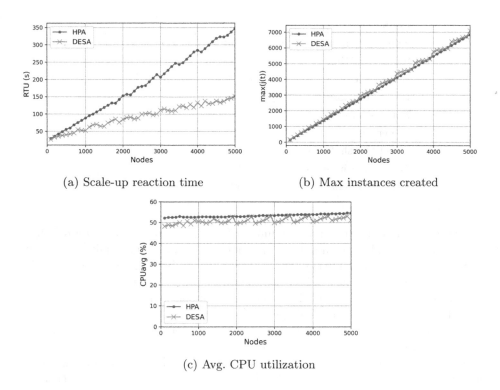

(a) Scale-up reaction time   (b) Max instances created

(c) Avg. CPU utilization

Fig. 4. Experimental Result of DESA and HPA

Note that we disregard the container startup time in measuring RTU. Therefore, in an actual system, RTU is expected to be slightly higher than the simulation result for both DESA and HPA. However, this increase is expected to be constant for both autoscalers, which means that disregarding container startup time does not influence the comparison of the two approaches.

Furthermore, for DESA, the MAPE loop in an instance should begin once the instance is cloned. This means that although the monitoring interval is set to equal values for all instances, instances that are cloned at different times should have different starting points for monitoring. However, due to the limitation of the simulator, the MAPE loop begins from the same point in time for all the microservice instances. However, we expect that having different starting points of monitoring will have a minor influence on the scaling reaction time and overall performance of scaling.

Also due to the limitation of the simulator, we disregard the computational overhead of the MAPE control loop running in each microservice instance. This overhead that exists in DESA, however, is similar in amount to the computational overhead of HPA. The difference exists in that DESA distributes this overhead across multiple instances while HPA handles the computation in the centralized controller. Therefore, we expect that this overhead does not influence the result of our work.

4.4   Discussion and Future Work

Although DESA successfully reduces the *RTU* after a burst occurs, scaling down after the burst is gradual, which means that the scale-down process requires more computing resources to be occupied briefly after the burst has ended. This is to ensure that child instances are not terminated simultaneously, which may result in repeated fluctuation of the metric value such that instances are repeatedly scaled up and down within a short period of time.

Also, it is typical for developers to set an upper limit for the number of instances to negotiate the operational costs during bursts. To apply this limit, the autoscaler should be aware of the total number of instances that are currently active. However, since DESA is fully decentralized, the total number of active instances can only be heuristically estimated. Otherwise, DESA requires an additional process to track the number of microservice instances. We leave the development of the method for limiting the number of total instances as future work.

We plan to expand DESA to consider the geographic locality of the requests from the end devices. To fully exploit the advantage of geographically distributed fog nodes, DESA may detect a burst of load in a specific region and clone microservice instances to the fog nodes close to the requesting end devices in the region. In that case, neighboring fog nodes would be defined in terms of geographical locations and may cooperate to make scaling decisions systematically.

In order to expand DESA to consider the geographic locality, the node selection process needs to be carefully considered. Currently, when the current node cannot place the cloned instance, DESA uses a simple round-robin method to select an alternative neighboring node. However, if all the resources in N_i are occupied and cannot host any additional microservice instance, the cloning command may repeatedly hover around the fog layer before finally reaching the cloud. While this limitation was not focused on in this work, we plan to consider such resource-constrained scenarios in selecting the appropriate neighboring node in future work.

5   Conclusion

Establishing service elasticity when microservices experience unpredictable bursts of load has been a challenge that must be addressed, especially for large-scale fog computing systems. Since these bursts of load are unpredictable, existing proactive approaches are insufficient. Furthermore, current reactive autoscalers lack scalability in fog computing systems due to their centralized components. In this work, we present DESA, a fully decentralized self-adaptive autoscaler that rapidly scales microservice instances across geographically distributed fog nodes. With a MAPE loop running in each microservice instance, DESA performs scaling of microservices without a centralized controller, reducing the network overhead of existing reactive autoscalers. Evaluation results show that DESA has a faster scale-up reaction time to bursts of load, especially as the number of fog nodes in the system increases. Moreover, DESA results in a similar maximum number of instances and average CPU utilization during burst compared to the baseline, showing a comparable performance of scaling despite its decentralized nature.

We plan to expand DESA to consider the geographic locality of the requests from the end devices. To fully exploit the advantage of geographically distributed fog nodes, DESA may detect a burst of load in a specific region and clone microservice instances to the fog nodes close to the requesting end devices in the region. In that case, neighboring fog nodes would be defined in terms of geographical locations and may cooperate to make scaling decisions systematically.

In the future, DESA can be expanded to address the geographic locality of the bursts of load, rapidly scaling microservice instances to clusters near the region of burst to minimize data transfer and latency. We will also expand upon the node selection process to consider scenarios in which regional clusters are resource-constrained.

Acknowledgements. This research was supported by the MSIT (Ministry of Science and ICT), Korea, under the ITRC (Information Technology Research Center) support program (IITP-2023-2020-0-01795) supervised by the IITP (Institute for Information & Communications Technology Planning & Evaluation)

References

1. Bonomi, F., Milito, R., Zhu, J., Addepalli, S.: Fog computing and its role in the internet of things. In: Proceedings of the First Edition of the MCC Workshop on Mobile Cloud Computing, MCC 2012, pp. 13–16. Association for Computing Machinery, New York (2012). https://doi.org/10.1145/2342509.2342513, https://doi-org.libra.kaist.ac.kr/10.1145/2342509.2342513
2. Casalicchio, E., Perciballi, V.: Auto-scaling of containers: the impact of relative and absolute metrics. In: 2017 IEEE 2nd International Workshops on Foundations and Applications of Self* Systems (FAS*W), pp. 207–214 (2017). https://doi.org/10.1109/FAS-W.2017.149
3. Computing, A., et al.: An architectural blueprint for autonomic computing. IBM White Pap. **31**(2006), 1–6 (2006)

4. Dupont, C., Giaffreda, R., Capra, L.: Edge computing in IoT context: horizontal and vertical Linux container migration. In: 2017 Global Internet of Things Summit (GIoTS), pp. 1–4 (2017). https://doi.org/10.1109/GIOTS.2017.8016218

5. Ismail, B.I., et al.: Evaluation of docker as edge computing platform. In: 2015 IEEE Conference on Open Systems (ICOS), pp. 130–135 (2015). https://doi.org/10.1109/ICOS.2015.7377291

6. Ju, L., Singh, P., Toor, S.: Proactive autoscaling for edge computing systems with kubernetes. In: Proceedings of the 14th IEEE/ACM International Conference on Utility and Cloud Computing Companion, UCC 2021. Association for Computing Machinery, New York (2022). https://doi.org/10.1145/3492323.3495588

7. López, M.R., Spillner, J.: Towards quantifiable boundaries for elastic horizontal scaling of microservices. In: Companion Proceedings of the10th International Conference on Utility and Cloud Computing, pp. 35–40 (2017)

8. Mahmud, R., Pallewatta, S., Goudarzi, M., Buyya, R.: iFogSim2: an extended iFogSim simulator for mobility, clustering, and microservice management in edge and fog computing environments (2021). https://doi.org/10.48550/ARXIV.2109.05636

9. Nguyen, H.X., Zhu, S., Liu, M.: Graph-PHPA: graph-based proactive horizontal pod autoscaling for microservices using LSTM-GNN. In: 2022 IEEE 11th International Conference on Cloud Networking (CloudNet), pp. 237–241 (2022). https://doi.org/10.1109/CloudNet55617.2022.9978781

10. Nunes, J., Bianchi, T., Iwasaki, A., Nakagawa, E.: State of the art on microservices autoscaling: an overview. In: Anais do XLVIII Seminário Integrado de Software e Hardware, pp. 30–38. SBC, Porto Alegre (2021). https://doi.org/10.5753/semish.2021.15804

11. Pallewatta, S., Kostakos, V., Buyya, R.: Microservices-based IoT applications scheduling in edge and fog computing: a taxonomy and future directions (2022). https://doi.org/10.48550/ARXIV.2207.05399

12. Rossi, F., Cardellini, V., Presti, F.L.: Self-adaptive threshold-based policy for microservices elasticity. In: 2020 28th International Symposium on Modeling, Analysis, and Simulation of Computer and Telecommunication Systems (MASCOTS), pp. 1–8 (2020). https://doi.org/10.1109/MASCOTS50786.2020.9285951

13. Taherizadeh, S., Jones, A.C., Taylor, I., Zhao, Z., Stankovski, V.: Monitoring self-adaptive applications within edge computing frameworks: a state-of-the-art review. J. Syst. Softw. **136**, 19–38 (2018). https://doi.org/10.1016/j.jss.2017.10.033

14. Tangari, G., Tuncer, D., Charalambides, M., Qi, Y., Pavlou, G.: Self-adaptive decentralized monitoring in software-defined networks. IEEE Trans. Netw. Serv. Manage. **15**(4), 1277–1291 (2018). https://doi.org/10.1109/TNSM.2018.2874813

15. Yan, M., Liang, X., Lu, Z., Wu, J., Zhang, W.: HANSEL: adaptive horizontal scaling of microservices using bi-LSTM. Appl. Soft Comput. **105**, 107216 (2021). https://doi.org/10.1016/j.asoc.2021.107216

16. Zhang, S., Zhang, M., Ni, L., Liu, P.: A multi-level self-adaptation approach for microservice systems. In: 2019 IEEE 4th International Conference on Cloud Computing and Big Data Analysis (ICCCBDA), pp. 498–502 (2019). https://doi.org/10.1109/ICCCBDA.2019.8725647

TiME: Time-Sensitive Multihop Data Transmission in Software-Defined Edge Networks for IoT

Simran Gurung[1](✉) and Ayan Mondal[2]

[1] Department of Computer Science, St. Xavier's College, Kolkata, India
simrangurung1501@gmail.com
[2] Department of Computer Science and Engineering, Indian Institute of Technology Indore, Indore, India
ayanm@iiti.ac.in

Abstract. This work addresses the problem of optimal data transmission in a multi-hop edge network. In edge networks, IoT devices need to transmit data to the local processing units. However, having a short-range communication capacity, it is hard for IoT devices to transmit the data to the concerned processing edge devices. Hence, they mostly rely on multi-hop communication. There is no such scheme for multi-hop communication at the edge while ensuring timeliness. We envision that software-defined networking can help in solving the aforementioned problem. Hence, we proposed a software-defined edge architecture and designed a game theoretic model for optimal multi-hop data transmission. We use a dynamic coalition game to identify the optimal paths for data transmission in edge networks for IoT. The performance of the proposed scheme is also evaluated and compared with the existing literature.

Keywords: Edge networks · Multi-hop · IoT · Coalition · Game Theory

1 Introduction

Software-Defined Networking (SDN) is envisioned to overcome the constraints of traditional networking. In conventional networking, each device is configured with low-level and frequent vendor-specific instructions. Fault dynamics and load fluctuations in the network environments follow this configuration complexity. Real-time reconfiguration and response mechanisms are almost nonexistent in IP networks. Therefore, the researchers mentioned that SDN can play a crucial role. SDN separates the data plane from the control plane, making the network switches simple forwarding devices. This results in implementing the control logic in a logically centralized controller [12]. SDN simplifies policy enforcement, network reconfiguration, and evolution by implementing the control logic in physical devices depending upon the application-specific requirements in real-time [4]. On

S. Casteleyn et al. (Eds.): ICWE 2023 Workshops, CCIS 1898, pp. 44–54, 2024.
https://doi.org/10.1007/978-3-031-50385-6_4

the other hand, in the presence of numerous Internet of Things (IoT) devices, the amount of data generated increases significantly, which is to be delivered with a predefined time duration in the edge network. This is one of the essential issues in software-defined edge networks (SDEN).

In the existing literature, Mondal et al. [18] considered that the IoT devices are directly connected with the switches at the data plane. However, in reality, it may not always be possible. Therefore, the IoT devices at the edge rely on multi-hop communication. In this scenario, the intermediate IoT devices act as relay nodes and forward packets to the SDN switches in multiple hops [1–6]. Additionally, multi-hop communication is essential for transferring data to the SDN switches from ad-hoc IoT devices while ensuring reduced energy consumption. However, IoT data transmission in edge networks is challenging and fails to provide a global overview of the network topology. The end-to-end delay in data transmission also varies significantly in edge networks in the presence of mobile IoT devices. Hence, there is a need to design a scheme for time-sensitive data transmission in SDEN.

As observed by Fedor and Collier [8], introducing multiple hops in the path increases the network lifetime of the IoT networks. Though IoT-based real-time applications mainly rely on the reception of IoT data in a timely manner, data arrival is an exogenous process with less control over its arrival. The network performance depends on the data generation rate and transmission path parameters. In the existing literature, viz. [1,4,8,25], the researchers studied the optimal data generation rate. However, the effects of optimal path selection on timely data transfer are not studied extensively. An ideal situation would be to receive an update at the destination the moment it was generated at a source, but this is not possible because of the fact that the other updates queued up waiting for their own transmission. Additionally, a stale data packet cannot be used [24]. Hence, we argue that high throughput and minimal delay are not enough to measure the timeliness of an update, so another metric was introduced by Kaul et al. [9,10] known as the Age of Information (AoI) that measures the time that has passed since the freshest generated packet of data. This motivates us to devise a scheme for optimal flow-rule placement in SDEN that ensures the timeliness of end-to-end data transfer. We propose a dynamic coalition formation game theoretic scheme for time-sensitive multi-hop data transmission in SDENs. To summarize, the contributions in this work are as follows:

1. We designed a time-sensitive multi-hop data transmission scheme, named TiME, for the software-defined edge networks. We used a dynamic coalition formation game to model the proposed scheme mathematically.
2. We evaluated the performance of TiME through simulation while comparing it with the existing scheme.

2   Related Work

The existing literature is divided into flow-rule placement and flow-space utilization which are discussed in this section.

2.1 Flow-Rule Placement

Bera *et al.* [2] devised an adaptive flow-rule placement scheme and solved as a max-flow-min-cost optimization problem using a greedy heuristic approach. They also used Integer Linear Programming (ILP) to select the optimal flow rules to minimize the number of exact-match flow rules in the network. Lastly, a rule distribution algorithm was formulated to assign a more significant number of flows in the network, thereby decreasing rule congestion in the network. In [17], Mondal *et al.* proposed a scheme, FlowMan, using generalized Nash bargaining game to ensure high throughput and low delay in a heterogeneous Software-Defined Internet of Things (SDIoT) environment. The authors observed that FlowMan could effectively boost network throughput while reducing network delay while optimizing the flows in each hop. In another work, Bera *et al.* [3] proposed a mobility-aware adaptive flow-rule placement scheme, Mobi-Flow, for Software Defined Access Networks (SDANs) that predicted the future location of users by using the Markov predictor. Based on these predicted locations, flow rules are installed at those access points (APs), minimizing delay, and controlling overhead, energy consumption, and cost in the network. In [11], Khoobbakht *et al.* proposed a hybrid rule placement algorithm to effectively utilize the flow table's limited space and decrease the controller's load. The proactive and reactive methods are combined in the algorithm to reduce the signaling overhead on the controller, reducing the network's reaction time to network changes. In Ref. [13], Kyung proposed a mobility-aware prioritized flow-rule placement scheme that classifies delay-sensitive flows in SDAN directly affecting the users' QoS experience. The prioritized delay-sensitive flows are pre-installed into the target forwarding devices minimizing unnecessary rule placement.

Nguyen *et al.* [19] applied deep reinforcement learning (DRL) to design an adaptive flow-rule placement system, DeepPlace, in SDIoT networks. This scheme provided a very detailed analysis on the network traffic along with increasing the QoS in traffic flows in the network. Another rule placement algorithm using Deep Reinforcement Learning (DRL) and traffic prediction is studied by Bouzid *et al.* [5]. The authors used Long Short-Term Memory (LSTM) prediction method and ILP to solve the flow-rule placement problem. Misra *et al.* [16] designed a traffic forwarding scheme for a software-defined healthcare network. They used machine learning to identify the criticality of the flow in the presence of mobile devices. In [22], Saha *et al.* devised a QoS-aware adaptive flow-rule aggregation scheme in SDIoT network. This scheme uses a Best-fit heuristic approach for fast aggregation and sufficient reduction in the number of flow rules without degrading the QoS of IoT traffic. In another work, Saha *et al.* [23] proposed a QoS-aware flow-rule aggregation scheme for a generic network topology for improving the QoS of IoT applications by aggregating the flow rules adaptively. The proposed scheme applies a path selection heuristic to increase the total number of flow rules that can be accommodated in the network and a flow-rule aggregation scheme, concurrently enhancing the QoS of fresh IoT flows. Mimidis-Kentis *et al.* [15] devised a flow-rule placement algorithm that utilized both the software and hardware flow tables. The authors devised a placement algorithm to implement for the Open Network Operating System (ONOS) SDN controller, and it was validated on an SDN testbed. A larger number of flows could be accommodated at the SDN switches without much degradation in the network performance and no packet loss. Saha *et al.* [21] proposed a traffic-aware QoS routing scheme in SDIoT network, which considers two types of routing techniques- delay-sensitive that deals with delay-sensitive flows and loss-sensitive, that deals with loss-sensitive flows for incoming packets from the applications. This scheme is proposed to reduce end-to-end delay and the percentage of flows. The optimal forwarding path is computed based on a greedy method, and the SDN controller implements sufficient flow rules at the forwarding devices in the network.

2.2   Flow-Space Utilization

Lu *et al.* [14] proposed a scheme known as TF-IdleTimeout that configures the flow entry lifecycle following the real-time traffic network in an SDN-based data center network. Two criteria- Flow Entry Missing Number and Flow Dropping Number were applied in this scheme to improve the utilization efficiency of ternary content-addressable memory (TCAM) capacity in SDN. In [20], Panda *et al.* proposed a dynamic way to allocate a hard timeout value for each flow entry. This flow entry considers both predictable and unpredictable flow properties. The dynamically assigned hard timeout method proves more effective than the statically assigned hard timeout. Chen and Lin [7] devised a scheme for flow-rule placement for maximum packet throughput. This can reduce the TCAM utilization as a whole but also increase the link bandwidth if the packet gets dropped before it reaches the switch where its associated rule is already placed. So, this study offers a trade-off between the space utilization of TCAM and bandwidth exhaustion in SDN. The authors in [26] presented a routing scheme to ensure minimal entries at the switches and high resource utilization.

Synthesis. After a detailed analysis of the existing research work, we observe a research gap in the flow-rule placement schemes while considering multiple hops in SDEN. Multiple hops in the network can reduce power consumption for distant transmissions. However, the existing literature has only focused on single-hop network transmissions. Therefore, we aim to devise an optimal flow-rule placement scheme that ensures end-to-end throughput and minimal delay in SDENs.

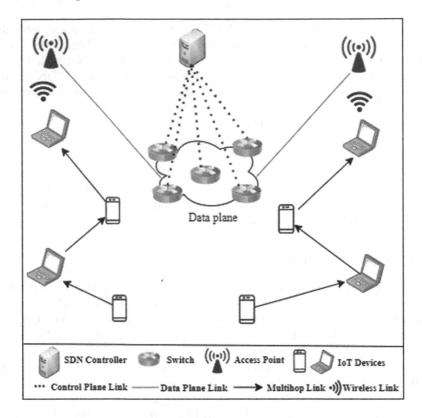

Fig. 1. Schematic Diagram of SDEN Architecture

3   System Model

We consider an SDEN to have a centralized controller that is connected with a set of switches S through the control plane. Figure 1 presents a multi-hop connection between the APs and the terminal IoT devices. We represent the flow association as $F(A, N)$, where A denotes the set of APs and N denotes the set of IoT devices present in the network. Each IoT device $n \in N$ is connected to a switch in the data plane through the APs where each of the APs $a \in A$ communicates with a set of switches s_a where s_a is a subset of S and set of switches is denoted by S. These APs forward the data traffic generated by each IoT device to the SDN switches, where the latter process the data according to the flow rules installed into them by the controller. After processing, the switches transmit the data to the backhaul network for additional processing. In case of a mismatch, metadata for the data traffic is sent to the controller for installing the corresponding flow rules at the switches.

We consider various parameters for each IoT device and the SDN switches, such as energy consumption, data rate, the capacity of each switch, the throughput of each flow, and the delay associated with it. Apart from maximizing the throughput and minimizing the delay associated with each flow, low energy consumption and optimal utilization of TCAM space of each SDN switch are also essential for ensuring the QoS of the network. We assume that each IoT device $n \in N$ generates $F_n(t)$ number of flows at time instant t. We consider that there is adequate space in switches S to accommodate $\sum_n F_n(t)$ number of flow rules so that $\sum_n F_n(t) \leq \sum_{s \in S} F_s^{max}$, where F_s^{max} is the maximum number of flow-rules that can be installed at switch s. It is also crucial to generate the optimal data rate to avoid clogging the network or delay in receiving network updates. If the rate of data generation for each flow $f_n(t) \in F_n(t)$ is $r_n(t)$, then the throughput of an SDN switch s can be represented as:

$$T_s(t) = \sum_{f_n(t) \in F_s(t)} r_n(t) \tag{1}$$

where $F_s(t)$ represents the flow rules installed at switch s.

We assume that for each IoT device n, there exists a communication range R_n. Hence, the nodes that lie within this range are considered the neighboring nodes. If the amount of energy a node requires to transmit data is E_n, the constraint — $E_n \leq E_r$ — should be satisfied, where E_r is the amount of residual energy of a node. Additionally, the end-to-end delay for each hop must satisfy the constraint — $[\sum_{N-1} d_{ij} \leq D_{N-1}]$, where d_{ij} is the delay associated with the edge that is formed by the ith and j^{th} nodes in the network and D_{N-1} is the delay threshold for a particular application with $N-1$ representing the total number of hops in the network with N as the set of nodes.

4   TiME: The Proposed Time-Sensitive Multihop Data Transmission Scheme

In TiME, we try to inculcate optimal flow-rule placement at the switches for time-bound data transfer. To accomplish the same, we use a dynamic coalition-formation game theoretic model. A coalition formation game is said to be dynamic when the nature of the game can alter due to environmental factors such as the mobility of the user nodes or the deployment of new users. We are utilizing a dynamic coalition-formation game theoretic model to control these changes. Two players can be in a particular coalition: the source node and the intermediate node. If cooperating with a user device, i.e., a node, can boost the overall payoff that the participating users can accomplish, then the merging occurs between the devices, starting with the nearest neighbor. If there are two coalitions and the distances of each of the coalitions from a particular AP with co-ordinates (a_x, a_y) are α_i and α_j respectively, applying the Euclidean distance formula, we get-

$$\alpha_i = \sqrt{(x_1 - a_x)^2 + (y_1 - a_y)^2}$$
$$\alpha_j = \sqrt{(x_2 - a_x)^2 + (y_2 - a_y)^2}$$

where (x_1, y_1) and (x_2, y_2) are the respective co-ordinates of the two coalitions. If $\alpha_i \geq \alpha_j$, then the first coalition is preferred; otherwise, the second coalition is preferred. We form a coalition structure that aims at maximizing the total utility keeping the following points in mind:

- The utility function of a node i where i is an intermediate node signifies the effect of latency incurred during transmission.
- The delay associated with the network has a negative impact on the utility function. The payoff decreases if the delay in the network increases.
- With the increase in the bandwidth-delay product, the payoff also increases, where δB_i represents the bandwidth-delay product associated with the intermediate node i.
- The payoff decreases with the increase in energy consumption associated with each hop.

Therefore, we construct utility function $U_i(t)$ as follows:

$$U_i(t) = \frac{B_{r,i}}{B_i} + \frac{D_{N-1}}{d_{ij}} + \frac{E_{r,i}}{E_i} \tag{2}$$

where $B_{r,i}$ and $E_{r,i}$ represent the residual bandwidth associated with the node i and the residual energy of the node i, respectively.

4.1   Proposed Algorithm

The proposed scheme, TiME, aims to ensure the timeliness of transferring data in SDENs through optimal placement of flow rules, as presented in Algorithm 1. A dynamic coalition-formation game theoretic approach is used for the above objective. The algorithm is formulated on the idea of the *Merge and Split* algorithm, where we merge the players to form a coalition that maximizes the utility function. If the utility is not maximized, we split the coalition and move on to other players for merging to ensure maximum utility in the game.

Complexity Analysis. In the algorithm, the time complexity of the outer *for* loop in line 1 is $O(N)$ as it runs for N times. For every iteration of this outer loop, the inner *for* loop in line 2 runs for $(N - i)$ times. The time complexity is $O(1)$ for all other lines. Therefore the overall time complexity of the algorithm is $O(N^2)$.

5   Performance Evaluation

The performance of the proposed scheme is measured by comparing it with the existing scheme, TROD [18]. In TROD, Mondal *et al.* proposed a scheme for dynamic data traffic management in SDNs in the presence of IoT devices ensuring optimal throughput and minimal latency in the network (Fig. 2).

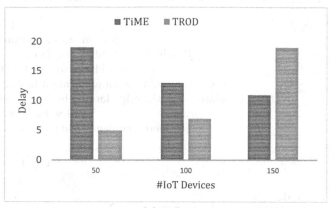

(a) Delay

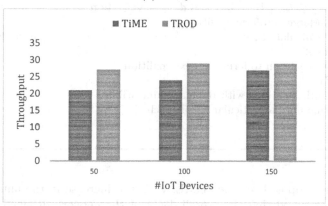

(b) Throughput

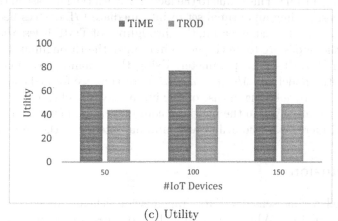

(c) Utility

Fig. 2. Performance Evaluation

Algorithm 1. Determining throughput ensuring optimal delay

INPUTS:

1: N ⊳ Set of nodes
2: R_i ⊳ Communication range of node i
3: $B_{r,i}$ ⊳ Residual bandwidth associated with the node i
4: B_i ⊳ Bandwidth associated with the node i
5: D_{N-1} ⊳ Delay threshold for an application having $N-1$ hops
6: $d_{i,j}$ ⊳ Delay associated with the edge formed by the ith and j^{th} nodes
7: $E_{r,i}$ ⊳ Residual energy of node i
8: E_i ⊳ Energy consumption associated with node i

OUTPUTS:

1: U_i ⊳ Payoff at equilibrium

METHOD:

1: **for** Each $i \in N$ **do**
2:     **for** Each $j \in N/\{i\}$ and j lies in R_i **do**
3:         **if** $E_j \leq E_{r,j}$, $B_j \leq B_{r,j}$ and $d_{ij} \leq D_{N-1}$ **then**
4:             Merge and form coalition
5:             Calculate U_i ⊳ using Equation (2)
6:         **end if**
7:         split coalition to form the next coalition
8:     **end for**
9:     Choose the coalition with the maximum utility
10:     Continue until a particular AP is reached.
11: **end for**
12: **return** U_i

Using the proposed scheme, TiME, with the increase in the number of IoT devices, we observed that the overall delay of the network dropped more compared to using TROD. This is due to the fact that with the increase in the number of IoT devices, finding an optimal set of intermediate IoT devices becomes efficient. However, for the same reason, the throughput of TiME is less than TROD. In TROD, the nodes are to be chosen to maximize the throughput, and delay is not considered a constraint parameter. Using the dynamic coalition-formation game-theoretic model and *Merge and Split* algorithm, we formed coalitions with the user devices by merging in case of maximum payoff and splitting in case of a decrease in overall payoff in the multihop communication network. This resulted in an overall increase in the utility and minimal latency in the network.

6   Conclusion

We proposed a time-sensitive data transmission scheme for edge networks in the presence of IoT. While considering IoT devices are connected with edge computing nodes in multi-hop communication, we evaluated the significance of SDN in edge networks for IoT. Thereafter, we proposed a game theory-based mathematical model, TiME, to identify the optimal path between the source and destination edge nodes. We highlighted the choice of a dynamic coalition game for the same. Thereafter, we evaluated the performance of the proposed scheme, TiME, while comparing it with the existing scheme. We observed that TiME improves the performance latency significantly while ensuring optimal throughput.

In the future, this work can be extended to improve the throughput of the multi-hop edge networks while serving delay-critical applications. This work also can be extended while considering the dependency among the edge devices.

Acknowledgement. This work was supported by the IIT Indore Young Faculty Research Seed Grant (YFRSG) Scheme (Grant No: IITI/YFRSG/2022-23/12).

References

1. Abdel Hamid, S., Hassanein, H.S., Takahara, G., Abdel Hamid, S., Hassanein, H.S., Takahara, G.: Introduction to wireless multi-hop networks. In: Routing for Wireless Multi-Hop Networks. SBCS, pp. 1–9. Springer, New York, NY (2013). https://doi.org/10.1007/978-1-4614-6357-3_1
2. Bera, S., Misra, S., Jamalipour, A.: Flowstat: adaptive flow-rule placement for per-flow statistics in SDN. IEEE J. Sel. Areas Commun. **37**(3), 530–539 (2019). https://doi.org/10.1109/JSAC.2019.2894239
3. Bera, S., Misra, S., Obaidat, M.S.: Mobi-flow: mobility-aware adaptive flow-rule placement in software-defined access network. IEEE Trans. Mob. Comput. **18**(8), 1831–1842 (2019). https://doi.org/10.1109/TMC.2018.2868932
4. Bera, S., Misra, S., Vasilakos, A.V.: Software-defined networking for internet of things: a survey. IEEE Internet Things J. **4**(6), 1994–2008 (2017). https://doi.org/10.1109/JIOT.2017.2746186
5. Bouzidi, E.H., Outtagarts, A., Langar, R.: Deep reinforcement learning application for network latency management in software defined networks. In: 2019 IEEE Global Communications Conference (GLOBECOM), pp. 1–6. IEEE (2019)
6. Braun, T., Kassler, A., Kihl, M., Rakocevic, V., Siris, V., Heijenk, G.: Multihop wireless networks. Traffic and QoS Management in Wireless Multimedia Networks: COST 290 Final Report, pp. 201–265 (2009)
7. Chen, Y.W., Lin, Y.H.: Study of rule placement schemes for minimizing TCAM space and effective bandwidth utilization in SDN. In: 2018 6th International Conference on Future Internet of Things and Cloud Workshops (FiCloudW), pp. 21–27. IEEE (2018)
8. Fedor, S., Collier, M.: On the problem of energy efficiency of multi-hop vs one-hop routing in wireless sensor networks. In: 21st International Conference on Advanced Information Networking and Applications Workshops (AINAW'07), vol. 2, pp. 380–385 (2007). https://doi.org/10.1109/AINAW.2007.272
9. Kaul, S., Gruteser, M., Rai, V., Kenney, J.: Minimizing age of information in vehicular networks. In: Proceedings of the 8th Annual IEEE Communications Society Conference on Sensor, Mesh and Ad Hoc Communications and Networks, pp. 350–358 (2011). https://doi.org/10.1109/SAHCN.2011.5984917
10. Kaul, S., Yates, R., Gruteser, M.: Real-time status: how often should one update? In: Proceedings of IEEE INFOCOM, pp. 2731–2735 (2012). https://doi.org/10.1109/INFCOM.2012.6195689

11. Khoobbakht, M., Noei, M., Parvizimosaed, M.: Hybrid flow-rule placement method of proactive and reactive in SDNs. In: Proceedings of the 11th International Conference on Computer Engineering and Knowledge (ICCKE), pp. 121–127 (2021). https://doi.org/10.1109/ICCKE54056.2021.9721507
12. Kreutz, D., Ramos, F.M.V., Veríssimo, P.E., Rothenberg, C.E., Azodolmolky, S., Uhlig, S.: Software-defined networking: a comprehensive survey. Proc. IEEE **103**(1), 14–76 (2015). https://doi.org/10.1109/JPROC.2014.2371999
13. Kyung, Y.: Mobility-aware prioritized flow rule placement in software-defined access networks. In: 2021 International Conference on Information Networking (ICOIN), pp. 59–61 (2021). https://doi.org/10.1109/ICOIN50884.2021.9333854
14. Lu, M., Deng, W., Shi, Y.: TF-Idletimeout: improving efficiency of TCAM in SDN by dynamically adjusting flow entry lifecycle. In: 2016 IEEE International Conference on Systems, Man, and Cybernetics (SMC), pp. 002681–002686. IEEE (2016)
15. Mimidis-Kentis, A., Pilimon, A., Soler, J., Berger, M., Ruepp, S.: A novel algorithm for flow-rule placement in SDN switches. In: Proceedings of the 4th IEEE Conference on Network Softwarization and Workshops (NetSoft), pp. 1–9 (2018). https://doi.org/10.1109/NETSOFT.2018.8459979
16. Misra, S., Saha, R., Ahmed, N.: Health-flow: criticality-aware flow control for SDN-based healthcare IoT. In: GLOBECOM 2020–2020 IEEE Global Communications Conference, pp. 1–6 (2020). https://doi.org/10.1109/GLOBECOM42002.2020.9348058
17. Mondal, A., Misra, S.: Flowman: QoS-aware dynamic data flow management in software-defined networks. IEEE J. Sel. Areas Commun. **38**(7), 1366–1373 (2020)
18. Mondal, A., Misra, S., Chakraborty, A.: TROD: throughput-optimal dynamic data traffic management in software-defined networks. In: 2018 IEEE Globecom Workshops (GC Wkshps), pp. 1–6. IEEE (2018)
19. Nguyen, T.G., Phan, T.V., Hoang, D.T., Nguyen, H.H., Le, D.T.: Deepplace: deep reinforcement learning for adaptive flow rule placement in software-defined IoT networks. Comput. Commun. **181**, 156–163 (2022). https://doi.org/10.1016/j.comcom.2021.10.006
20. Panda, A., Samal, S.S., Turuk, A.K., Panda, A., Venkatesh, V.C.: Dynamic hard timeout based flow table management in openflow enabled SDN. In: 2019 International Conference on Vision Towards Emerging Trends in Communication and Networking (ViTECoN), pp. 1–6. IEEE (2019)
21. Saha, N., Bera, S., Misra, S.: Sway: traffic-aware QoS routing in software-defined IoT. IEEE Trans. Emerg. Top. Comput. **9**(1), 390–401 (2018)
22. Saha, N., Misra, S., Bera, S.: QoS-aware adaptive flow-rule aggregation in software-defined IoT. In: 2018 IEEE Global Communications Conference (GLOBECOM), pp. 206–212. IEEE (2018)
23. Saha, N., Misra, S., Bera, S.: Q-flag: qos-aware flow-rule aggregation in software-defined IoT networks. IEEE Internet Things J. **9**(7), 4899–4906 (2022). https://doi.org/10.1109/JIOT.2021.3113777
24. Talak, R., Karaman, S., Modiano, E.: Optimizing information freshness in wireless networks under general interference constraints. IEEE/ACM Trans. Netw. **28**(1), 15–28 (2020). https://doi.org/10.1109/TNET.2019.2946481
25. Zeng, K., Lou, W., Li, M.: Multihop Wireless Networks: Opportunistic Routing, vol. 25. John Wiley & Sons, Hoboken (2011)
26. Zhang, S.Q., et al.: TCAM space-efficient routing in a software defined network. Comput. Netw. **125**, 26–40 (2017)

DELCAS: Deep Reinforcement Learning Based GPU CaaS Packet Scheduling for Stabilizing QoE in 5G Multi-Access Edge Computing

Changha Lee(✉)(iD), Kyungchae Lee(iD), Gyusang Cho(iD), and Chan-Hyun Youn(iD)

School of Electrical Engineering, KAIST, Daejeon, Republic of Korea
{changha.lee,kyungchae.lee,gyusang.cho,chyoun}@kaist.ac.kr

Abstract. Recently, Docker Container as a Service (CaaS) has been provided for multi-user services in the 5G Multi-Access Edge Computing (MEC) environment, and servers that support accelerators such as GPUs, not conventional CPU servers, are being considered. In addition, as the number of AI services is increasing and the computation power required by deep neural network model increases, offloading to edge servers is required due to insufficient computational capacity and heat problem of user devices (UE). However, there is a resource scheduling problem because all users' packets cannot be offloaded to the edge server due to resource limitations. To address this problem, we suggest deep reinforcement learning-based GPU CaaS Packet scheduling named as *Delcas* for stabilizing quality of AI experience. First, we design the architecture using containerized target AI application on MEC GPUs and multiple users send video stream to MEC server. We evaluate video stream to identify the dynamic amount of resource requirement among each users using optical flow and adjust user task queue. To satisfy equal latency quality of experience, we apply lower quality first serve approach and respond hand pose estimation results to each user. Finally, we evaluate our approach and compare to conventional scheduling method in the aspect of both accuracy and latency quality.

Keywords: 5G MEC · Task Offloading · Deep Reinforcement Learning

1 Introduction

The rise of 5G networks has unlocked new opportunities for communication and computing, enabling ultra-low latency, high bandwidth, and massive connectivity. This has paved the way for advancements in various domains, including edge computing, virtualization, the Internet of Things (IoT), and immersive user experiences. In particular, the integration of 5G with multi-access edge computing (MEC) and virtualization has emerged as a promising paradigm for efficient

---

Supported by Samsung Network (SNIC) and BK21.

and scalable computing at the network edge, with the potential to revolution-
ize applications that require real-time interaction between humans and artificial
intelligence (AI) [1, 2].

The concept of the metaverse, a virtual universe where users can interact
with digital environments and virtual beings, has gained significant attention
in recent years. As the metaverse continues to evolve and expand, realistic and
natural human interaction within this virtual space becomes crucial for creating
immersive and engaging experiences [3]. Hand pose estimation, which involves
estimating the 3D position and configuration of a user's hand in real-time, plays a
pivotal role in enabling realistic hand gestures and interactions in the metaverse
[4]. Hand pose estimation has numerous practical applications, including virtual and augmented reality, gaming, human-computer interaction, sign language
recognition, and robotics, among others [5]. The ability to accurately estimate
hand poses in real-time is critical for enabling natural and intuitive interactions
between humans and AI systems in immersive virtual environments, where users
can interact with virtual objects and manipulate them using hand gestures [6–8].

To achieve real-time and accurate hand pose estimation in immersive user
experiences, the integration of 5G, MEC, virtualization (with a focus on
containerization), and COTS hardware, including Graphics Processing Units
(GPUs), has become a topic of significant interest [9]. The advent of **5G networks** has brought about significant advancements in the field of communication
and computing, enabling ultra-low latency, high bandwidth, and massive connectivity [10,11]. **Multi-access edge computing (MEC)** refers to the deployment
of computing resources, including servers, storage, and networking, at the edge
of the communication network, closer to the end-users and devices. This allows
for the processing and analysis of data in close proximity to the source, reducing latency, bandwidth consumption, and reliance on centralized cloud resources
[12,13]. **Virtualization** involves the abstraction of physical resources into virtualized instances that can be dynamically allocated and managed, providing
flexibility, scalability, and resource optimization [14,15]. **Commercial off-the-
shelf (COTS)** hardware, which includes standard computing components and
systems, has gained significant attention as a cost-effective and scalable solution
for implementing MEC and virtualization in 5G networks [16]. COTS hardware
offers the advantage of leveraging widely available and affordable off-the-shelf
components, which can be easily deployed and scaled in diverse environments
[17]. COTS-based solutions can foster innovation, interoperability, and vendor-
agnostic platform, enabling a vibrant ecosystem of applications and services.
Containerization, specifically container as a service (CaaS), is an emerging
virtualization technology that allows for lightweight and portable deployment
of software applications, encapsulating them in self-contained containers that
can be easily deployed, scaled, and managed across different COTS computing
environments [18].

In this paper, we aim to investigate of the multi-user offloading packet inter-
gpu scheduling for our target AI application to satisfy service level objective in
5G multi-access edge computing. Inspired by DRL-based previous work, we ana-

lyze multi-user AI application offloading task and suggest a deep reinforcement learning based scheduling algorithm for stable quality of experience in terms of accuracy and latency. We evaluate our proposed method in experiment section and conclude the paper.

2   Related Work

Optical Flow Computation. To identify the amount of offloading resources in hand pose estimation, we need to extract movement information in the first person view because if the hand moves quickly, more resources must be served to process more frames to increase accuracy. Therefore, we are going to refer to optical flow computation. Optical flow estimation has been extensively studied in computer vision literature, with numerous techniques proposed over the years. Traditional techniques [19,20], are based on classical optimization or differential techniques and are widely used due to their simplicity and low computational requirements.

Resource Controller Based on Deep Reinforcement Learning. Deep reinforcement learning has shown promising results in resource scheduling and resource allocation problems, where the goal is to optimize the allocation of limited resources, such as CPU, GPU, or memory, to different tasks or processes to achieve a specific objective, such as maximizing performance, minimizing energy consumption, or reducing computation time. The previous research [21,22], which combined Q-learning with deep neural networks and genetic algorithms to learn optimal control policies in an end-to-end manner. However, applying deep reinforcement learning to utilize MEC services for large-scale users is very difficult due to resource limitations and trade-off between accuracy and latency in real-world case. To address these challenges, we carefully design the AI application system using MEC and introduce how to provide stable QoE with accuracy and latency in the next section.

3   Methodology

3.1   System Overview

Figure 1 shows an proposed architecture that can estimate the computing resources required for multi-user hand posture estimation. For each user equipment UE_i send video stream to MEC server through 5G base station (gNB) and user plane function (UPF). Based on this, we propose task scheduling to provide stable quality of experience for multiple requests of deep learning model computation in a containerized GPU Pool in a 5G MEC environment.

First, we need to train deep reinforcement learning-based network to predict the urgency score, which depicts the relative amount of computing resource requirements among multiple user input streams to stabilize accuracy quality in *Phase 1*. After training urgency prediction network in phase-1, we use DRL-based model inference results to adjust served resource ratio according to multiple user in *Phase 2*. We will explain details in the next phase sections.

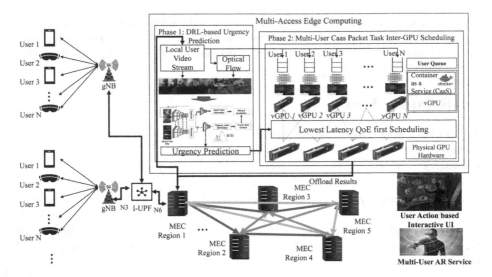

Fig. 1. The overview of the proposed architecture. Phase 1 predicts the urgency score, which depicts the relative amount of computing resource requirements among multiple user input streams and Phase 2 shows multi-user CaaS Packet Inter-GPU scheduling

3.2 Problem Setting

In this paper, some of the environmental conditions for target applications (hand posture estimation) of extended reality (XR) through 5G MEC offloading service are assumed as follows:

1. The amount of computational resources required to provide the same QoE varies according to the dynamically changing movement of multiple users.
2. 5G MEC GPU servers are computationally more powerful than XR devices, but computing resources may be limited.
3. The 5G MEC GPU server supports container-based virtualization and can provide CaaS to users by virtualizing GPU resources.

In the assumption above, multiple user equipment $UE = \{ue_1, ..., ue_N\}$ send video stream $X = \{x_1, ..., x_N\}$ to edge server and call for DL model-based estimation of their hand pose in the first person view. This paper proposes adaptive GPU resource scheduling, focusing on offloading scenarios of 5G MEC in the task of estimating hand posture.

3.3 Hand Pose Estimation and Optical Flow

Hand Pose Estimation CaaS. For hand pose estimation container as a service, we refer to a lightweight hand pose estimation model based on deep neural network [23], denoted by f_{hpe}. Let the hand pose result is Y_i, then the result is presented by the point set $\{k^1, ..., k^m\}$ where $k \in \mathbb{R}^3$ representing three dimensional coordinates and m means the number of hand joint. Due to end-to-end running in DL application, we can obtain the result from input stream $Y_i = f_{hpe}(X_i) = \{k^1, ..., k^m\}$ where i is a user index and X_i is input data of the user. This hand pose estimation application is deployed on the nvidia-docker container.

Optical Flow Application. To predict the workload of hand pose estimation for stable QoE, we utilize optical flow function f_{of} with reference to [24]. When input image X_i for each user i is given, we tried to extract magnitude m and direction v of the pixel displacement by the optical flow function, $(m, v) = f_{of}(X_i, X_{i-1})$.

3.4   Urgency Score

To demonstrate the workload relation between optical flow and hand pose estimation, we conducted preliminary experiment to figure out the relation between the magnitude of optical flow and two metrics.

Figure 2 shows the result of linear regression according to magnitude of optical flow. X-axis shows magnitude of optical flow and Y-axis presents two metrics, required resources and mean square error (MSE) of hand pose estimation. Our observation through experiment means that the magnitude of optical flow is positively correlated to both required resources and the quality of hand pose estimation. Therefore, we proposed an urgency predictor as follows:

$$\mu = f_\mu(f_{of}(X_i, X_{i-1}); \theta) \tag{1}$$

where θ is trainable parameters to reduce the MSE of hand pose estimation by adjusting allocated resources according to urgency score for each user.

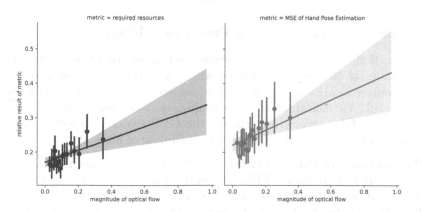

Fig. 2. The linear regression result according to optical flow. X-axis shows the normalized magnitude of optical flow and Y-axis presents the normalized metric of both required resources (blue) and the hand pose estimation error (orange). The light colored region around the each line represents 95% confidence interval. (Color figure online)

3.5   Phase 1: DRL-Based Multi-User Input Stream Control

In this section, we first introduce the deep reinforcement learning based Multi-Agent Resource Coordination (MARCO) agent proposed in our previous works [25,26] to dynamically allocate computational resources to multiple users based on their urgency scores, which results in heterogeneous user inference rates.

This phase aims to control the user inference rates where users with relatively high urgency (e.g. fast movements in object detection or hand-pose estimation) gets higher inference rate capacity given the limited amount of the edge-server resources, thus improving the user experience. We enable options such as optical flow-based motion information, golden baseline, and static-scheduling baseline in the MARCO agent's reward function to improve its training stability and performance.

Here, the golden baseline refers to the accuracy achieved when the server can handle all frame requests under the ideal assumption of an infinite resource situation. We defined a reward function that minimizes the decrease in accuracy obtained during the finite resource scheduling in our experiment, as shown in the Eq. (2). Additionally, we also used the relative reward advantage compared to the static-scheduling case as our objective to further ensure better convergence as following Eq. (3). Details of the reward formulation can be found in [25].

$$R_{golden} = \frac{1}{m} \frac{\sum_{i=1}^{m} (Y_i - \hat{Y_i^*})^2 - (Y_i - \hat{Y_i})^2}{\sum_{i=1}^{m} (Y_i - \hat{Y_i^*})^2} \tag{2}$$

$$\begin{aligned} R_{final} &= R_{golden} - R_{static} \\ &= \frac{1}{m} \frac{\sum_{i=1}^{m} (Y_i - \hat{Y_i^s})^2 - (Y_i - \hat{Y_i})^2}{\sum_{i=1}^{m} (Y_i - \hat{Y_i^*})^2} \end{aligned} \tag{3}$$

3.6   Phase 2: Multi-User CaaS Packet Scheduling

In this section, we introduce containerized AI application task scheduling for equal quality of latency. Following assumption in this paper, we have limited GPU resources in MEC server. Therefore, we need to apply GPU virtualization because GPU virtualization allows multiple users or containers to share the same physical GPU, effectively utilizing the GPU resources. Figure 3 shows an illustration of the proposed CaaS packet scheduling of phase 2.

GPU Containerization. To virtualize GPU resources using Docker containers [27], a technology called *NVIDIA Docker* can be used. NVIDIA Docker is an extension of the Docker containerization platform that provides GPU virtualization capabilities. It allows Docker containers to access and utilize GPUs on the host system, enabling GPU-accelerated computing within containers. The NVIDIA Docker runtime includes the necessary GPU drivers, libraries, and tools required for GPU-accelerated computing. Docker containers with GPU support can be deployed to a host system with NVIDIA Docker runtime installed. The containers can specify the required GPU resources, such as the number of GPUs,

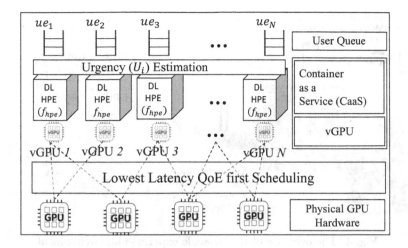

Fig. 3. Illustration of multi-user CaaS packet scheduling in phase 2.

GPU memory, and GPU device IDs, using Docker command line options. In this paper, for full GPU utilization, main scheduler container possesses all GPU and has the permission to allocate GPU to each users. Each user AI application container has its owned queue denoted by $vGPUReq_{ue_i}$.

The best way to improve accuracy is always calculating the hand joint position, but due to the prior assumption that the resource is insufficient, it is impossible to measure the hand joint position in all users' video streams. To allocate resource efficiently, we utilize the urgency obtained by the DRL network. From the urgency μ_i, we compute the urgency ratio set U as follows:

$$U = \{U_1, ..., U_i, ..., U_N\}$$
$$= \{\frac{e^{\mu_1}}{\sum_{i=1}^{N} e^{\mu_i}}, ..., \frac{e^{\mu_i}}{\sum_{i=1}^{N} e^{\mu_i}}, ..., \frac{e^{\mu_N}}{\sum_{i=1}^{N} e^{\mu_i}}\} \tag{4}$$

where the sum of urgency ratio element is $\sum_i U_i = 1$ and $U_i \leq 1$.

As the hand pose estimation service can not be provided among all video stream $X = \{X_1, ..., X_i\}$, the efficient input stream $\hat{X}_i^*$ in which the hand joint is to be predicted is adjusted according to the ratio as follows:

$$\hat{X}_i^* = U_i \times X_i \tag{5}$$

where $\hat{X}_i^* \leq X_i$. This efficient input stream will be pushed into virtualized request queue $vGPUReq_{ue_i}$. Then, the length of the user queue is given by $|vGPUReq_{ue_i}| = \hat{X}_i^*$.

Lowest Latency QoE First Scheduling. To provide the equal latency-QoE in the hand pose estimation application for multiple user, the user packet having larger queue length should be served first than the others. We define the Latency QoE, l_{qoe}^i as follows:

$$l_{qoe}^i = \alpha_i / |vGPUReq_{ue_i}| \tag{6}$$

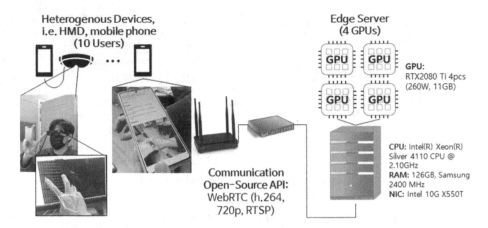

Fig. 4. The overview of the lab-scale experimental environment

where α_i presents a priority coefficient for user i. Equation (6) means that when a user i has larger queue length than the other users, the latency QoE will be the lowest and will be served first in our proposed architecture.

4   Experiment and Evaluation

In order to evaluate the performance of our proposed architecture, we implemented hand pose estimation model [23] on the nvidia-docker with Pytorch framework [28]. For real-time communication and supporting heterogeneous user device, we apply Web Real-Time Communication (Web-RTC), which is an open-source technology that enables real-time communication between browsers and mobile applications without the need for external plugins or software. By using WebRTC, video stream protocol follows Real Time Streaming Protocol (RTSP) in the format of H.264 and 720p. Figure 4 shows our lab experimental environment.

Comparable Method. Our proposed approach is compared and evaluated against a static scheduling method satisfying latency and a golden case method maximizing accuracy, in the aspect of both accuracy and latency. Static scheduling is designed by the best-effort to satisfy latency objective.

CaaS Objective. As following [29], the response delay of hand pose estimation is required to be less than 20 ms after physical hand movement. Therefore, our target service level objective in latency is 20 ms. Accuracy is to provide as high as possible by the refinement of the hand-pose observation model based on deep reinforcement learning, however the accuracy of our proposed method depends on the pre-trained model [23]. Therefore, we measured the relative average accuracy drop from the golden case.

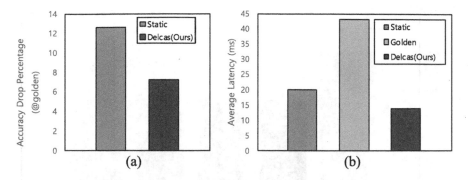

Fig. 5. Performance Result. **(a)** presents the average accuracy drop from the golden case. **(b)** shows the average latency among 10 users.

4.1   Evaluation Metric

We measure the accuracy according to the curve area under the percentage correct keypoints as known as AUC of PCK with the range of 20 mm to 50 mm by following [23]. For the latency measurement, we measure the elapsed time at edge server side because it is hard to evaluate exact time in client devices in video streaming via WebRTC. Although the frame rate may be slightly lower than that of the edge server on the client device, we measured the processing time per frame at the server stage because we confirmed that it was almost the same.

4.2   Performance Evaluation and Discussion

In this section, we discuss test results to evaluate the proposed method. The 10 users are served by 4 GPUs to predict their own hand pose. Figure 5 shows performance results on our target application.

Figure 5(a) shows the relative accuracy drop from golden case which estimates hand pose for every user inputs. In static scheduling, it shows average accuracy drop in 12.58%. This result is achieved by the best-effort scheduling to satisfy latency objective. However, the average accuracy drop in Delcas shows 7.24%, which is smaller than static scheduling.

Figure 5(b) represents the average latency among 10 users. The golden case meaning no accuracy drop shows 43.1 ms which is the largest response delay. However, the static scheduling and Delcas show that the latency is lower than 20 ms and the latency objective is satisfied. In static scheduling, the target latency is set to 20 ms, and the best-effort algorithm aims to maximize the served user images within the computational constraints. Delcas method shows average latency 13.75 ms which is faster than static scheduling. According to Fig. 5, our proposed method can achieve both lower accuracy drop and faster response delay than the best-effort scheduling.

To verify the standard deviation of latency for each physical GPU, we repeatedly evaluated the latency according to each GPUs. Figure 6 shows that the

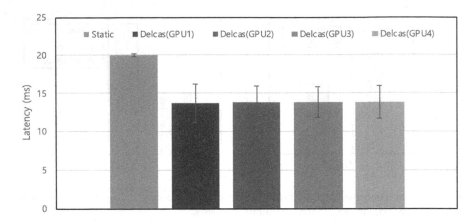

Fig. 6. The latency result for each physical resources (GPU). Orange bar represents the averaged latency according to each GPU in static scheduling method. Blue bar shows the latency and standard deviation of Delcas according to each GPUs. (Color figure online)

average latency among physical 4 GPUs. The averaged standard deviation of the latency in Best-effort scheduling shows 0.19 which is under 1% of average latency. Averaged standard deviation of Delcas is 2.19 which is 15.93% of average latency. This implies that the latency in Delcas dynamically varies significantly based on the specific circumstances of user input, as it is handled dynamically to accommodate different optical flow and hand pose movement.

5   Conclusion

In conclusion, we propose a novel approach for deep reinforcement learning-based GPU Container as a Service (CaaS) packet scheduling to enhance the quality of AI experience. With the increasing demand for AI services and the limitations of user devices in terms of computational capacity and heat dissipation, offloading to edge servers with accelerators such as GPUs has become crucial. However, due to resource constraints, not all users' packets can be offloaded to the edge server. To tackle this issue, we utilize optical flow-based evaluation of video stream to dynamically adjust the resource allocation for each user's task queue, while maintaining stable latency quality of experience through a lower quality first serve approach. Our approach is compared to conventional scheduling methods in terms of accuracy and latency quality, and the results demonstrate its effectiveness in stabilizing the quality of AI experience in the 5G MEC environment.

Acknowledgements. This work is supported in part by Samsung Electronics Co., Ltd and in part by BK21.

References

1. Cheng, R., Wu, N., Chen, S., Han, B.: Will metaverse be NextG internet? Vision, hype, and reality. IEEE Netw. **36**(5), 197–204 (2022)
2. Huang, Z., Xiong, C., Ni, H., Wang, D., Tao, Y., Sun, T.: Standard evolution of 5G-advanced and future mobile network for extended reality and metaverse. IEEE Internet Things Mag. **6**(1), 20–25 (2023)
3. Kozinets, R.V.: Immersive netnography: a novel method for service experience research in virtual reality, augmented reality and metaverse contexts. J. Serv. Manag. **34**(1), 100–125 (2023)
4. Park, S.M., Kim, Y.G.: A metaverse: taxonomy, components, applications, and open challenges. IEEE Access **10**, 4209–4251 (2022)
5. Chakraborty, B.K., Sarma, D., Bhuyan, M.K., MacDorman, K.F.: Review of constraints on vision-based gesture recognition for human-computer interaction. IET Comput. Vis. **12**(1), 3–15 (2018)
6. O'Hagan, R., Zelinsky, A., Rougeaux, S.: Visual gesture interfaces for virtual environments. Interact. Comput. **14**(3), 231–250 (2002)
7. Oprea, S., Martinez-Gonzalez, P., Garcia-Garcia, A., Castro-Vargas, J.A., Orts-Escolano, S., Garcia-Rodriguez, J.: A visually realistic grasping system for object manipulation and interaction in virtual reality environments. Comput. Graph. **83**, 77–86 (2019)
8. Yin, R., Wang, D., Zhao, S., Lou, Z., Shen, G.: Wearable sensors-enabled human-machine interaction systems: from design to application. Adv. Funct. Mater. **31**(11), 2008936 (2021)
9. Raj, P., Saini, K., Surianarayanan, C.: Edge/Fog Computing Paradigm: The Concept, Platforms and Applications. Academic Press, Cambridge (2022)
10. Attaran, M.: The impact of 5G on the evolution of intelligent automation and industry digitization. J. Ambient Intell. Humaniz. Comput. 1–17 (2021)
11. Sukhmani, S., Sadeghi, M., Erol-Kantarci, M., El Saddik, A.: Edge caching and computing in 5G for mobile AR/VR and tactile internet. IEEE Multimed. **26**(1), 21–30 (2018)
12. Premsankar, G., Di Francesco, M., Taleb, T.: Edge computing for the internet of things: a case study. IEEE Internet Things J. **5**(2), 1275–1284 (2018)
13. Marjanović, M., Antonić, A., Žarko, I.P.: Edge computing architecture for mobile crowdsensing. IEEE Access **6**, 10662–10674 (2018)
14. Gavrilovska, L., Rakovic, V., Denkovski, D.: From cloud ran to open ran. Wirel. Pers. Commun. **113**, 1523–1539 (2020)
15. Bonati, L., Polese, M., DOro, S., Basagni, S., Melodia, T.: Open, programmable, and virtualized 5G networks: state-of-the-art and the road ahead. Comput. Netw. **182**, 107516 (2020)
16. Iqbal, S., Hamamreh, J.M.: A comprehensive tutorial on how to practically build and deploy 5G networks using open-source software and general-purpose, off-the-shelf hardware. RS Open J. Innov. Commun. Tech **2**(6), 1–28 (2021)
17. Gallipeau, D., Kudrle, S.: Microservices: building blocks to new workflows and virtualization. SMPTE Motion Imaging J. **127**(4), 21–31 (2018)
18. Goniwada, S.R., Goniwada, S.R.: Containerization and virtualization. Cloud Native Architecture and Design: A Handbook for Modern Day Architecture and Design with Enterprise-Grade Examples, pp. 573–617 (2022)
19. Horn, B.K., Schunck, B.G.: Determining optical flow. Artif. Intell. **17**(1–3), 185–203 (1981)

20. Lucas, B.D., Kanade, T.: An iterative image registration technique with an application to stereo vision. In: IJCAI'81: 7th International Joint Conference on Artificial Intelligence, vol. 2, pp. 674–679 (1981)

21. Xue, F., Hai, Q., Dong, T., Cui, Z., Gong, Y.: A deep reinforcement learning based hybrid algorithm for efficient resource scheduling in edge computing environment. Inf. Sci. **608**, 362–374 (2022)

22. Yang, T., Hu, Y., Gursoy, M.C., Schmeink, A., Mathar, R.: Deep reinforcement learning based resource allocation in low latency edge computing networks. In: 2018 15th International Symposium on Wireless Communication Systems (ISWCS), pp. 1–5. IEEE (2018)

23. Zhou, Y., Habermann, M., Xu, W., Habibie, I., Theobalt, C., Xu, F.: Monocular real-time hand shape and motion capture using multi-modal data. In: Proceedings of the IEEE/CVF Conference on Computer Vision and Pattern Recognition, pp. 5346–5355 (2020)

24. Farnebäck, G.: Two-frame motion estimation based on polynomial expansion. In: Bigun, J., Gustavsson, T. (eds.) Image Analysis. SCIA 2003. LNCS, vol. 2749, pp. 363–370. Springer, Berlin, Heidelberg (2003). https://doi.org/10.1007/3-540-45103-X_50

25. Lee, K., Youn, C.H.: Reinforcement learning based adaptive resource allocation scheme for multi-user augmented reality service. In: 2022 13th International Conference on Information and Communication Technology Convergence (ICTC), pp. 1989–1994 (2022). https://doi.org/10.1109/ICTC55196.2022.9952934

26. Lee, K., Youn, C.H.: Reindear: reinforcement learning agent for dynamic system control in edge-assisted augmented reality service. In: 2020 International Conference on Information and Communication Technology Convergence (ICTC), pp. 949–954. IEEE (2020)

27. Merkel, D., et al.: Docker: lightweight Linux containers for consistent development and deployment. Linux j **239**(2), 2 (2014)

28. Paszke, A., et al.: Pytorch: an imperative style, high-performance deep learning library. Adv. Neural Inf. Process. Syst. **32** (2019)

29. Zhang, C., Zhou, G., Li, J., Chang, F., Ding, K., Ma, D.: A multi-access edge computing enabled framework for the construction of a knowledge-sharing intelligent machine tool swarm in industry 4.0. J. Manuf. Syst. **66**, 56–70 (2023)

Towards the Integration of Digital Avatars in Urban Digital Twins on the Cloud-to-Thing Continuum

Lorenzo Toro-Gálvez[(✉)] [ID], Rafael García-Luque [ID], Javier Troya [ID], Carlos Canal [ID], and Ernesto Pimentel [ID]

ITIS Software, Universidad de Málaga, Málaga, Spain
{lorenzotoro,rafagarcialuque,jtroya,carloscanal,epimentel}@uma.es

Abstract. Urban Digital Twins (UDTs) represent a powerful tool to effectively make cities smart. Over the last few years, the interest in the social aspects of smart cities is growing fast. For this reason, citizens must be considered as first-class entities in UDTs. At the same time, citizens' privacy cannot be compromised. In this paper, we propose to integrate citizens through their digital avatars (DAs) into UDTs. DAs allow to exploit citizens' information, behavioral habits and personal preferences, while allowing them to have full control of their own data. We present our envisioned architecture that makes use of the Cloud-to-Thing Continuum for optimizing the available processing resources. We focus on a case study of the public transformation service of the city of Malaga (Spain) and describe how we are addressing its implementation.

Keywords: Urban Digital Twin · Digital Avatar · Cloud-to-Thing Continuum

1 Introduction

Smart cities use technology to try to offer solutions to global problems such as climate change or resource depletion, and aim to provide useful services to their citizens and to solve specific urban problems, such as transportation and accessibility. The concept of Digital Twin City [6], also known as Urban Digital Twin (UDT), has been defined as a way to effectively make cities smart. A UDT is a digital twin capable of modeling specific city aspects such as transportation, heat maps of population density or environmental factors. Similar to other digital twins, UDTs facilitate two-way feedback between the model and the physical entities represented in it. These digital twins cannot only enable real-time remote monitoring for cities, but also suggest adaptation policies and enhance decision-making processes in areas such as improved urban governance, smart healthcare or smart transportation.

This work was partially funded by the Spanish Government (FEDER/Ministerio de Ciencia e Innovación–Agencia Estatal de Investigación) under projects PID2021-125527NB-I00 and TED2021-130523B-I00, as well as by UMA.

S. Casteleyn et al. (Eds.): ICWE 2023 Workshops, CCIS 1898, pp. 67–74, 2024.
https://doi.org/10.1007/978-3-031-50385-6_6

Over the last few years, the interest in the social aspects of smart cities is growing fast. For this reason, citizens must be considered as first-class entities of the UDT, since they are the fundamental key to this ecosystem. However, the role of people has often been ignored, treating them as a crowd and not as individuals. And if citizens are to be considered as individuals, then their privacy would be compromised [2]. In previous works [3,4,13,14], we presented the concept of *Digital Avatar (DA)*, which represents a virtual representation of its user and through which the latter can decide which personal information to share. The DA resides in the smartphone of its user.

In this paper we propose to integrate citizens through their DAs into UDTs. The idea is to exploit citizens' information, behavioral habits and personal preferences, at the same time allowing them to have full control of their own data, including access control and storage location. Citizens who share specific information can benefit from better services from the organizations to which they entrust their data.

In addition to addressing the integration of citizens into UDTs, our proposal also aims to face the challenge of managing the large number of devices involved in these systems, that can require high computing capacity. To this end, we envision the development of a framework which takes advantage of the Cloud-to-Thing Continuum [9–11] for optimizing the available processing resources. For this, we propose a distributed architecture based on four layers, namely *mist*, *edge*, *fog* and *cloud*, and define the devices and services to be placed in each layer by focusing on a case study of the public transportation service of the city of Malaga (Spain). We also present the technology stack with which we plan to implement our framework, and give a glimpse of the implementation centered on digital twins.

The remainder of this paper is structured as follows. Section 2 gives an insight into the basics needed to understand our approach. Then, Sect. 3 presents a case study of a UDT dealing with public transportation that motivates our proposal. Sections 4 and 5 present the architecture to be applied to our envisioned framework and the implementation centered on digital twins that we are carrying out, respectively. Finally, Sect. 6 concludes the paper with an insight to future work.

2 Background

2.1 Urban Digital Twins

A Digital Twin (DT) is a comprehensive digital representation of a real system, service or product (the Physical Twin, PT), synchronized at a specified frequency and fidelity [1]. The DT includes the properties, conditions, and behavior of the physical entity through models and data, and is continuously updated with real-time data about the PT's performance, maintenance, and health status throughout its entire lifetime [5,7].

One specific type of DT is the Urban Digital Twin (UDT), which is a virtual representation of a city's physical assets that utilizes data, analytics, and machine learning to create real-time, adaptable simulation models. The digital twin describes the reality (and the history of it), while it is the additional applications that bring the real intelligence and help create the common picture of reality that is the added value of an urban digital twin. UDTs enable more informed decision-making, participatory governance, and improved urban planning by offering a risk-free testing environment for long-term predictions and impact assessments.

2.2 Digital Avatars

A Digital Avatar (DA) [4,13] is a virtual entity residing in an individual's smartphone or tablet that records information about its owner and offers different services for interacting with their surroundings and other users' DAs. This concept arises from the People as a Service (PeaaS) [8] paradigm, which provides a conceptual model for application development focused on the smartphone as a representative and interface to its owner. The main purpose of a DA is to serve as a digital representation of a person, facilitating their participation in collaborative social computing applications. In this context, the DA of a user is designed to collect data about the user and their habits, integrate this information with external sensor data or open data sources, and interact with both the environment and other users' DAs.

Additionally, a DA is responsible for representing the user in responding to requests coming from other avatars or social computing applications, as well as adjusting its records and anticipated behavior as needed. Consequently, DAs empower users by enabling them to (i) take control of the information and contents they create, (ii) manage how all that information is accessed and exploited in a secure manner by third parties, and (iii) be in control of their changes and adaptations. Thus, privacy and security can be ensured [12], since users can have the control over their own data and decide whether or not they want to share it, and with whom. However, there are limitations to the capabilities of DAs, such as lack of support for global decision making and comprehensive planning, which are key elements of any smart city application.

3 Case Study

The case study we are dealing with is urban transportation in smart cities, specifically in the city of Malaga (Spain). We have access to real-time information about the use of buses in the city: transport lines, stops and schedules, GPS position of the buses, traffic status, among others, provided by the City Council as open data[1].

Our main goal is to develop an urban digital twin with the ability to use all the information about the transportation network to make predictions about peak occupancy hours, recognize usage patterns and allocate the resources for

---

[1] https://datosabiertos.malaga.eu/group/transporte.

optimal use. The digital twin can also monitor the current state of transport and react or adapt to unexpected peaks or incidents.

Furthermore, the UDT would be improved if it was connected to the citizens' DAs. Thus, one of our goals is also to infer information from them: how individuals use the transportation system, their habits and routines in relation to it, or their behavioral patterns for commuting to work or moving around the city. This will allow for more accurate predictions made on individuals. In this manner, citizens may get improved and personalized services.

Another benefit of DAs is that personal preferences could be taken into consideration to suggest alternative transportation methods more suited to citizens' likings and needs. Knowing their preferences could be very useful in deciding about the overall transport solutions to be implemented.

4   Architecture

To carry out the above case study, we rely on the Cloud-to-Thing Continuum [9,15]. This concept refers to a highly distributed, decentralized, and dynamic environment spanning from IoT devices to the cloud. The continuum helps us to solve the problem of computing capacity since it is designed to address the challenges of next-generation IoT systems that involve a large number of heterogeneous devices generating massive amounts of data and require real-time processing, low service response times, and enhanced reliability and security.

Following the continuum model, we propose a four-tier architecture where each layer offloads the upper layer by taking over some of its functionalities. Next, we present the four layers starting from the lowest layer of the architecture: mist, edge, fog and cloud computing [11]. A snapshot of our architecture is shown in Fig. 1.

Mist represents the layer closest to the citizens, and we place here the citizens' smartphones that include their DAs. Therefore, all citizens' data coming from their DAs is collected at this level: positioning, information on their habits and routines, personal preferences, etc., always ensuring their privacy and data anonymization and allowing users to decide with whom they share them. Recall that citizens' information resides in their smartphones, from where they decide what to share and with whom [13]. *Mist* is also the layer through which citizens receive individualized and personalized information, coming from the processing in the upper layers, based on their virtual profiles.

The next layer is *edge* computing. This layer processes data directly coming from the mist as well as data gathered in this layer. Here, we consider that the bus stops and buses can gather and process information depending on the environment and different situations. Thus, this architecture makes it possible to run specific applications in a fixed location providing direct data transmission. Specifically, the inclusion of tracking and processing devices such as Bluetooth beacons in the different buses or bus stops makes it possible to send notifications to citizens and provide significant information, e.g., about the bus being late, overcrowded, or skipping a particular stop.

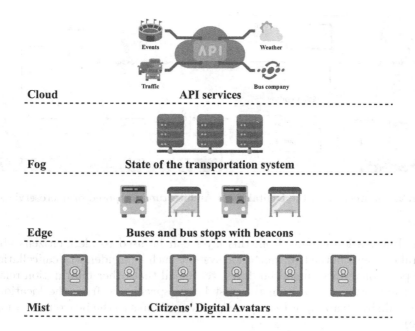

Fig. 1. Proposed architecture for the transportation system based on the continuum.

The third layer is *fog* computing, which enables ubiquitous access to a shared range of scalable computing resources. In the context of the proposed scenario, the *fog* layer will include the state of the transportation system including relevant factors organized in city areas. By using fog computing to process and analyze real-time data from the transportation system and citizens, we can gain valuable insights into factors such as traffic congestion, passenger load and route optimization, all of which can help improve the overall efficiency and reliability of the transportation system. Furthermore, this layer is essential for making predictions. By analyzing real-time and historical data, we can predict transportation costs, identify potential traffic bottlenecks and crowded areas, forecast peak demand times, and recognize popular routes and transit hubs.

The *cloud* layer, as the top tier of our proposed architecture, provides access to a range of services and real-time data that can have a direct effect in both the current and future state of the transportation system. This information is directly translated to the fog layer for analysis. Examples of services that can have an effect in the state of the transportation system include weather information and forecast, events taking place in the city (sport games, concerts or festivals) and real-time traffic information—for instance, the TomTom API offers information on the current traffic status. All these services offer information that can be crucial for optimizing transportation routes and reducing travel time for commuters.

Note that some information on the urban public transportation system is also accessible from the cloud layer, such as the route or position of the different

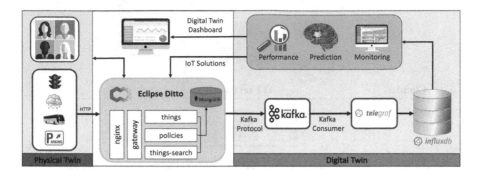

Fig. 2. An overview of the Digital Twin Architecture composed of microservices.

buses. Information coming from this layer can be used to alert citizens about general incidents in the transportation system, such as accidents or cancellations, non-operational lines on special days, etc. Recall that other information related to transportation comes from the mist layer (specifically from the location of citizens' digital avatars) or from the edge layer (thanks to the beacons mentioned above).

5   Implementation

For materializing the architecture described before, we employ Eclipse Ditto[2], an open-source domain-agnostic framework that helps build digital twins. Figure 2 shows our envisioned architecture from a digital twins point of view. It is composed of independent microservices that communicate with one another in real time, using protocols such as AMQP or Apache Kafka. Each of these services is encapsulated in containers managed by Docker, ensuring isolation for both, which in turn enables portability and guarantees correct execution.

The physical twin in our system is comprised of real-world entities providing information to the digital twin, with the Eclipse Ditto platform situated between them. The physical twin is scalable, since more entities can be added, and so is the digital twin. We also include the citizens, through their digital avatars, as part of the physical twin, since they are an integral part in any smart city.

At the current point of the implementation, we are gathering information from the entities of the physical twin. For this, we have implemented a Java application, using Maven, that makes requests to the different APIs and collects the information through Eclipse Ditto. However, Ditto is only responsible for storing and updating the most recent state of each entity in its database, implemented in MongoDB, which prevents having historical records. For this reason, we use, as part of the digital twin, InfluxDB[3], an open-source database

---

[2] https://www.eclipse.org/ditto/intro-overview.html.

[3] https://www.influxdata.com/products/influxdb-overview/.

that enables fast storage and retrieval of time series data, with high availability. Since Ditto requires an intermediary in the connection to InfluxDB, we use Telegraf[4], which plays the role of a server-based agent responsible for collecting and sending metrics to databases, IoT systems, etc.

The information stored as time series data can be used for different purposes, such as obtaining performance insights, monitoring and doing predictions. All these can be used to improve or correct the service offered by the different entities of the physical twin. Some of this information can also be used to improve and create easy-to-understand recommendations to citizens through their digital avatars, such as suggesting alternative routes when commuting to work or avoiding traffic congestion in rush hours.

As for the data we are collecting so far from the services of the physical entities, we are making periodic requests to the APIs of (i) Malaga City Council, (ii) OpenWeatherMap, and (iii) Tomtom. This means we are storing information about real-time buses location, parking occupancy, urban traffic and meteorological parameters of the city of Malaga. For instance, regarding information from public buses, our framework has currently collected around 79k documents containing the geolocation of all buses in each time interval (requests are made every minute). This data-base knowledge allows to set the location of each bus with respect to its established stop and, thus, estimate the duration of all the routes.

The combination of the times taken by the buses, together with the climatic aspects, parking occupancy and traffic congestion, will pave the way for establishing patterns that infer the performance of buses and, based on this, adapt it to the preferences and needs of the citizens.

6   Conclusions and Future Work

This contribution describes the architecture for our envisioned framework in which we propose to integrate citizens through their DAs into UDTs, making use of the Cloud-to-Thing Continuum to arrange different components in each of the four proposed layers: *mist, edge, fog* and *cloud*.

As a proof of concept of the proposed approach, we have developed an initial version of the UDT based on Eclipse Ditto, that takes into consideration real-time data of services such as bus transportation, traffic status and weather information.

This work can be continued in several directions. First, we plan to integrate the UDT with citizens' custom information to know how citizens use the transportation system for moving around the city, their daily routines and their preferences, among others. We also aim to expand the UDT by including other elements such as beacons and processing devices on the buses to collect more data and provide a more comprehensive analysis of the transportation system. Furthermore, we plan to incorporate data on specific events happening in the city,

---

[4] https://www.influxdata.com/time-series-platform/telegraf/.

such as festivals or sports events, which may have an impact on the transportation system. Finally, we also plan to explore the integration of other techniques like ML and AI to further improve the system's performance and accuracy in its predictions.

Overall, this proposed framework has the potential to significantly improve the transportation system of the city of Malaga by providing real-time data and analysis that can optimize routes, reduce travel time, and enhance the efficiency and reliability of the system.

References

1. Digital Twin Consortium. 2021. Glossary of Digital Twins
2. Badii, C., Bellini, P., Difino, A., Nesi, P.: Smart city IoT platform respecting GDPR privacy and security aspects. IEEE Access **8**, 23601–23623 (2020)
3. Bandera, D., Pozas, N., Bertoa, M.F., Álvarez, J.M., Canal, C., Pimentel, E.: Extensión de Digital Avatars para crowdsensing distribuido. In: Sistedes JCIS (2021)
4. Bertoa, M.F., Moreno, N., Pérez-Vereda, A., Bandera, D., Álvarez-Palomo, J.M., Canal, C.: Digital avatars: promoting independent living for older adults. Wirel. Commun. Mob. Comput. **2020**, 1–11 (2020)
5. Bordeleau, F., Combemale, B., Eramo, R., van den Brand, M., Wimmer, M.: Towards model-driven digital twin engineering: current opportunities and future challenges. In: ICSMM Proceedings, vol. 1262, pp. 43–54 (2020)
6. Deng, T., Zhang, K., Shen, Z.J.M.: A systematic review of a digital twin city: a new pattern of urban governance toward smart cities. MSC J. **6**(2), 125–134 (2021)
7. Grieves, M.: Digital twin: manufacturing excellence through virtual factory replication **1**, 1–7 (2014)
8. Guillén, J., Miranda, J., Berrocal, J., García-Alonso, J., Murillo, J.M., Canal, C.: People as a service: a mobile-centric model for providing collective sociological profiles. IEEE Softw. **31**(2), 48–53 (2014)
9. Herrera, J.L., Galán-Jiménez, J., Garcia-Alonso, J., Berrocal, J., Murillo, J.M.: Joint optimization of response time and deployment cost in next-gen IoT applications. IEEE IoT J. **10**(5), 3968–3981 (2023)
10. Laso, S., et al.: Elastic data analytics for the cloud-to-things continuum. IEEE IC **26**(6), 42–49 (2022)
11. Lynn, T., Mooney, J.G., Lee, B., Endo, P.T.: The Cloud-to-Thing Continuum: Opportunities and Challenges in Cloud, Fog and Edge Computing (2020)
12. Muñoz, P., Pérez-Vereda, A., Moreno, N., Troya, J., Vallecillo, A.: Incorporating trust into collaborative social computing applications. In: Proceedings of the EDOC'21, October 2021
13. Pérez-Vereda, A., Canal, C., Pimentel, E.: Modelling digital avatars: a tuple space approach. Sci. Comput. Program. **203**, 102583 (2021)
14. Pérez-Vereda, A., Murillo, J.M., Canal, C.: Dynamically programmable virtual profiles as a service. In: 2019 IEEE SmartWorld/SCALCOM/UIC/ATC/CBDCom/IOP/SCI, pp. 1789–1794 (2019)
15. Čilić, I., Žarko, I.P., Kušek, M.: Towards service orchestration for the cloud-to-thing continuum. In: 2021 6th SpliTech, pp. 01–07 (2021)

Exploring the Feasibility of ChatGPT for Improving the Quality of Ansible Scripts in Edge-Cloud Infrastructures Through Code Recommendation

Sunjae Kwon[1], Sungu Lee[1], Taehyoun Kim[1], Duksan Ryu[2], and Jongmoon Baik[1(✉)]

[1] Korea Advanced Institute of Science and Technology, Daejeon, Republic of Korea
jbaik@kaist.ac.kr
[2] Jeonbuk National University, Jeonju, Republic of Korea

Abstract. Edge-cloud system aims to reduce the processing time of Big data by bringing massive infrastructures closer to the source of data. Infrastructure as Code (IaC) supports the automatic deployment and management of these infrastructures through reusable code, and Ansible is the most popular IaC tool. As the quality of Ansible script directly influences the quality of Edge-cloud system, many researchers have studied improving the quality of Ansible scripts. However, there has yet to be an attempt to leverage the power of ChatGPT. Thus, we study to explore the feasibility of ChatGPT to improve the quality of Ansible scripts. Three raters evaluate ChatGPT's code recommendation ability on 48 code revision cases from 25 Ansible project GitHub repositories, and we analyze the rating results. As a result, we can confirm that ChatGPT can recognize and understand Ansible script. However, its ability largely depends on how to user formulates the questions. Thus, we can confirm the need for prompt engineering for ChatGPT to acquire stable code recommendation results.

Keywords: Edge-cloud · Ansible · ChatGPT · Code Recommendation

1 Introduction

Edge-cloud system plays a crucial role in processing Big data with low latency through massive distributed infrastructures [1, 2]. Infrastructure-as-Code (IaC) [10] is a tool that enables automatic provisioning and management of infrastructure using reusable code instead of manual labor. While IaC can assist in implementing and managing the distributed infrastructures of the Edge-cloud system, as IaC itself consists of code, the correctness of the IaC code is vital for the smooth functioning of entire Edge-cloud system. Ansible is the most popular IaC tool [5, 9]; due to its popularity, various studies have explored the method for ensuring the correctness of Ansible [3, 6, 11, 13].

ChatGPT is one of the most advanced Large Language Models (LLMs) and has shown impressive performance across various fields. Researchers in Software Engineering (SE) have attempted to use ChatGPT to automate SE tasks such as code recommendation and code repairing [14–16]. While they have confirmed the decent performance

S. Casteleyn et al. (Eds.): ICWE 2023 Workshops, CCIS 1898, pp. 75–83, 2024.
https://doi.org/10.1007/978-3-031-50385-6_7

of ChatGPT, their research has mainly focused on Java or C languages, and no study has focused on IaC code. Therefore, we investigate ChatGPT's code recommendation ability for the correctness of Ansible code.

To evaluate ChatGPT's ability, we collected 48 code revision cases from 25 Ansible project repositories on GitHub using the GitHub Pull-Request (GHPR), a novel approach to collecting issue resolving information from GitHub. Three raters evaluated ChatGPT's code recommendation ability on the 48 collected cases, and we analyzed the rating results using the Kappa statistic, which measures the degree of agreement between different raters. The results indicate that ChatGPT can recognize Ansible scripts and understand their grammar. However, how each user generates a prompt for ChatGPT to get the recommendation largely influences the quality of its response.

2   Background and Related Work

2.1   Edge-Cloud System and Ansible

Edge-cloud system is an essential computing infrastructure for collecting and processing Big data with low latency using distributed infrastructure that is geographically and conceptually dispersed [1, 2]. However, manually provisioning and managing such a complex system can be laborious and prone to errors. IaC is a framework that enables system administrators to provision and manage infrastructure automatically, using reusable code instead of manual labor. Due to the benefits of IaC, it has become a critical factor in Edge-cloud system. However, the quality of IaC is directly related to the quality of the entire system.

Among various IaC tools, Ansible is widely regarded as the most popular thanks to its simple functions and Python-based system [5, 9]. However, ensuring the correctness of Ansible script is crucial because defects in the code have been linked to various cloud service outages [3, 11]. Several studies have studied Ansible to reduce the outages by improving the quality of Ansible script. For example, Opdebeeck et al. [11] used graph algorithms to analyze *smelly variables* in the script, while Dalla Palma et al. [3] attempted to predict defect-prone script using machine learning algorithms. In this paper, for the first time, we leverage the power of an LLM, which has demonstrated outstanding performance in various fields, to fix Ansible script by utilizing information from GitHub issues.

2.2   Software Engineering Tasks Using ChatGPT

ChatGPT, developed by OpenAI, is among the most advanced chatbot technologies based on LLM. Since its release, it has been applied in various fields, including software engineering. For instance, Sobania et al. [14] analyzed the automatic bug-fixing capabilities of ChatGPT, while Chunqiu Steven Xia et al. [16] proposed ChatRepair, an automated program repair approach based on ChatGPT that utilizes conversation. However, their studies mainly focused on *Java* or *C* languages, which provide sufficient training data for ChatGPT to learn from. In this paper, we seek to determine whether ChatGPT can improve the quality of Ansible scripts, which are relatively scarce compared to other languages.

3 Approach

3.1 Collecting Cases Using GitHub Pull-Request (GHPR)

GitHub Pull-Request (GHPR) is a novel approach to acquiring code change information based on issues in a repository; additionally, various studies have employed it to collect training data for studying SE tasks [7, 8, 17]. We selected 48 Ansible code change cases to evaluate ChatGPT's code recommendation ability using the GHPR, and the overall case selection process consisted of two parts, as shown in Fig. 1. Firstly, we selected 25 actively developing Ansible project GitHub repositories from the Andromeda dataset [12] containing metadata of 25K Ansible projects, using three criteria, as shown in the figure. Secondly, we collected cases that resolved an issue by modifying a single Ansible script to ensure accurate evaluations of ChatGPT's code recommendation ability through GHPR process. As shown in the figure, when an issue arises on a main branch, a developer generates a separate branch to address the issue. After resolving the issue, the developer sends a Pull-Request (PR) message to the main branch maintainers for reviewing the changed code. If the maintainers approve the PR, the change is merged into the main branch. We assume the merged changes are reliable, as the repository's maintainers have reviewed and approved them. Thus, we use the merged code as Ground-truth for evaluating ChatGPT's code recommendation ability.

Through the GHPR process, we can gather the original source code, issue information (i.e., Symptoms of the issue), PR information (i.e., How to resolve the issue), and the changed code to address the issue (i.e., *Git_diff* information). Each case has those four types of information.

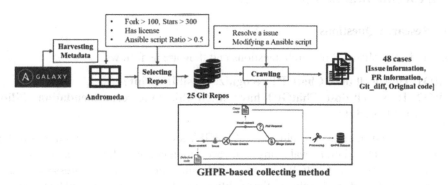

GHPR-based collecting method

Fig. 1. Overall process for collecting cases using GHPR

3.2 Three Tasks to Evaluate the Code Recommendation Ability of ChatGPT

Three Ph.D. students evaluated ChatGPT's code recommendation ability through 3 tasks on the 48 cases. Figure 2 depicts the 3 tasks as follows; 1) *Task #1* checks how accurately ChatGPT could understand Ansible scripts. A rater inputs an Ansible script to ChatGPT, and ChatGPT shows the description of the script. 2) *Task #2* checks how well ChatGPT could recommend a revision code similar to a human-modified code based on the original script and issue information. A rater gives ChatGPT the original code and the generated prompt (i.e., Question to ChatGPT) based on issue information, and ChatGPT shows the revision code to solve the issue. 3) *Task #3* is the same as the *Task #2*, but the inputted information is the PR rather than the issue information. A rater gives ChatGPT the original code and the generated prompt based on the PR information, and ChatGPT shows the revision code reflecting the PR. In order to reflect the actual usage environment, the raters were permitted freely ask questions to ChatGPT using the information of each case, but the number of questions was limited to once for each task.

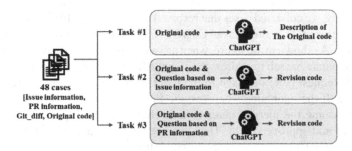

Fig. 2. Three tasks to evaluate code recommendation ability of ChatGPT

4   Experimental Setup

4.1   Research Questions

This study establishes 2 research questions and they are as follows.

1. **RQ1: How well dose ChatGPT recognize Ansible script**?
2. **RQ2: How well dose ChatGPT have acceptable code recommendation ability for Ansible script?**

It is the first attempt to evaluate the ChatGPT's code recommendation ability for Ansible script. Thus, before evaluating code recommendation performance, we establish RQ1 to confirm whether ChatGPT understands Ansible script well. To address RQ1, each rater executes *Task #1* and evaluates the quality of the description generated by ChatGPT on a 5-point scale (i.e., 5: Very satisfied, 4: satisfied, 3: Neither satisfied nor dissatisfied, 2: dissatisfied, 1: Very dissatisfied) based on following 2 questions; 1) *Does ChatGPT recognize an inputted Ansible script as Ansible script?* 2) *Does the generated description sufficiently reflect the inputted Ansible script?*

To address RQ2, each rater executes *Task #2* first, and if the response is not acceptable, performs *Task #3*. This process reflects the real-word situation of continuously asking questions with more specific information until the user gets a satisfactory answer. Finally, each rater evaluates the quality of ChatGPT's revision code on a 5-point scale based on the following questions; 1) *Does ChatGPT modify the same code line as the human-modified code?* 2) *Does ChatGPT properly reflect the issue and PR information provided?* 3) *Is ChatGPT's revision code match the human-modified code?* or *can the rater infer the human-modified code through ChatGPT's revision code?*

4.2 Measuring Reliability of Raters' Rating Result

Three raters independently evaluate 48 common cases, and if their rating results are reliable (i.e., having a high degree of agreement between different raters), we can expect similar results from other users. The degree of agreement between different raters can be measured using the Kappa statistic, which calculates the Kappa coefficient based on the evaluation results of different evaluators. We utilize Fleiss' kappa [4], which evaluates the reliability of the three or more raters' rating results. The interpretation according to Fleiss' kappa coefficient is as follows; *Poor Agreement* (< 0), *Slight Agreement* (0.01 ~ 0.20), *Fair Agreement* (0.21 ~ 0.40), *Moderate Agreement* (0.41 ~ 0.60), *Substantial Agreement* (0.61 ~ 0.80), and *Almost Perfect Agreement* (0.61 ~ 0.80).

5 Experimental Result

5.1 RQ1: How Well Does ChatGPT Recognize Ansible Script?

Table 1. The number of cases according to the score given by each rater on RQ1

	1	2	3	4	5	AVG
Rater #1	0	0	0	5	43	4.9
Rater #2	0	0	0	5	43	4.9
Rater #3	0	0	0	4	44	4.92

Table 1 shows the number of cases according to the score given by each rater. Most cases received a rating of 5 from all raters, resulting in an average rating of 4.9 (i.e., Very satisfied). The Fleiss' Kappa coefficient for the ratings is 0.683, indicating substantial agreement among the raters that ChatGPT provides descriptions that sufficiently reflect the content of the inputted Ansible script.

Figure 3 shows the result of the #17 case where Fig. 3-(a) is Ansible script inputted to ChatGPT, and Fig. 3-(b) is ChatGPT's output for the inputted Ansible script. Ansible script follows *YAML* file format and consists of a unit called task starting with '-*name*' tag. As shown in Fig. 3-(b), ChatGPT recognizes the inputted script as an Ansible script without any additional information, which is consistent across all cases. Additionally, ChatGPT provides a summary of the entire script and an explanation for each task. In conclusion, ChatGPT can recognize Ansible scripts and comprehend their grammar.

| (a) Inputted script | (b) Generated description |

Fig. 3. Inputted Ansible script and generated description by ChatGPT for #17 case.

5.2 RQ2: How Well Does ChatGPT Have Acceptable Code Recommendation Ability for Ansible Script?

Table 2 shows the number of cases according to the score given by each rater. The distribution of scores given by each rater is different and the overall average rating is 3.49 (i.e., Neither satisfied nor dissatisfied). In addition, the Fleiss' Kappa coefficient is 0.02 indicating inconsistency among raters in evaluating the satisfaction level of ChatGPT's code revision. Based on the fact that each rater has the same information to generate a prompt for Chat GPR, the inconsistency assumes to be caused by the difference in the questioning method of each evaluator.

For example, Table 3-(a) shows the #15 case's issue title, issue body, PR tile, and PR body, where each rater gives 5, 1, and 3 points, respectively. Table 3-(b) shows the questions posed by each rater, referring to the contents of Table 3-(a), to enable ChatGPT to resolve the issue, as well as the points awarded by each rater.

Rater #1 generated the question based on the contents of the issue body with emphasis on important words (i.e., *main_push_enable* and *main_upload_enable*), and ChatGPT provided the revision code that exactly matched the human-modified code without the PR information. *Rater #2* generated the first question based on the issue title and the

Table 2. The number of cases according to the score given by each rater on RQ2

	1	2	3	4	5	AVG
Rater #1	6	4	9	10	19	**3.67**
Rater #2	3	4	7	11	23	**3.98**
Rater #3	14	6	10	10	8	**2.83**

Table 3. Issue and PR information of #15 case & Each rater's question and rating result

Issue Title	Ansible role fails when trying to upload an NGINX configuration file
Issue Body	Two different variables main_push_enable and main_upload_enable are used throughout the role interchangeably This leads to an error when trying to run a playbook that uploads an NGINX configuration file
PR Title	Replace *_upload_enable with *_push_enable
PR Body	-

(a) Issue and PR information of #15 case

Rater	Question	Rate
#1	1) Two different variables '*main_push_enable*' and '*main_upload_enable*' are used throughout the role interchangeably. This leads to an error when trying to run a playbook that uploads a NGINX configuration file. how to fix it?	5
#2	1) The Ansible role fails when we try to upload an NGINX configuration file. Can you fix that? Show only relevant part of the code 2) Change the when condition from "*main_upload_enable*" so that the problem resolves	1
#3	1) Fix issue, [*issue title*] 2) [*PR title*]	3

(b) Each rater's question to ChatGPT and the rating result

second question based on the PR title. However, ChatGPT modified lines of script that are different from the human-modified code lines, and *Rater #2* cannot infer the human-modified code using ChatGPT's revision script. Lastly, *Rater #3* provided issue title and PR body information without editing. ChatGPT modified the code to be similar to the human-modified code but also modified the lines other than the human-modified part. In conclusion, even if the same information is provided, ChatGPT's code recommendation ability largely depends on how the users formulate their question using the provided information.

6 Threats to Validity

Internal Validity is the inconsistency of ChatGPT's recommendations for the same question, which could affect the evaluation results depending on the timing of the recommendation. To mitigate this threat, we limited the number of questions for each case to one during the evaluation process.

External Validity; The evaluation of ChatGPT's code recommendation ability on Ansible script only involved 3 raters. While the small number of raters may limit the generalizability of our findings, we tried to address this limitation by assessing the consistency of the evaluations using Fleiss' Kappa statistic. In future work, we plan to improve external validity by involving more than five raters.

7 Conclusion

IaC supports effective infrastructure management in edge-cloud system through automated processes. Ansible is one of the popular tools for IaC, and as interest in Ansible increases, the quality of Ansible scripts becomes more important. Recently, ChatGPT has shown excellent performance in various fields, and researchers in SE have attempted to utilize it to improve SE tasks. Thus, we evaluate ChatGPT's code recommendation ability on 48 code revision cases from 25 Ansible repositories to explore the feasibility of ChatGPT in improving the quality of Ansible scripts. As a result, we can confirm that ChatGPT can recognize Ansible scripts and comprehend their grammar. However, ChatGPT's code recommendations are largely influenced by how the users formulate their questions. In future work, we plan to study efficient questioning methods to obtain satisfactory code recommendation results through further case analysis (i.e., Prompt engineering for ChatGPT).

Acknowledgment. This research was supported by Information Technology Research Center (ITRC) support program supervised by the Institute of Information & Communications Technology Planning & Evaluation (IITP-2023–2020-0–01795), and the Basic Science Research Program through the National Research Foundation of Korea (NRF) funded by the Ministry of Education (NRF- 2022R1I1A3069233).

References

1. Agapito, G., et al.: Current trends in web engineering. In: ICWE 2022 International Workshops, BECS, Bari, Italy, Revised Selected Papers. Springer, Cham (2023). https://doi.org/10.1007/978-3-031-25380-5
2. Buyya, R., et al.: Fog and Edge Computing: Principles and Paradigms. Wiley, Hoboken (2019)
3. Palma, D., et al.: Within-project defect prediction of infrastructure-as-code using product and process metrics. IEEE Trans. Software Eng. **14**(8), 1 (2020)
4. Fleiss, J.L.: Measuring nominal scale agreement among many raters. Psychol. Bull. **76**(5), 378 (1971)
5. Guerriero, M, et al.: Adoption, support, and challenges of infrastructure-as-code: insights from industry. In: 2019 IEEE International Conference on Software Maintenance and Evolution (ICSME), pp. 580–589.IEEE (2019)
6. Kokuryo, S., Kondo, M., Mizuno, O.: An empirical study of utilization of imperative modules in ansible. In: 2020 IEEE 20Th International Conference on Software Quality, Reliability and Security (QRS), pp. 442–449. IEEE (2020)
7. Kwon, S., et al.: Codebert based software defect prediction for edge-cloud systems. In: Agapito, G., et al. Current Trends in Web Engineering: ICWE2022 Communications in Computer and Information Science, vol. 1668, pp. 11–21. Springer, Cham (2023). https://doi.org/10.1007/978-3-031-25380-5_1
8. Li, Z., et al.: Codereviewer: Pre-training for automating codereview activities. arXiv preprint arXiv:2203.09095 (2022)
9. Meijer, B., et al.: Ansible: Up and Running. O'Reilly Media Inc, Sebastopol (2022)
10. Morris, K.: Infrastructure as Code: Managing Servers. O'Reilly Media, Inc Sebastopol (2016)
11. Opdebeeck, R., et al.: Andromeda: a dataset of ansible galaxy roles and their evolution. In: 2021 IEEE/ACM 18th International Conference on Mining Software Repositories (MSR), pp. 580–584. IEEE (2021)

12. Opdebeeck, R., et al.: Smelly variables in ansible infrastructure code: detection, prevalence, and lifetime. In: Proceedings of the 19th International Conference on Mining Software Repositories, pp. 61–72 (2022)
13. Rahman, A., et al.: Security smells in ansible and chef scripts: a replication study. ACM Trans. Softw. Eng. Methodol. (TOSEM) **30**(1), 1–31 (2021)
14. Sobania, D., Briesch, M., Hanna, C., Petke, J.: An analysis of the automatic bug fixing performance of ChatGPT. arXiv preprint arXiv:2301.08653 (2023)
15. White, J et al.: ChatGPT prompt patterns for improving code quality, refactoring, requirements elicitation, and softwaredesign. arXiv preprint arXiv:2303.07839 (2023)
16. Xia, C.S., Zhang, L.: Keep the conversation going: Fixing 162 out of 337 bugs for $0.42 each using chatGPT. arXiv preprint arXiv:2304.00385 (2023)
17. Xu, J., Yan, L., Wang, F., Ai, J.: A github-based data collection method for software defect prediction. In: 2019 6th International Conference on Dependable Systems and Their Applications (DSA), pp. 100–108. IEEE (2020)

Second International Workshop on the Semantic WEb of Everything (SWEET 2023)

2nd International Workshop on the Semantic WEb of EveryThing (SWEET 2023) - Preface

Giuseppe Loseto[1], Hasan Ali Khattak[2], Agnese Pinto[3], Michele Ruta[3]
and Floriano Scioscia[3]

[1] LUM "Giuseppe Degennaro" University, Italy
loseto@lum.it
[2] Faculty of Computing and Information Technology, Sohar University,
Sohar Oman
hasan.alikhattak@ieee.org
[3] Polytechnic University of Bari, Italy
{agnese.pinto,michele.ruta,floriano.scioscia}@poliba.it

The Second International Workshop on the Semantic WEb of EveryThing (SWEET 2023) was held in Alicante (Spain) on July 6th, 2023, in conjunction with the 23rd International Conference on Web Engineering (ICWE 2023).

SWEET was organized to give researchers and practitioners an opportunity to discuss and interact about realistic penetration of Artificial Intelligence techniques and technologies in the Internet of Things (IoT) and the Web of Things, with particular attention to pervasive contexts. Three presentations and an invited talk were given in the two technical sessions of the workshop, for a total of 12 authors from 4 institutions. All presentations were given in person according to ICWE 2023 guidelines.

A range of innovative architectures, algorithms and applications was presented, including strategies for optimizing knowledge graph construction and data integration. The discussions following each presentation were very fruitful, allowing the participants to explore current and future perspectives with respect to the following problems:

- How can we integrate the Web of Things with Semantic Web technologies and tools?
- How can we use ontologies and semantic annotations to enhance real world pervasive devices, applications and services?
- How can we exploit reasoning and planning in Web of Things scenarios?
- How can we integrate machine learning efficiently in pervasive large-scale scenarios with high volumes of data?
- What IoT technologies are able to support the Semantic Web of Everything evolution?

Knowledge representation technologies for mobile, embedded and ubiquitous computing were the focus of most talks. Further contributions concerned other Artificial Intelligence (AI) areas, including machine learning and non-standard reasoning. The proposed approaches often integrated AI with other research fields, such as ambient intelligence, sensor networks, and data protection. Discussed application areas included smart tourism, precision farming, and smart financial services.

We were pleased with the quality of the submitted papers, the oral presentations and the discussions emerged during the workshop. We also received a good feedback from the attendees about their satisfaction with the experience. We are sincerely grateful to all contributors for their participation. Special thanks go to ICWE 2023 organizers, and particularly to the Workshop Tommi Mikkonen and Sven Casteleyn, for their constant support before, during and after the event.

We hope to continue and improve on every aspect of the workshop in future SWEET editions, in order to promote the mutual exchange of ideas and possibly even new research collaborations to bring Semantic Web and AI technologies everywhere and to everything.

A Framework for Automatic Knowledge Base Generation from Observation Data Sets

Agnese Pinto[1], Saverio Ieva[1], Arnaldo Tomasino[1], Giuseppe Loseto[2],
Floriano Scioscia[1(✉)], Michele Ruta[1], and Francesco De Feudis[1]

[1] Polytechnic University of Bari, 70125 Bari, Italy
{agnese.pinto,saverio.ieva,arnaldo.tomasino,floriano.scioscia,
michele.ruta,francesco.defeudis}@poliba.it
[2] LUM University "Giuseppe Degennaro", 70010 Casamassima, BA, Italy
loseto@lum.it

Abstract. In the Semantic Web of Everything, observation data collected from sensors and devices disseminated in smart environments must be annotated in order to produce a Knowledge Base (KB) or Knowledge Graph (KG) which can be used subsequently for inference. Available approaches allow defining complex data models for mapping tabular data to KBs/KGs: while granting high flexibility, they can be difficult to use. This paper introduces a framework for automatic KB generation in Web Ontology Language (OWL) 2 from observation data sets. It aims at simplicity both in usage and in expressiveness of generated KBs, in order to enable reasoning with SWoE inference engines in pervasive and embedded devices. An illustrative example from a precision farming case study clarifies the approach and early performance results support its computational sustainability.

Keywords: Knowledge Representation · Web Ontology Language · Knowledge Graph Construction · Machine Learning

1 Introduction and Motivation

The Semantic Web of Everything (SWoE) vision aims to bring interoperable technologies for knowledge representation and reasoning to all scales of computing, from the World Wide Web (WWW) to nanodevices with strict processing, memory, and energy constraints. Distributed infrastructures for data stream gathering, analysis and interpretation can greatly benefit from knowledge-based methods and techniques, as commonly adopted Machine Learning (ML) methods have optimal performance only for very large and well-curated datasets. Dataset transformation into a usable Knowledge Base (KB) or Knowledge Graph (KG) requires overcoming the *impedance mismatch* of the Resource Description Framework (RDF) [26] and Web Ontology Language (OWL) [22] data models with respect to most data sources [20]. Data governance and curation are complex

© The Author(s), under exclusive license to Springer Nature Switzerland AG 2024
S. Casteleyn et al. (Eds.): ICWE 2023 Workshops, CCIS 1898, pp. 89–100, 2024.
https://doi.org/10.1007/978-3-031-50385-6_8

problems for the majority of real-world infrastructures [28] based on wireless sensor networks, embedded devices and wearables, which generate high-volume and high-velocity streams of noisy and uncertain data.

When starting from raw observation data sets, the currently prevalent approaches to the generation of a KB/KG rely on cloud-based *Data Lakes*. Though flexible, this approach is too complex and cumbersome for SWoE scenarios, not only because it requires huge storage resources, but also because it prevents agents running on pervasive devices from discovering and detecting relevant information autonomously. A wide body of research concerns mapping tabular data to KBs and KGs, which can cover many practical use cases: several methods, systems, and evaluation benchmarks exist [18]. They allow flexible mapping definitions beyond the simple "entity-per-row" assumption, in order to meet the requirements of advanced data management applications. For this reason, they often exhibit a steep learning curve and require significant expertise with Semantic Web technologies. In many SWoE contexts, however, observations represent events gathered from heterogeneous independent sources, such as sensors, Internet of Things (IoT) devices and objects populating a smart environment. Every event –either periodic or triggered by a condition– is an individual entity, with a specific value for each one of its attributes. As data models are kept relatively simple and regular, these contexts can benefit from leaner data processing frameworks for KB/KG construction.

This paper introduces a framework for automatic generation of OWL 2 KBs from observation data sets. The method consists in three phases: (i) data preparation and modeling of an upper ontology including classes for each type of observation (*i.e.*, relevant event in the problem domain) and for each feature; (ii) automatic Terminological Box (TBox) generation; (iii) automatic Assertion Box (ABox) generation, creating an OWL individual for each observation instance. By keeping logical expressiveness relatively simple, the KB generation approach is amenable to event classification and detection problems based on semantic matchmaking, [25] which can be executed on pervasive devices by means of optimized reasoning engines [24]. The correctness of the approach has been validated in a precision farming case study, while preliminary performance tests have evaluated the sustainability of the proposal.

The remainder of the paper is as follows. Relevant related work is recalled in Sect. 2. Section 3 describes in detail the framework architecture and processing steps. Section 4 reports on an illustrative example taken from the precision farming case study, while performance results are in Sect. 5, before conclusion.

2   Related Work

The *RDF Mapping Language* (RML) [11] has extended the *Relational database-to-RDF* (R2RML) [8] World Wide Web Consortium (W3C) recommendation for a declarative mapping language from tabular data to RDF. RML adds support for the integration of multiple data sources and for various structured data formats in addition to relational databases. R2RML and RML are still among the most widely adopted approaches for KG construction. RML has been further extended by *RML-star* [10] in order to support the *RDF-star* [27] language for annotating RDF statements with other RDF statements. These approaches, however, require writing a configuration document manually to specify mapping definitions. *Morph-KGC* [3] is an R2RML and RML interpreter focusing on performance and scalability: it groups rules in the input mapping documents, in order to guarantee the generation of disjoint sets of RDF triples by each group.

Several systems use popular Linked Open Data sources to annotate tabular data automatically. The architecture of *JenTab* [1] consists in a pool of modular processing tasks, which are combined in different pipelines for each type of table semantic annotation problem; it uses *Wikidata* [30] for entity resolution. In addition to Wikidata, *DAGOBAH* [19] queries four other services, including DBpedia [17] and Wikipedia API. Machine learning combined with probabilistic [31] and constraint programming [9] methods have also been exploited to assign a semantic model to tabular data sources automatically.

Whereas the above approaches produce RDF output, systems targeting OWL include *Mapping Master* [21] and *BootOX* [16]. Mapping Master provides a language to define mappings of complex spreadsheets to OWL ontologies. BootOX interprets R2RML mappings by encoding relational database features to OWL 2 axioms: the three phases of the *bootstrapping* problem as formulated in BootOX –vocabulary and ontology generation, mapping generation, importing– are conceptually similar to the processing phases of the approach presented in this paper, although the latter focuses on data-driven applications.

3 Framework Architecture

The main goal of the proposed framework is to automate the construction of a Knowledge Base starting from a reference dataset consisting of observation data. In this way, a dataset can be easily mapped into a conceptual model related to a specific domain through which every observation can be annotated. As shown in Fig. 1, the process of KB generation consists of three sub-tasks: (a) data preparation and upper ontology modeling; (b) TBox generation; (c) ABox generation. The following paragraphs provide a top-down description of the approach.

3.1 Data Preparation and Upper Ontology Modeling

The first step towards the definition of the Knowledge Base is the dataset analysis, aiming to identify the following information:

- list of *features* of observations, denoted as $\mathcal{F} = (F_1, F_2, \ldots, F_N)$; each feature has a (numerical or categorical) domain;
- list of *tuples*, denoted as $\mathcal{R} = (R_1, R_2, \ldots, R_M)$. Each tuple R_i is a set of attribute values $\langle v_{i,1}, v_{i,2}, \ldots, v_{i,N} \rangle$ representing an observation collected for the specific scenario;

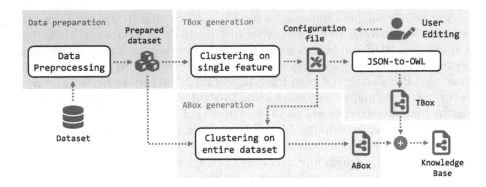

Fig. 1. Workflow of the proposed framework

– list of *events* of interest, denoted as $\mathcal{E} = (E_1, E_2, \ldots, E_P)$ and representing the set of class labels associated to the observations. Each tuple R_i can be associated to one or more events.

The upper layers of the reference ontology $\mathcal{T}$ should model the domain conceptualization along the specific patterns detailed hereinafter, in order to support semantic-based data annotation and interpretation. $\mathcal{T}$ is assumed as acyclic and expressed in the moderately complex $\mathcal{ALN}$ (Attributive Language with unqualified Number restrictions) Description Logic [4]. This is required to be compliant with nonstandard, nonmonotonic inferences provided by reasoning engines designed for SWoE applications (*e.g.*, *Tiny-ME* [24]). For each feature in $\mathcal{F}$, $\mathcal{T}$ must include a hierarchy of concepts derived from a reference class, selected by the user typically by referring to a well-known upper ontology, forming a partonomy of the topmost concept. For example, in Fig. 2 the *FeatureOfInterest* class defined in the *SOSA (Sensor, Observation, Sample, and Actuator)* ontology [15] is used as an upper layer for the TBox section related to the features. This subphase must deal with any *impedance mismatch* between the dataset model and (the available expressiveness of) the selected OWL sublanguage [23]. In this way, each dataset attribute F_i is represented by means of a class/subclass taxonomy featuring all significant value ranges and configurations it can take in the domain of interest. The breadth of each sublevel will be determined automatically during the TBox generation task described in Sect. 3.2. In that step, each subclass $F_{i,j}$ will be also associated with contextual parameters by means of specific *OWL Annotation Properties*. Similarly, the events in $\mathcal{E}$ are modeled as subclasses of an output concept identified by the user (*e.g.*, the *Observation* class in Fig. 2).

3.2   TBox Generation

The next step of the framework consists in processing the prepared dataset to generate the TBox. This task is composed of two distinct sub-tasks:

1. generation of a configuration file, storing the ontology metadata and all features parameters required to create and characterize the concept hierarchy;

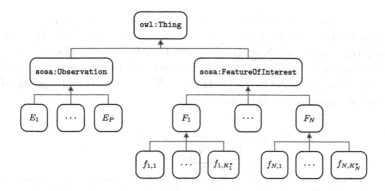

Fig. 2. TBox hierarchy

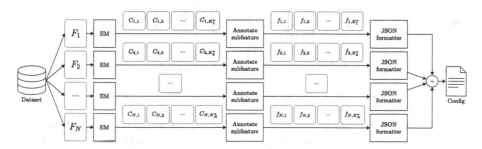

Fig. 3. Generation of the configuration file

2. serialization of the TBox, according to one of the available OWL 2 syntaxes, guided by the configuration file.

The main advantage of this two-step approach lies in the fact that the user can customize the configuration file (*e.g.*, to include further contextual information) before proceeding with the generation of the TBox. In this way, the proposed workflow can be adapted and reused for the generation of ontologies in a wide variety of domains of interest. Given a properly prepared dataset as input, the process of building the configuration file is illustrated in Fig. 3. The prepared dataset is processed via the *K-means* clustering algorithm, which has been chosen due to computational complexity amenable to SWoE contexts [2]. For each feature $F_i \in \mathcal{F}$, the *Elbow Method* (EM) [29] is used to compute the optimal number K_i^* of clusters to partition the values contained in the dataset for each i-th feature. Denoting as $\mathcal{C}_i = \{C_{i,1}, C_{i,2}, \ldots, C_{i,K_i^*}\}$ the set of clusters obtained from the feature F_i, for each cluster $C_{i,j} \in \mathcal{C}$ a new subclass $f_{i,j}$ (for $i = 1..N$ and $j = 1..K_i^*$) is added to the TBox. The name of each subclass of a given feature is obtained by combining a cluster *prefix* with the feature *name*, *e.g.*, *Low* + *Temperature* = *LowTemperature*). Up to 7 different prefixes are currently supported to partition a feature: *ExtremelyLow, VeryLow, Low, Medium, High, VeryHigh, ExtremelyHigh*. As shown in Fig. 4, if the number of clusters K_i^* associated to F_i is odd, then the prefix *Medium* will be assigned to the subclass $f_{i,m}$ with $m = (K_i^* + 1)/2$. On the contrary, if K_i^* is even then the prefix *Medium* will not be assigned to any subclass.

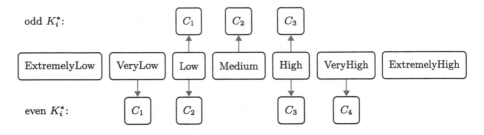

Fig. 4. Example of prefix assignment

Table 1. List of supported OWL annotation properties

Metadata	Annotation Property IRI	Short IRI	Range
Title	http://purl.org/dc/terms/title	`dcterms:title`	`xsd:string`
Description	http://purl.org/dc/terms/description	`dcterms:description`	`xsd:string`
Creator	http://purl.org/dc/terms/creator	`dcterms:creator`	`xsd:string`
Version	http://www.w3.org/2002/07/owl#versionIRI	`owl:versionIRI`	`xsd:string`
Centroid	http://swot.sisinflab.poliba.it/onto/kbgen/centroid	`kbg:centroid`	`xsd:float`
Min Value	http://schema.org/minValue	`schema:minValue`	`xsd:float`
Max Value	http://schema.org/maxValue	`schema:maxValue`	`xsd:float`

Each subclass $f_{i,j}$ is also characterized by the *centroid* ($c_{i,j}$) and the *range* of values associated to the $C_{i,j}$ cluster computed via K-means. The *kbg:centroid* annotation property associates the centroid to the subclass, while minimum and maximum values are specified as a pair of annotation properties –borrowed from the *Schema.org* vocabulary [12]– named *schema:minValue* and *schema:maxValue*, respectively. This facilitates associating the features of individual dataset observations to specific clusters and mapping each of them to the related subclass. The final configuration is then created by including the definition of all computed OWL classes and their annotated values. Basic ontology metadata (detailed in Table 1) is also specified by the user to further characterize the reference Knowledge Base. Finally, the configuration file is generated according to JSON (JavaScript Object Notation) syntax [5] representing a self-describing and easy-to-parse data format.

In the second step, domain experts can modify the configuration file both to refine results obtained by the clustering procedure and introduce additional elements (*e.g.*, classes, properties) not included in the original dataset. The refined configuration is parsed by a dedicated software module implemented in Java in order to generate the corresponding ontology. OWL API (version 3.4.10) library [13] is used as reference implementation providing several functionalities for creating, manipulating and serializing OWL ontologies.

3.3 ABox Generation

The ABox generation process is shown in Fig. 5. The same dataset used to generate the TBox is annotated to generate OWL individuals. In particular, an instance of the ABox can represent:

- a single tuple of the dataset whose values are mapped to elements of the TBox. In this way, a generic data corpus can be translated to an OWL KB, where each record corresponds to an instance;
- an aggregate event description derived from a clustering procedure considering all attributes simultaneously rather than individual features.

In the latter case, K-means algorithm takes the whole dataset in input, in order to identify different partitions of collected observations into K clusters. Each cluster represents an OWL individual to be modeled within the KB with a reference class expression, which can be used to label new observations. The EM is used also in this case for defining the optimal number K^* of clusters to partition the whole dataset. Since the clustering is performed on a dataset with N attributes, each cluster $D_i \in \mathcal{D} = \{D_1, D_2, \ldots, D_{K^*}\}$ will be associated to a list of centroids $d_i = (d_{i,1}, d_{i,2}, \ldots, d_{i,N}) \in \mathbb{R}^N$, where the value $d_{i,j}$ represents the reference centroid for the feature $F_j \in \mathcal{F}$. In particular, let ϕ_j be the set of partitions $\{f_{j,1}, f_{j,2}, \ldots, f_{j,K_j^*}\}$ computed for the feature F_j; each value $d_{i,j} \in d_i$, $\forall j = 1..N$ is mapped to the corresponding subclass defined in the TBox associated with the partition $f_{j,h} \in \phi_j$ if and only if $minValue(f_{j,h}) < d_{i,j} \leq maxValue(f_{j,h})$. After mapping all values $d_{i,j} \in D_i$ into OWL classes defined in the TBox, an OWL named individual will be created as a conjunctive expression of ontology axioms. Two different modeling approaches have been investigated to represent the generated instances, which can be selected by means of the configuration file. In the first approach, each individual description is modeled as a simple conjunction of atomic concepts corresponding to the subclasses $f_{j,h}$. In the other one, individuals are modeled combining OWL object properties with each subclass. The latter approach preserves the hierarchy of concepts, a further explicit semantics is given and each ontology axiom is expressed by means of a universal and an existential quantifier. Finally, individuals are associated to a specific event selected among the output classes in the ontology. This process is applied for each cluster D_i to populate the ABox of the KB.

4 Illustrative Example in Precision Farming

In this section, a simple example is described in order to highlight peculiarities of the proposed framework. The reference dataset derives from on-site measurements of several parameters characterizing wheat, olive and grapevine crops in

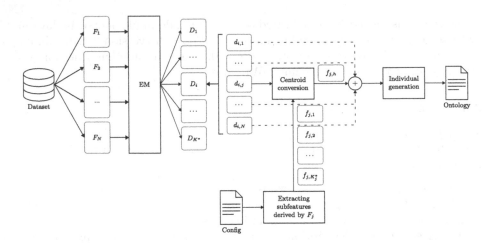

Fig. 5. ABox generation process

the Apulia region, exploiting IoT device networks as well as hyperspectral images taken from Unmanned Aerial Vehicle (UAV), manned aircraft, and satellite constellations. Each crop is described by a set of attributes related to health status, growth factors and phenological phases. Quantitative data are processed according to the workflow in Fig. 1 and the generated KB is reported in what follows. For the sake of readability, OWL statements are expressed in *Manchester* syntax [14] but all OWL 2 serializations are supported and the reference syntax can be selected in the configuration file.

$SAREF4AGRI^1$ is used as upper ontology representing an extension of the *Smart Applications REFerence ontology* (SAREF) [7] for the agriculture and food domain. This ontology includes two concepts *saref:Property* and *s4agri:Crop* configured as reference class for the subtrees related to crop parameters and observed events, respectively.

```
Prefix: : <https://www.example.com/crop-onto#>
Prefix: saref: <https://saref.etsi.org/core/>
Prefix: s4agri: <https://saref.etsi.org/saref4agri/>
Class: saref:Property
Class: s4agri:Crop
```

The TBox generation task produces the following results. For each feature F_i within the dataset (*e.g.*, petiole height), a new OWL class is created as subclass of *saref:Property*. As mentioned in Sect. 3.2, F_i is also partitioned in multiple subclasses $f_{i,j}$ (*e.g.*, low petiole height), according to the clustering algorithm executed on the single attribute, and characterized by means of OWL annotation properties. An OWL object property is also generated as subproperty of *saref:hasProperty*.

---

1 https://saref.etsi.org/saref4agri/.

```
Prefix: xsd: <http://www.w3.org/2001/XMLSchema#>
Prefix: schema: <https://schema.org/>
Prefix: kbg: <http://swot.sisinflab.poliba.it/onto/kbgen/>
Class: PetioleHeight
  SubClassOf: saref:Property
Class: LowPetioleHeight
  SubClassOf: PetioleHeight
  Annotations: kbg:centroid "3.57"^^xsd:float,
    schema:minValue "3.1"^^xsd:float,
    schema:maxValue "3.8"^^xsd:float
ObjectProperty: hasPetioleHeight
  SubPropertyOf: saref:hasProperty
  Range: PetioleHeight
```

Three OWL classes are defined as subclasses of *Crop* to model the cultivations observed during the measurement procedure: *Grapevine*, *OliveTree* and *Wheat*.

```
Prefix: rdf: <http://www.w3.org/1999/02/22-rdf-syntax-ns#>
Class: GrapeVine
  SubClassOf: s4agri:Crop
Class: OliveTree
  SubClassOf: s4agri:Crop
Class: Wheat
  SubClassOf: s4agri:Crop
AnnotationProperty: cropType
  SubPropertyOf: rdf:value
  Range: s4agri:Crop
```

Finally, the ABox is generated as described in Sect. 3.3. The following example reports an OWL named individual representing an olive tree observation. The individual description is obtained by means of the K-means algorithm applied on the whole dataset. All numeric values in the cluster are mapped to concepts and properties defined during the previous step.

```
Individual: OliveTreeObservation
  Annotations: cropType OliveTree
  Types: (hasPetioleHeight only LowPetioleHeight) and (hasPetioleArea
    only MediumPetioleArea) and (hasTemperature only VeryLowTemperature)
    and (hasHumidity only HighHumidity) ... and (hasTreeDensity only
    HighTreeDensity)
```

5   Performance Evaluation

As a preliminary feasibility assessment of the proposed approach, computational performance has been evaluated exploiting a reference dataset [6] consisting of 10000 observations, each characterized by 48 features (specifically, 22 Boolean, 3 continuous numeric, 16 discrete numeric and 7 categorial features). Tests have been carried out on a desktop PC equipped with Intel Core i7-4790 quad-core

CPU at 3.6 GHz, 16 GB DDR3 RAM at 1600 MT/s, 2 TB SATA storage memory at 7200 RPM, Windows 10 Home 64-bit. Performed tests regard the turnaround time of the KB generation procedure, which is composed of the following subtasks: (a) dataset preprocessing; (b) features clustering; (c) configuration file creation; (d) TBox generation; (e) dataset clustering; (f) ABox generation (atomic concepts conjunction); (g) ABox generation (atomic concepts with object properties). Tests have been repeated five times and average values have been reported. As shown in Fig. 6, steps (b) and (e) require on average a higher processing time due to the clustering procedures. In particular, the execution time of task (b) strongly correlates with on the number of distinct values collected for each feature (Fig. 7). The two modeling approaches (f) and (g) for the generation of the ABox require similar processing time. Users can select the most suitable approach according to the tasks that will be performed on the generated output without worrying about particular performance issues.

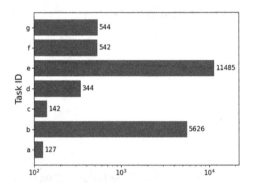

Fig. 6. Processing time (ms)   **Fig. 7.** Clustering time - Task *b*

6   Conclusion and Future Work

This paper has presented an approach for generation of OWL 2 KBs from observation data sets. The proposal aims to automate annotation of data gathered by sensing devices in pervasive computing contexts, fostering usage of semantic-enhanced machine learning in the SWoE. K-means clustering is exploited on each data set feature to create the TBox along partonomy patterns; K-means is applied to individuals as well, in order to model (i) clusters across all features as concept expressions, representing the reference model in a training set, and (ii) single records in a test set for evaluation. The correctness of the approach has been validated empirically in a case study on precision farming, while preliminary performance of a prototype implementation supports its computational feasibility.

Future work includes adapting the framework implementation to embedded, wearable and single-board computer platforms, followed by experimental evaluations of the computational efficiency and the quality of the generated KB w.r.t. state-of-the-art methods on available reference benchmarks. Moreover, the exploitation of generated KBs in a variety of real SWoE case studies will allow to fully validate the suitability of the approach. Further investigation includes integration with RML or RML-derived languages to provide both ease-of-use for typical applications and flexibility when needed.

Acknowledgments. This work has been supported by project TEBAKA (TErritorial BAsic Knowledge Acquisition), funded by the Italian Ministry of University and Research.

References

1. Abdelmageed, N., Schindler, S.: JenTab: matching tabular data to knowledge graphs. In: Semantic Web Challenge on Tabular Data to Knowledge Graph Matching Workshop, International Semantic Web Conference, 40–49 (2020)
2. Ahmed, M., Seraj, R., Islam, S.M.S.: The K-means algorithm: a comprehensive survey and performance evaluation. Electronics 9(8), 1295 (2020)
3. Arenas-Guerrero, J., Chaves-Fraga, D., Toledo, J., Pérez, M.S., Corcho, O.: Morph-KGC: Scalable knowledge graph materialization with mapping partitions. Semantic Web, pp. 1–20 (2022)
4. Baader, F., Calvanese, D., McGuinness, D., Patel-Schneider, P., Nardi, D., et al.: The Description Logic Handbook: Theory. Implementation and Applications. Cambridge University Press, Cambridge (2003)
5. Bray, T.: RFC 8259: The JavaScript object notation (JSON) data interchange format (2017)
6. Chiew, K.L., Tan, C.L., Wong, K., Yong, K.S., Tiong, W.K.: A new hybrid ensemble feature selection framework for machine learning-based phishing detection system. Inf. Sci. 484(C), 153–166 (2019)
7. Daniele, L., den Hartog, F., Roes, J.: Created in close interaction with the industry: the smart appliances REFerence (SAREF) ontology. In: Cuel, R., Young, R. (eds.) FOMI 2015. LNBIP, vol. 225, pp. 100–112. Springer, Cham (2015). https://doi.org/10.1007/978-3-319-21545-7_9
8. Das, S., Sundara, S., Cyganiak, R.: R2RML: RDB to RDF Mapping Language. Recommendation, W3C (2012). https://www.w3.org/TR/r2rml/
9. De Una, D., Rümmele, N., Gange, G., Schachte, P., Stuckey, P.J.: Machine learning and constraint programming for relational-to-ontology schema mapping. In: International Joint Conference on Artificial Intelligence, pp. 1277–1283 (2018)
10. Delva, T., Arenas-Guerrero, J., Iglesias-Molina, A., Corcho, O., Chaves-Fraga, D., Dimou, A.: RML-star: a declarative mapping language for RDF-star generation. In: ISWC2021, the International Semantic Web Conference, vol. 2980. CEUR (2021)
11. Dimou, A., Vander Sande, M., Colpaert, P., Verborgh, R., Mannens, E., Van de Walle, R.: RML: a generic language for integrated RDF mappings of heterogeneous data. In: Workshop on Linked Data on the Web, 23rd International World Wide Web Conference, pp. 1–5 (2014)
12. Guha, R.V., Brickley, D., Macbeth, S.: Schema Org.: evolution of structured data on the web. Commun. ACM 59(2), 44–51 (2016)

13. Horridge, M., Bechhofer, S.: The OWL API: a java API for OWL ontologies. Semant. Web **2**(1), 11–21 (2011)
14. Horridge, M., Patel-Schneider, P.: OWL 2 Web Ontology Language Manchester Syntax (Second Edition). W3C note, W3C (2012). https://www.w3.org/TR/owl2-manchester-syntax/
15. Janowicz, K., Haller, A., Cox, S.J., Le Phuoc, D., Lefrançois, M.: SOSA: a lightweight ontology for sensors, observations, samples, and actuators. J. Web Semant. **56**, 1–10 (2019)
16. Jiménez-Ruiz, E., et al.: BOOTOX: practical mapping of RDBs to OWL 2. In: Arenas, M., et al. (eds.) ISWC 2015. LNCS, vol. 9367, pp. 113–132. Springer, Cham (2015). https://doi.org/10.1007/978-3-319-25010-6_7
17. Lehmann, J., et al.: DBpedia-a large-scale, multilingual knowledge base extracted from Wikipedia. Semant. web **6**(2), 167–195 (2015)
18. Liu, J., Chabot, Y., Troncy, R., Huynh, V.P., Labbé, T., Monnin, P.: From tabular data to knowledge graphs: a survey of semantic table interpretation tasks and methods. J. Web Semant. **76**, 100761 (2022)
19. Liu, J., Troncy, R.: Dagobah: an end-to-end context-free tabular data semantic annotation system. In: Semantic Web Challenge on Tabular Data to Knowledge Graph Matching Workshop, International Semantic Web Conference, pp. 41–48 (2019)
20. Modoni, G.E., Sacco, M.: Discovering critical factors affecting RDF stores success. In: Pandey, R., Paprzycki, M., Srivastava, N., Bhalla, S., Wasielewska-Michniewska, K. (eds.) Semantic IoT: Theory and Applications. SCI, vol. 941, pp. 193–206. Springer, Cham (2021). https://doi.org/10.1007/978-3-030-64619-6_8
21. O'Connor, M.J., Halaschek-Wiener, C., Musen, M.A.: Mapping master: a flexible approach for mapping spreadsheets to OWL. In: Patel-Schneider, P.F., et al. (eds.) ISWC 2010. LNCS, vol. 6497, pp. 194–208. Springer, Heidelberg (2010). https://doi.org/10.1007/978-3-642-17749-1_13
22. Parsia, B., Rudolph, S., Krötzsch, M., Patel-Schneider, P., Hitzler, P.: OWL 2 Web Ontology Language Primer (Second Edition). W3C Recommendation, W3C (2012). https://www.w3.org/TR/owl2-primer
23. Pinkel, C., et al.: RODI: benchmarking relational-to-ontology mapping generation quality. Semant. Web **9**(1), 25–52 (2018)
24. Ruta, M., et al.: A multiplatform reasoning engine for the semantic web of everything. J. Web Semant. **73**, 100709 (2022)
25. Ruta, M., Scioscia, F., Loseto, G., Pinto, A., Di Sciascio, E.: Machine learning in the internet of things: a semantic-enhanced approach. Semant. Web **10**(1), 183–204 (2019)
26. Schreiber, G., Gandon, F.: RDF 1.1 XML syntax. Recommendation, W3C (2014). https://www.w3.org/TR/rdf-syntax-grammar/
27. Schreiber, G., Gandon, F.: RDF-star and SPARQL-star. Draft community group report, W3C (2023). https://w3c.github.io/rdf-star/cg-spec/editors_draft.html
28. Talburt, J.R., Ehrlinger, L., Magruder, J.: Automated data curation and data governance automation. Front. Big Data **6**, 1148331 (2023)
29. Thorndike, R.: Who belongs in the family? Psychometrika **18**(4), 267–276 (1953)
30. Van Veen, T.: Wikidata: from "an" identifier to "the" identifier. Inf. Technol. Libr. **38**(2), 72–81 (2019)
31. Vu, B., Knoblock, C., Pujara, J.: Learning semantic models of data sources using probabilistic graphical models. In: The World Wide Web Conference, pp. 1944–1953 (2019)

Exploring Knowledge-Based Systems for Commercial Mortgage Underwriting

K. Patricia Cannon and Simon J. Preis[✉]

OTH Amberg-Weiden, Hetzenrichter Weg 15, 92637 Weiden i.d.OPf., Germany
{k.cannon,s.preis}@oth-aw.de

Abstract. While the residential mortgage industry has benefited from automated mortgage applications and underwriting, the commercial mortgage industry still relies heavily on manual underwriting. The paper aims to present the state of research in the domain of knowledge-based systems (KBS) and commercial mortgage underwriting and to identify the challenges in commercial mortgage underwriting by conducting a systematic literature review (SLR). The SLR uses the review process outlined by Kitchenham and includes a hybrid coding approach to analyze the data. The paper finds that KBS and ontologies to automate commercial mortgage underwriting were not studied yet. It also identifies several challenges in mortgage underwriting in data, process, and underwriting categories. The findings of this paper can be used for further research in the field of commercial mortgage underwriting and KBS. KBS appear suitable to address the identified challenges and can be integrated into information system automation or artificial intelligence (AI) implementations for commercial mortgage underwriting.

Keywords: Ontology · knowledge-based system · commercial mortgage underwriting · underwriting challenges

1 Introduction

The US residential mortgage industry has seen technological innovation in automated, simplified, and faster mortgage processing. In 2015, Rocket Mortgage by Quicken Loans launched online mortgage applications, which were approved in as little as 8 min [1]. Automated mortgage applications and underwriting were groundbreaking as the residential mortgage industry has experienced little technology adoption through information systems standards until then [2]. Residential and insurance underwriting experienced a high degree of information system support and thus automation due to the structured data, as outlined in multiple studies [1, 3–9].

Not only can residential automated mortgage applications and underwriting save time, the automation can also reduce cost and lead to a lower default rate. A recent survey on lender cost drivers and the impact of digitalization efforts on cost efficiency stated that back-end operational employees (underwriters, processors, and closers) are the top cost-increase drivers. In contrast, back-end process technologies are the top cost-decrease drivers [10]. Fintech mortgage lenders process mortgages on average 20% faster

S. Casteleyn et al. (Eds.): ICWE 2023 Workshops, CCIS 1898, pp. 101–113, 2024.
https://doi.org/10.1007/978-3-031-50385-6_9

with their end-to-end online and automated mortgage and processing business model. At the same time, Fintech mortgage lenders maintain a default rate of about 25% lower than traditional lenders [1].

Unlike residential mortgages, commercial mortgages are still mostly manually underwritten with spreadsheets and an essentially paper-based process to analyze the dynamic data of non-standard loans, including non-standard properties or income [6, 11].

This research aims to explore the state of research on commercial mortgage underwriting and to identify commercial underwriting challenges. Ontologies and KBS will be explored as a possible solution for challenges and a basis for further development when building automation information systems or AI implementations. The specified research questions that the literature review aims to answer are the following:

R1:_What is the state of research regarding KBS to automate mortgage underwriting?_

R2: _What challenges exist in commercial mortgage underwriting?_

The paper is structured as follows. Section 2 discusses the theoretical background regarding the different dimensions of mortgage underwriting and KBS relevant to the research aims. Section 3 explains the research methodology utilized to answer RQ1 and RQ2. We present the results in Sect. 4, where we identify a research gap and mortgage underwriting challenges. We discuss the results and outline recommendations for future research in Sect. 5. Finally, we summarize the findings of the research in Sect. 6.

2 Theoretical Background

2.1 Mortgage Underwriting

Mortgage underwriting is the risk assessment of a proposed mortgage loan performed by an underwriter based on a due diligence study. The underwriter approves or denies a mortgage loan application based on the applicant and property information [12]. Underwriters analyze large amounts of dynamic information to better comprehend the collateral on loan applications and evaluate risk [11]. Underwriting is tedious and labor-intensive and relies heavily on the skill and experience of the underwriter [13].

Residential mortgage underwriting is generally limited to information about the applicant or applicants (verification of income and debts credit report, verification of identity) and the property in a primarily structured data format [14].

Commercial Mortgage Underwriting. Commercial mortgages are non-standard loans requiring a detailed analysis of the various aspects of the transaction. Lenders mainly use manual underwriting to underwrite non-standard loans, including those involving property or non-standard income [6]. Within the commercial underwriting domain, a challenge is combining qualitative and quantitative information incorporated into the underwriting decision. The quantitative information contains the commercial loan underwriting analysis of historical financial data and projections for the future. Furthermore, financial ratios are analyzed by showing the relationships between financial variables and evaluating the state of the business operations. This data is mainly structured data.

However, data about the management team and market, for instance, is qualitative and thus unstructured. Even subjective data such as a 'feel' of the operations through site visits and talking to staff needs becomes part of the commercial underwriting decision [15]. Commercial mortgages are largely manually underwritten using spreadsheets and a paper-based process that relies on underwriters to evaluate mortgage applications by analyzing large volumes of dynamic data [11].

Automated Mortgage Underwriting. Automating underwriting does not eliminate the position of human underwriters, but it does reduce the labor intensity of mortgage processing [1]. The benefits of an automated underwriting process are improved service quality and timing, reduced risk of losing submitted documents, immediate moving applications to the next step, and improved risk management in some instances [8].

The automation of residential mortgage underwriting and the first steps in mortgage underwriting AI started in the mid-1990s [4, 16, 17]. Since then, Fintech lenders have begun to emerge and offer faster online mortgage application processes without sacrificing risk assessment outcomes. Fintech mortgage lenders reduce the average processing time by 20% (about ten days) while keeping the default rates approximately 25% lower than traditional lenders. Moreover, Fintech lenders respond to market changes more efficiently, with their processing time increasing by merely 7.5 days after doubling the application volume, as opposed to the 13.5-day increase observed among traditional lenders [1].

The key to developing the systems mentioned above was the Mortgage Bankers Association of America's vendor-neutral Extensible Markup Language (XML)-based MISMO data standards for data sharing data both within mortgage companies and external participants of the lending process [2, 18]. MISMO has been slowly releasing some commercial mortgage standards based on industry demand and through volunteer participation. However, the commercial MISMO standards adoption has yet to happen within the commercial mortgage industry (R. Russo, personal communication, February 10, 2023).

The adoption problems might be due to the different data formats. MISMO represents a unified structured data standard, while most of the commercial mortgage data is in an unstructured format.

2.2 Ontologies and KBS

Semantics is the study of meaning in language or data and the meaning of words, phrases, and sentences [19–21]. Ontologies originate in the semantic web, which extends the world wide web. The semantic web represents machine-readable and machine-understandable information, thus being more meaningful for computers and humans [22]. Within the semantic web architecture consisting of components such as RDF, OWL, and SPARQL, as shown in Fig. 1, ontologies are an extension of XML.

The semantic web provides a standardized structure for data representation and reasoning. The data is organized in ontologies to provide inference power over the stored data. Machine interpretable semantics to handle textual information is a requirement of the semantic web. Natural language techniques such as information extraction and term recognition give unstructured data or text meaning. The mixture of semantic web

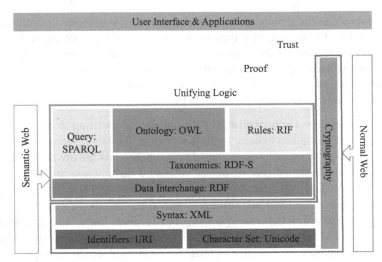

Fig. 1. Adopted from semantic web architecture [23]

technologies with NLP provides an infrastructure for complex queries and the ability to fetch actual logical answers [24].

Ontologies. Formally defined knowledge is based on conceptualizing objects, concepts, and other items representing a knowledge base or KBS [26]. Making an ontology is like creating a set of data and specifying its structure for use by other programs. Domain-independent applications, software agents, and problem-solving techniques all employ ontologies and knowledge bases created from ontologies as data [27]. The explicit specification of a formal language is used for practical applications and human communication [28].

Accordingly, an ontology provides a standard vocabulary to share knowledge within a domain. It offers relationships and machine-interpretable definitions of critical terms in the domain. Ontologies connect people, organizations, and application systems. They are tools to assist human-machine communication and help realize interoperability between software systems to make them more resilient and robust [29]. Ontologies and semantic technologies are the main technologies in some banks since they increase the efficiency of bank processes and help the integration of electronic services [25].

Ontologies are commonly expressed in the formal Web Ontology Language (OWL). Its current version is also called "OWL 2", which has an RDF/XML syntax [30]. While XML Schema language restricts the structure of XML documents with an extension of datatypes, OWL adds more vocabulary. The vocabulary describes classes and properties, relations between classes (e.g., disjointness), cardinality (e.g., exactly one), and equality, among others [31]. OWL is a powerful general-purpose modeling language for certain parts of human knowledge. The results of the OWL modeling processes are ontologies. Human thinking draws consequences from knowledge. OWL captures this aspect of human intelligence through knowledge it can represent [32].

Related and Relevant Existing Ontologies and Data Standards. A central idea of ontologies is providing a standard vocabulary to share knowledge within a domain and having machine-interpretable definitions of key terms in the domain [29]. Therefore, existing and applicable ontologies should be utilized whenever possible. Within the finance industry, there are several ontologies, including the Financial Industry Business Ontology (FIBO) [33], Financial Regulation Ontology (FRO) [34], Financial Industry Regulatory Ontology (FIRO) [35], and OntoFINE, an Ontology Network in Finance and Economics [36]. These are general finance ontology concepts, whereas FIBO contains some residential mortgage ontologies. Additionally, there is a partial XML schema for commercial mortgages by the Mortgage Industry Standards Maintenance Organization (MISMO).

Within the semantic web architecture, XML is part of the standard web languages and a basis of the semantic web languages such as RDF, SPARQL, and OWL, see Fig. 1. Table 1 compares the MISMO and FIBO standards and their uses and applications.

Table 1. Adopted comparison between MISMO and FIBO [37]

MISMO (datasets)	FIBO (ontology)
Mortgage Industry	Finance Industry
Data needed for transactions	All financial market concepts
A defined sender and receiver	Used to interpret disparate info
XML Schema Based	RDF/OWL Based
Used to create structured messages	Used to interpret unstructured data
Uses classic data modeling concepts	Uses a series of assertions
Transmits a transaction	Conducts reasoning

As outlined in Table 1, the MISMO data standards are sufficient to create structured messages and transmit data. In contrast, ontologies are crucial to interpret unstructured data. While the finance industry has a comprehensive ontology with FIBO, the mortgage ontologies within FIBO are still under development and limited to the residential mortgage domain. The commercial mortgage domain does have some MISMO data standards that could be utilized for future commercial mortgage ontology development.

This research seeks to determine to which extent KBS and ontologies for commercial mortgage underwriting were studied and what underwriting challenges require ontological KBS.

3 Research Methodology

Literature reviews are the basis for IS research [38]. We conducted a systematic literature review (SLR) to confirm a suspected literature gap and to answer R1 and R2. The research scope is defined based on Vom Brocke's adaption of Cooper's taxonomy for categorizing literature reviews [39, 40]. The research scope consists of an iterative process, bibliographic databases, and publication sources to provide a representative and seminal works coverage by utilizing keyword, forward, and backward searches. The SLR uses the review process outlined by Kitchenham for the SLR [41]. The research process was adjusted for the scope of this research regarding the review team.

The initial keywords were chosen based on the research's title, aims, and objectives and expanded during the iterative search to include the following search string: (mortgag* OR underwrit* OR credit risk) AND (expert system OR ontolog* OR knowledge based OR KBS OR graph). The databases searched were Science Direct, Springer Link, IEEE Xplore Digital Library, and ACM Digital Library.

Given the limited research in the field, we included relevant papers published between 1995 and 2022 in the SLR to ensure a comprehensive search. The included research had to be in English and from peer-reviewed publications with a minimum citation count of 1 as the quality criteria. All articles were screened for general applicability within title, keywords, and abstract, producing 37 results for further analysis. Following a full-text review, quality criteria exclusions, and rating, a final pool of 22 studies emerged. A research protocol documents and outlines all steps of the SLR.

For RQ1, the journal articles and conference papers from the SLR were tabulated and analyzed for content relating to the different dimensions of the research. These dimensions consist of two technology and four business area dimensions. We systematically mapped the extracted data and results for further analysis in Sect. 4.

For the data analysis to answer RQ2, we utilized a hybrid coding approach to code and analyze the data. Firstly, deductive codes were derived from the Infranodus text network analysis [42]. The text sections identifying mortgage underwriting challenges and problems in the reviewed literature were extracted and cleaned for further analysis. In text network analysis, the thematic clusters consist of nodes (words) that tend to appear together (side by side) in the same context. Secondly, the research followed an inductive approach and used the most influential elements, data, process, and underwriting (describing and in the following referred to as human factor), as coding categories. We manually coded text excerpts describing underwriting challenges and further categorized and iteratively specified them.

4 Results

We completed an SLR to answer RQ1 and RQ2. The rationale behind RQ1 is to describe and understand the state of KBS research in the context of automating commercial mortgage underwriting to identify a suspected research gap. Additionally, we answered RQ2 and identified the underwriting challenges with the information derived from the literature of the SLR.

4.1 State of Research

Commercial mortgage underwriting covers multiple aspects researched in academia in the past. Table 2 provides an overview of the SLR results following Webster and Watson [38].

Table 2. Concept Matrix of SLR

No	Source	Year	ES, KBS, KG*	Ontologies	Mortgage	Underwriting	Commercial	Finance
1	[6]	2019	X			X		X
2	[43]	2022			X			
3	[44]	2010		X	X			
4	[45]	2007	X			X		
5	[46]	2015	X			X	X	
6	[15]	2006	X			X	X	
7	[47]	2022	X			X	X	
8	[16]	1995	X		X	X		
9	[48]	2008	X	X		X		X
10	[49]	2020			X	X		
11	[50]	2009		X		X		
12	[51]	2022		X				
13	[52]	2012		X				X
14	[53]	2010	X		X			
15	[54]	2013		X				X
16	[55]	2020	X	X		X		X
17	[56]	2022	X		X			
18	[57]	2014		X				X
19	[36]	2022		X				X
20	[58]	2017		X				X
21	[59]	2015	X					X
22	[60]	2014	X		X			
	Our research		**X**	**X**	**X**	**X**	**X**	**X**

*Expert System, Knowledge-based System, Knowledge Graph

KBS and ontologies have been studied generally in finance and within the research areas of mortgages, underwriting, and within a commercial context. However, based on the content analysis of these dimensions, commercial mortgage underwriting has not been studied in the context of KBS or, more specifically, ontologies. The analysis indicates a research gap justifying our research. Additionally, we noticed that the literature frequently mentions and describes underwriting challenges. However, we could not find any empirical studies on underwriting challenges within the scope of the SLR.

4.2 Underwriting Challenges

RQ2 seeks to identify and analyze the challenges in mortgage underwriting from the existing literature. There is not enough literature to focus only on commercial mortgage underwriting, so the focus range was extended to mortgage underwriting in general. Table 3 shows the results of the categorization and coding process as summarized challenges within the categories of data, process, and human factor.

Table 3. Analysis of underwriting challenges

Data		Process		Human Factor	
Semantics & heterogeneity	17	Complexity	9	Skill & experience	14
Consistency & accuracy	11	Time	7	Error	6
Volume	7	Manual underwriting	3	Bias	2
Interdependence	5	Transparency	1		
Completeness	2	Compliance	2		
Validation	1				
Total	**43**		**22**		**22**

Data semantics and heterogeneity-related challenges were noted 17 times in the literature, compared to data validation and human bias challenges which were noted one and two times, respectively. The data challenges totaling 43 equals almost as many mentions as the combined process and human factor challenges. It should be noted that challenges are often interdependent. For example, many external parties in a mortgage transaction result in multiple challenges, such as interdependence, complexity, and timing.

Data Challenges. The underwriting challenges related to data are tied to semantics, heterogeneity, consistency, and accuracy. These are challenges with heterogeneous data sources and forms, including financial or non-financial information, quantitative and qualitative underwriting criteria, and even subjective information [15, 45]. Problems caused by using different concepts for semantically equivalent information lead to data conflicts as data becomes inconsistent. Additionally, calculation errors and incorrect entries are other sources of data quality problems. Inaccurate data leads to slow and expensive loan processing, weak underwriting, inadequate portfolio management, and other costs to lenders and mortgage investors [52].

Additional underwriting issues relating to data are volume, interdependence, completeness, and validation. The data volume becomes increasingly challenging in combination with semantic and heterogeneity aspects, such as different meanings of the underwritten real-world objects and data entities within the organization's information systems [57]. The mortgage lending process involves interactions with many external entities providing information, leading to interdependence challenges [49].

Process Challenges. The challenges in the underwriting process are mainly complexity and timing but also compliance, manual underwriting, and transparency.

Process complexity has been described in interdepartmental file circulation with the lending company [6, 57] and in the context of processing time and data volume [49, 56]. Processing time has been described in the same context and as the consequence of complex and manual processes [16, 46]. As a document-intensive business, the operational nature leads to extensive manual verification, thus adding process complexity [49].

Human Factor Challenges. Narrowing in on the human factor in underwriting, the underwriter's skill and experience were noticeable patterns in the challenge descriptions. Quality underwriting requires careful attention to detail. The underwriter's decision-making process is complex and requires numerous input variables to reflect the underwriters' knowledge and guidelines [6]. Underwriters are highly qualified individuals with many years of mortgage lending experience. Underwriters are experts who use heuristic knowledge gained through years of experience and learning [6, 13]. Underwriters must know hundreds of product-specific underwriting guidelines to determine if a loan profile meets the lender's and eventual investor's requirements [16]. Finally, underwriting errors and bias were subcategories in the description of underwriting challenges.

5 Discussion

Most literature is published in the financial services field, and the mortgage lending literature only applies to residential mortgages. The data structure in these studies mainly comprises structured data inputs and a significantly smaller data pool than commercial mortgages. These studies do not address the aspects of unstructured and qualitative data, which are predominant in commercial underwriting. Therefore, the literature on KBS and ontologies for mortgage underwriting lacks a representation of the semantics, volume, and complexity of commercial mortgages and underwriting.

In our research, we identified data challenges, particularly semantics and heterogeneity, and a general interdependence of underwriting challenges. KBS and ontologies could be promising solutions to resolve these challenges. Ontologies offer a standardized structure for representing and reasoning with data and the ability to handle machine-interpretable semantics for textual information. At the same time, integrating semantic web technologies with NLP enables complex querying and the retrieval of logical answers from unstructured data. Therefore, we recommend future research to focus on prototyping and evaluating a sample ontology to determine if ontologies can solve underwriting challenges.

Finally, there has been no empirical research on the underwriting challenges discovered during this research. The underwriting challenges described in the literature primarily state these challenges but contain little explanation of why these challenges exist. Future research should include empirical research on underwriting challenges. Although there is no formal study on the difficulties of the automation of commercial mortgage underwriting, the multitude of challenges identified by this research and the lack of descriptive challenge detail of prior studies suggest being contributing factors.

6 Conclusion

In conclusion, the residential mortgage industry has witnessed impressive technological innovation, resulting in automated, simplified, and faster mortgage processing. However, commercial mortgages are still mostly manually underwritten, which is costly and slow. The SLR confirmed the existence of a literature gap for KBS and ontologies to automate commercial mortgage underwriting. The research further identified the challenges that exist in mortgage underwriting.

We categorized and identified the challenges in data, process, and human factor categories. Data challenges account for nearly as many challenges as process and human factor challenges combined. Within the data challenges, data semantics, heterogeneity, consistency, and accuracy are mentioned most.

The semantic capabilities of KBS and, more specifically, OWL-based ontologies could address various of the identified underwriting challenges, particularly for the semantics and heterogeneity challenges of unstructured and qualitative data prominent in commercial mortgage underwriting. KBS can further be the foundation for building automation information systems or AI implementations. As such, this study contributes to future research in mortgage underwriting automation and the development of KBS to improve commercial mortgage underwriting efficiency.

Because of the above mentioned, future work should focus on prototyping and evaluating a sample ontology to determine if ontologies can solve the underwriting challenges. Finally, this research was limited by the fact that there was insufficient existing literature to identify commercial underwriting challenges exclusively. For this reason and because there is no empirical research on underwriter challenges, future research should include an empirical study on commercial mortgage underwriting challenges.

References

1. Fuster, A., Plosser, M., Schnabl, P., Vickery, J.: The role of technology in mortgage lending. Rev. Finan. Stud. **32**, 1854–1899 (2019). https://doi.org/10.1093/rfs/hhz018
2. Markus, M.L., Steinfield, C.W., Wigand, R.T.: The evolution of vertical IS standards : electronic interchange standards in the us home mortgage industry. In: International conference on IS Special Workshop on Standard Making sponsored by MISQ, pp. 80–91 (2003)
3. Yan, W., Bonissone, P.P.: Designing a neural network decision system for automated insurance underwriting. In: IEEE International Conference on Neural Networks - Conference Proceedings, pp. 2106–2113 (2006). https://doi.org/10.1109/IJCNN.2006.246981
4. Krovvidy, S., Landsman, R., Opdahl, S., Templeton, N., Smalera, S.: Custom DU - A web-based business user-driven automated underwriting system. AI Mag. **29**, 41–51 (2008)
5. Dubey, A., Parida, T., Birajdar, A., Prajapati, A.K., Rane, S.: Smart underwriting system: an intelligent decision support system for insurance approval risk assessment. In: 2018 3rd International Conference for Convergence in Technology, I2CT 2018. (2018). https://doi.org/10.1109/I2CT.2018.8529792
6. Sachan, S., Yang, J.-B., Xu, D.-L., Benavides, D.E., Li, Y.: An explainable AI decision-support-system to automate loan underwriting. Expert Syst. Appl. **144**, 113100 (2020). https://doi.org/10.1016/j.eswa.2019.113100
7. Wigand, R.T., Steinfield, C.W., Markus, M.L.: Information technology standards choices and industry structure outcomes: the case of the US home mortgage industry. J. Manag. Inf. Syst. **22**(2), 165–191 (2005). https://doi.org/10.1080/07421222.2005.11045843

8. Lee, R.C.M., Mark, K.P., Chiu, D.K.W.: Enhancing workflow automation in insurance underwriting processes with Web services and alerts. In: Proceedings of the Annual Hawaii International Conference on System Sciences. (2007) https://doi.org/10.1109/HICSS.2007.208

9. Wilson, T.C.: Risk Underwriting – Technical Tools. In: Value and Capital Management: A Handbook for the Finance and Risk Functions of Financial Institutions, pp. 527–548. Wiley, Hoboken (2015). https://doi.org/10.1002/9781118774359.CH24

10. Duncan, D.: Lenders Discuss Loan Costs and Efficacy of Recent Tech Investments | Fannie Mae. https://www.fanniemae.com/research-and-insights/perspectives/lenders-discuss-loan-costs-and-efficacy-recent-tech-investments. Accessed 02 Jan 2023

11. Peterson, D.: How Automation Can Improve Your Loan Origination Process. https://www.moodysanalytics.com/articles/2018/maximize-efficiency-how-automation-can-improve-your-loan-origination-process. Accessed 18 Oct 2022

12. Friedman, J.P., Harris, J.C., Lindeman, J.B.: Dictionary of Real Estate Terms. Barron's, Hauppauge, NY (2004)

13. Li, Q., et al.: Causal-aware generative imputation for automated underwriting; causal-aware generative imputation for automated underwriting. In: Virtual Event, QLD, Australia (2021). https://doi.org/10.1145/3459637.3481900

14. Liston, J., Ringuette, S.: Application Threshold Decision Model and White paper (2022)

15. Kumra, R., Stein, R.M., Assersohn, I.: Assessing a knowledge-based approach to commercial loan underwriting. Expert Syst. Appl. **30**, 507–518 (2006). https://doi.org/10.1016/j.eswa.2005.10.013

16. Talebzadeh, H., Mandutianu, S., Winner, C.: Countrywide loan-underwriting expert system. AI Mag. (1995). https://doi.org/10.1609/AIMAG.V16I1.1123

17. Mcdonald, D.W., Pepe, C.O., Bowers, H.M., Dombroski, E.J.: Desktop underwriter: fannie mae's automated mortgage underwriting expert system. In: AAAI/IAAI. (1997)

18. Wigand, R.T., Steinfield, C.W., Markus, M.L.: Impacts of vertical IS standards: the case of the US home mortgage industry. In: Proceedings of the Annual Hawaii International Conference on System Sciences (2005). https://doi.org/10.1109/hicss.2005.304

19. Nazari Bagha, K.: A short introduction to semantics. J. Lang. Teach. Res. **2**, 1411–1419 (2011). https://doi.org/10.4304/jltr.2.6.1411-1419

20. Yule, G.: Semantics. In: The Study of Language, pp. 100–111. Cambridge University Press (2005). https://doi.org/10.1017/CBO9780511819742.011

21. Schewe, K.-D., Thalheim, B.: Semantics in data and knowledge bases. In: Schewe, K.-D., Thalheim, B. (eds.) SDKB 2008. LNCS, vol. 4925, pp. 1–25. Springer, Heidelberg (2008). https://doi.org/10.1007/978-3-540-88594-8_1

22. Taye, M.M.: Understanding semantic web and ontologies: theory and applications. J. Comput. **2**, 182–192 (2010)

23. Gerber, A., van der Merwe, A., Barnard, A.: A functional semantic web architecture. In: Bechhofer, S., Hauswirth, M., Hoffmann, J., Koubarakis, M. (eds.) ESWC 2008. LNCS, vol. 5021, pp. 273–287. Springer, Heidelberg (2008). https://doi.org/10.1007/978-3-540-68234-9_22

24. Patel, A., Jain, S.: Present and future of semantic web technologies: a research statement. Int. J. Comput. Appl. **43**, 413–422 (2019). https://doi.org/10.1080/1206212X.2019.1570666

25. Mizintseva, M.F., Gerbina, T.V.: Knowledge management practice: application in commercial banks (a Review). Sci. Tech. Inf. Process. **36**(6), 309–318 (2009). https://doi.org/10.3103/S0147688220906001X

26. Gruber, T.R.: A translation approach to portable ontology specifications. Knowl. Acquis. **5**, 199–220 (1993). https://doi.org/10.1006/KNAC.1993.1008

27. Noy, N.F., McGuinness, D.L.: Ontology development 101: a guide to creating your first ontology (2001)

28. Guarino, N., Oberle, D., Staab, S.: What is an ontology? In: Staab, S., Studer, R. (eds.) Handbook on Ontologies. IHIS, pp. 1–17. Springer, Heidelberg (2009). https://doi.org/10. 1007/978-3-540-92673-3_0

29. Jain, N., Sharma, L.: Sen: LoanOnt-a rule based ontology for personal loan eligibility evaluation. Int. J. Web Semant. Technol. **7**, 9–19 (2016). https://doi.org/10.5121/ijwest.2016. 7402

30. W3C OWL Working Group: OWL 2 Web Ontology Language Document Overview (Second Edition). https://www.w3.org/TR/2012/REC-owl2-overview-20121211/#Documentation_R oadmap. Accessed 06 Jan 2023/01/06

31. McGuinness, D.L., van Harmelen, F.: OWL web ontology language overview. http://www. w3.org/TR/2003/PR-owl-features-20031215/. Accessed 12 Apr 2023

32. Hitzler, P., Markus Krötzsch, Patel-Schneider, P.F., Sebastian Rudolph, A.-L.: OWL 2 web ontology language primer w3c proposed recommendation. http://www.w3.org/TR/2009/PR-owl2-primer-20090922/. Accessed 12 Apr 2023

33. EDMCouncil: FIBO Mortgage Loans Ontology(2022). https://spec.edmcouncil.org/fibo/ont ology/LOAN/RealEstateLoans/MortgageLoans/

34. Ziemer, J.: About FRO - financial regulation ontology. https://finregont.com/about-fro/. Accessed 12 Apr 2023

35. Ceci, M.: GRCTC/FIRO: financial industry regulatory ontology. https://github.com/GRCTC/ FIRO. Accessed 12 Apr 2023

36. Amaral, G., Sales, T.P., Guizzardi, G.: Towards an ontology network in finance and economics. In: Aveiro, D., Proper, H.A., Guerreiro, S., de Vries, M. (eds.) Advances in Enterprise Engineering XV. EEWC 2021 LNBIP, vol. 441, pp. 42–57 (2022). https://doi.org/10.1007/978-3-031-11520-2_4

37. Uschold, M., Calahan, L., Uschold, M.: Data Gizmos in the Loans Industry. https://www.you tube.com/watch?v=-eQpODIG5Zc. Accessed 05 Jan 2023

38. Webster, J., Watson, R.T.: Analyzing the past to prepare for the future: writing a literature review (2002)

39. vom Brocke, J., Simons, A., Riemer, K., Niehaves, B., Plattfaut, R., Cleven, A.: Standing on the shoulders of giants: challenges and recommendations of literature search in information systems research. Commun. Assoc. Inf. Syst. **37**, 205–224 (2015). https://doi.org/10.17705/ 1cais.03709

40. Cooper, H.M.: Organizing knowledge syntheses: a taxonomy of literature reviews. Knowl. Soc. **1**(1), 104 (1988). https://doi.org/10.1007/BF03177550

41. Kitchenham, B.A., Budgen, D., Brereton, P.: Evidence-Based Software Engineering and Systematic Reviews. Chapman and Hall/CRC, New York (2015). https://doi.org/10.1201/ b19467

42. Paranyushkin, D.: InfraNodus: generating insight using text network analysis. In: The Web Conference 2019 - Proceedings of the World Wide Web Conference, WWW 2019, pp. 3584–3589. Association for Computing Machinery, Inc (2019). https://doi.org/10.1145/3308558. 3314123

43. van Zetten, W., Ramackers, G.J., Hoos, H.H.: Increasing trust and fairness in machine learning applications within the mortgage industry. Mach. Learn. Appl. **10**, 100406 (2022). https://doi. org/10.1016/J.MLWA.2022.100406

44. Tsai, W.T., Shao, Q., Li, W.: OIC: Ontology-based intelligent customization framework for SaaS. In: Proceedings - 2010 IEEE International Conference on Service-Oriented Computing and Applications, SOCA 2010. (2010). https://doi.org/10.1109/SOCA.2010.5707139

45. Houshmand, M., Kakhki, M.D.: Presenting a rule based loan evaluation expert system. In: Proceedings - International Conference on Information Technology-New Generations, ITNG 2007, pp. 495–502 (2007). https://doi.org/10.1109/ITNG.2007.155

46. Roychoudhury, S., Kulkarni, V., Bellarykar, N.: Analyzing document intensive business processes using ontology. Presented at the (2015). https://doi.org/10.1145/2806416.2806638
47. Sachan, S.: Fintech lending decisions: an interpretable knowledge-base system for retail and commercial loans. In: Ciucci, D., et al. Information Processing and Management of Uncertainty in Knowledge-Based Systems. IPMU 2022. Communications in Computer and Information Science, vol. 1602, pp. 128–140 (2022). https://doi.org/10.1007/978-3-031-08974-9_10
48. Mahmoud, M., Algadi, N., Ali, A.: Expert system for banking credit decision. In: Proceedings of the International Conference on Computer Science and Information Technology, ICCSIT 2008, pp. 813–819 (2008) https://doi.org/10.1109/ICCSIT.2008.31
49. Brahma, A., Goldberg, D.M., Zaman, N., Aloiso, M.: Automated mortgage origination delay detection from textual conversations. Decis. Support. Syst. **140**, 1–11 (2021). https://doi.org/10.1016/J.DSS.2020.113433
50. Kotsiantis, S.B., Kanellopoulos, D., Karioti, V., Tampakas, V.: An ontology-based portal for credit risk analysis. In: Proceedings - 2009 2nd IEEE International Conference on Computer Science and Information Technology, ICCSIT 2009, pp. 165–169 (2009). https://doi.org/10.1109/ICCSIT.2009.5234452
51. Bellucci, M., Delestre, N., Malandain, N., Zanni-Merk, C.: Combining an explainable model based on ontologies with an explanation interface to classify images. Procedia Comput Sci. **207**, 2395–2403 (2022). https://doi.org/10.1016/J.PROCS.2022.09.298
52. Du, J., Zhou, L.: Improving financial data quality using ontologies. Decis. Support. Syst. **54**, 76–86 (2012). https://doi.org/10.1016/J.DSS.2012.04.016
53. Noguera, M., Hurtado, M.V., Rodríguez, M.L., Chung, L., Garrido, J.L.: Ontology-driven analysis of UML-based collaborative processes using OWL-DL and CPN. Sci. Comput. Program. **75**, 726–760 (2010). https://doi.org/10.1016/J.SCICO.2009.05.002
54. Bennett, M.: The financial industry business ontology: best practice for big data. J. Bank. Regul. **14**(3–4), 255–268 (2013). https://doi.org/10.1057/JBR.2013.13
55. Bhatore, S., Mohan, L., Reddy, Y.R.: Machine learning techniques for credit risk evaluation: a systematic literature review. J. Bank. Finan. Technol. **4**, 111–138 (2020). https://doi.org/10.1007/s42786-020-00020-3
56. Adla, A., Djamila, B., Ould-Mahraz, A.: A Knowledge-based recommender system for mortgage lending. In: Kacprzyk, J., Balas, V.E., Ezziyyani, M. (eds.) Advanced Intelligent Systems for Sustainable Development (AI2SD'2020), pp. 774–784. Springer, Cham (2022). https://doi.org/10.1007/978-3-030-90639-9_64
57. Butler, T., Abi-Lahoud, E.: A mechanism-based explanation of the institutionalization of semantic technologies in the financial industry. In: Bergvall-Kåreborn, B., Nielsen, P.A. (eds.) Creating Value for All Through IT. TDIT 2014 IFIP Advances in Information and Communication Technology, vol. 429, pp. 277–294. Springer, Heidelberg (2014). https://doi.org/10.1007/978-3-662-43459-8_17/COVER
58. Fischer-Pauzenberger, C., Schwaiger, W.S.A.: The OntoREA© accounting and finance model: ontological conceptualization of the accounting and finance domain. In: Mayr, H.C., Guizzardi, G., Ma, H., Pastor, O. (eds.) ER 2017. LNCS, vol. 10650, pp. 506–519. Springer, Cham (2017). https://doi.org/10.1007/978-3-319-69904-2_38
59. Ruiz-Martínez, J.M., Valencia-García, R., García-Sánchez, F.: An ontology-based opinion mining approach for the financial domain. In: Simperl, E., Norton, B., Mladenic, D., Della Valle, E., Fundulaki, I., Passant, A., Troncy, R. (eds.) ESWC 2012. LNCS, vol. 7540, pp. 73–86. Springer, Heidelberg (2015). https://doi.org/10.1007/978-3-662-46641-4_6
60. Naik, M.V., Mohanty, R.: An expert system approach for legal reasoning in acquire immovable property. In: First International Conference on Networks and Soft Computing (ICNSC 2014), pp. 370–374 (2014). https://doi.org/10.1109/CNSC.2014.6906664

Tiny-ME Wasm: Description Logics Reasoning in Your Browser

Giuseppe Loseto[1] , Ivano Bilenchi[2] , Filippo Gramegna[2] ,
Davide Loconte[2] , Floriano Scioscia[2(✉)] , and Michele Ruta[2]

[1] LUM University "Giuseppe Degennaro", 70010 Casamassima, BA, Italy
loseto@lum.it
[2] Polytechnic University of Bari, 70125 Bari, Italy
{ivano.bilenchi,filippo.gramegna,davide.loconte,floriano.scioscia,
michele.ruta}@poliba.it

Abstract. The World Wide Web is increasingly adopted as an application development platform in desktop and mobile contexts. As a building block of the Semantic Web of Everything vision, reasoning engines should be able to run in the client side of Web applications without resorting to remote servers for inference tasks. In order to fill a gap in the availability of such systems, this paper proposes Tiny-ME Wasm, a WebAssembly port of the Tiny-ME Description Logics reasoning and matchmaking engine. Tiny-ME Wasm exposes standard and non-standard inference services through a JavaScript API on top of the Tiny-ME core compiled to WebAssembly. A privacy-oriented service discovery case study highlights the usefulness of the proposed solution and a preliminary performance analysis demonstrates its usability on laptop and mobile devices.

Keywords: Semantic Web of EveryThing · Description Logics Reasoning · WebAssembly · Mobile Web

1 Introduction

World Wide Web (WWW) technologies are currently adopted as universal interoperability standards to allow sharing, aggregation, and composition of information and services in distributed computing environments comprising heterogeneous platforms. The Web has become a dominant deployment environment for new software systems and applications and the browser has become the default interface for many relevant applications [14]. The Web of Things (WoT) [8] aims to extend the reach of the WWW to physical objects and environments, countering the fragmentation of Internet of Things (IoT) technologies. The WoT enables access to the digital counterparts of physical entities, exposing data and/or services as addressable resources. Nevertheless, mobile and pervasive computing require more advanced approaches than traditional WWW solutions for information storage, discovery, management, and integration, to cope with device and resource volatility issues generated by location dependency, intermittent connectivity, performance limitations and energy consumption constraints.

S. Casteleyn et al. (Eds.): ICWE 2023 Workshops, CCIS 1898, pp. 114–126, 2024.
https://doi.org/10.1007/978-3-031-50385-6_10

The Semantic Web of Everything (SWoE) vision promotes the integration of Semantic Web languages and technologies for knowledge representation and automated inference on mobile, embedded and pervasive autonomous devices, enabling scalable interactions among people, things, environments and processes [10]. In order to fully include the Web as an application platform in this vision, reasoning engines should be able to run inside Web browsers at the client side of Web applications. Unfortunately, this has happened very rarely so far, due to the performance penalty of traditional JavaScript (JS) interpreters embedded in Web browsers w.r.t. native implementations. On the other hand, depending on remote servers for reasoning is not feasible in mobile and ubiquitous contexts due to the aforementioned issues, while exploiting local servers is forbidden by security policies of prevalent mobile and embedded operating systems.

This paper presents *Tiny-ME Wasm*, a port of the *Tiny Matchmaking Engine* [10] Description Logics (DL) reasoner, which can run in the *WebAssembly* (Wasm) [9] virtual machine embedded in major modern desktop and mobile Web browsers. It supports *standard* (satisfiability, subsumption, coherence, and classification) and *non-standard* (compatibility, abduction, contraction, bonus, difference, and covering) inference services; the latter are particularly useful for on-the-fly resource discovery and query processing in SWoE scenarios. Web developers can use these capabilities through a straightforward JS Application Programming Interface (API) mapping Tiny-ME's original C++ API. In order to demonstrate the usability and usefulness of the proposal, a mobile Web case study on a privacy-oriented local event finder is described. Since user experience in Web applications is particularly sensitive to latency [5], a performance evaluation has been carried out on both standard and non-standard inferences to assess reasoning times on macOS, iOS and Android devices.

The remainder of the paper is as follows. Section 2 discusses relevant related work, while Sect. 3 outlines the architecture and implementation of the proposed system. The case study is in Sect. 4, and experiments in Sect. 5 precede conclusions.

2   Related Work

The wide majority of Description Logics inference engines has been designed and developed for specific computing platforms, which support the required programming languages and runtime libraries. Due to inferior performance optimization, the Web-oriented JavaScript language has been seldom chosen. For this reason, Web applications typically exploit remote services for DL reasoning. A large number of semantic-enabled Web applications for conventional desktop clients follow this approach, covering a wide range of domains; unfortunately, both technological and user interface design choices prevent their adaptation to mobile and ubiquitous contexts. Notable semantic-enabled mobile-oriented Web apps include the *DBpedia Mobile* [2] and *LOD4AR* [18] location-based discovery clients for mobile devices. *OntoWiki Mobile* [4] is a mobile knowledge management applications exploiting HTML5 and jQuery Mobile to locally store knowledge annotated by users in the field, even without Internet connection, and synchronize it with a remote server when a connection becomes available. Overall, the survey in [20] on semantic-enabled mobile apps has found that only 4 out of 36 apps had been developed with Web-based cross-platform technologies.

Efforts on using Web technologies for cross-platform reasoning engines are sparse. The *EYE* (Euler Yet another proof Engine) [17] reasoner, implementing forward and backward rule chaining over Euler paths, has been ported to JS-based environments like the Web and *Node.js*[1] by leveraging a JS implementation of the *SWI Prolog* [19] engine. The *MobiBench* mobile semantic rule engine evaluation framework [16] supports integration with rule engines written in JS for the Web and further platforms, by means of the *Apache Cordova*[2] Software Development Kit (SDK). *HyLAR+*[3] [15] is a hybrid OWL 2 EL reasoner: both the server side and the client side can execute reasoning tasks by running the same JS code with Node.js and *AngularJS*[4], respectively. It leverages the *JSW* semantic technology framework for JS[5], which includes the *BrandT* browser-hosted OWL 2 EL inference engine [13].

WebAssembly discloses a viable path to developing or porting reasoning engines to Web applications and stand-alone runtime environments like Node.js with minimal performance penalty. Proposals, however, are in very early stages. *EYE JS*[6] is an initial WebAssembly port of EYE. A prototypical port of the *Tiny-ME* DL reasoner and matchmaker [10] has been included in a Web application for semantic-based quality of experience adaptation in Web multimedia [6].

3   Architecture and Implementation

The design and development of the Tiny-ME OWL reasoner and matchmaking engine [10] have been guided by architectural and technological choices aimed at ensuring support for a wide range of target platforms, one of the key requirements of the SWoE. System architecture comprises a shared core, which efficiently implements data structures and inference procedures, along with a set of high-level APIs that facilitate development for supported platforms. The core is written in the C programming language, which ensures a high degree of portability, as most programming languages and platforms provide some form of interoperability with C code. Web browser environments are no exception, as C programs and libraries can be cross-compiled for the WebAssembly runtime through the *Emscripten*[7] toolchain, and then invoked from JS. Emscripten does

---

[1] Node.js: https://nodejs.org/.
[2] Apache Cordova home: https://cordova.apache.org/.
[3] HyLAR GitHub repository: https://github.com/ucbl/HyLAR-Reasoner.
[4] AngularJS home: https://angularjs.org/.
[5] JSW GitHub repository: https://github.com/JavaScript-WindowFramework/JSW.
[6] EYE JS GitHub repository: https://github.com/eyereasoner/eye-js.
[7] Emscripten home: https://emscripten.org.

provide mechanisms to call C functions from JS[8], but they are cumbersome and bug-prone, as they rely either on specifying function signatures via strings, or on manually marshalling parameters to appropriate types. A better alternative involves creating JS wrappers for all exported C functions, though this results in a procedural API, which is rather unnatural for JS development, and leaves most native memory management to the programmer. A third method consists in providing a thin object-oriented C++ wrapping layer and generating bindings to JS classes through *Embind*.[9]. This results in a more natural object-oriented JS API, and allows delegating most native memory management to the C++ runtime.

Thus, the porting workflow of Tiny-ME Wasm, illustrated in Fig. 1, has involved the following steps:

- implementing an object-oriented C++ API by wrapping the Tiny-ME core component and the Cowl [3] library, which is used by the reasoner to access and parse Web Ontology Language 2 (OWL) ontologies;
- providing appropriate binding annotations, so allowing Embind to generate a JS interface that directly maps the low-level C++ API;
- configuring the *CMake*[10] build system to use Emscripten and invoking it to cross-compile the system for the WebAssembly runtime.

Emscripten generates two output artifacts: a Wasm module containing byte-code for the WebAssembly virtual machine, and a JS file responsible for loading the module and setting up the runtime environment. The latter can be imported in any Web application by means of HTML `script` tags or *JS modules*[11], allowing client-side code to use all the functionalities of the reasoner as a regular JS library.

Figure 2 summarizes the low-level system architecture. The object-oriented design of the C API of the reasoner [10] has resulted in a relatively straightforward mapping of C structures and related functions to C++ classes and methods. One friction point was due to the significantly different memory management paradigms of the underlying libraries, as the Tiny-ME core follows the traditional `malloc/free` approach, while Cowl adopts *reference counting*. Care has been devoted to standardizing object lifecycles under the *Resource Acquisition is Initialization* (*RAII*) paradigm, by encapsulating C pointers in a `CPtr<T>` template type, that implements type-specific memory management logic. This approach simplifies the handling of dynamic memory by delegating it to the C++ runtime, and allows the resulting JS bindings to correctly dispose of unneeded allocations.

---

[8] Connecting C and Javascript: https://emscripten.org/docs/porting/connecting_cpp_and_javascript/embind.html.

[9] Embind documentation: https://emscripten.org/docs/porting/connecting_cpp_and_JS/embind.html.

[10] CMake home: https://cmake.org.

[11] JS modules: https://developer.mozilla.org/en-US/docs/Web/JavaScript/Guide/Modules.

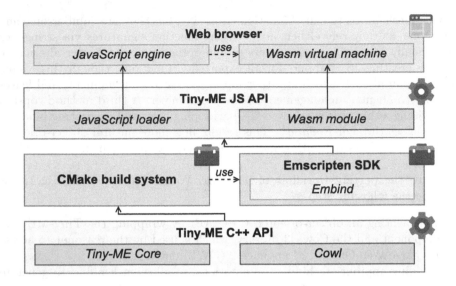

Fig. 1. Porting workflow and high-level architecture of Tiny-ME Wasm

The library entry point is the `Reasoner` object, which provides access to all Tiny-ME's standard (satisfiability, subsumption, coherence, and classification) and non-standard (compatibility, abduction, contraction, bonus, difference, and covering) inference services, which are recalled in [10]. Non-standard inferences are particularly useful in SWoE scenarios, as they go beyond the boolean answers of standard ones by allowing approximated matches and semantic-based (dis)similarity measures, making them suitable to be composed into more sophisticated reasoning tasks. One such task is *semantic matchmaking*, where semantic-based annotations of domain resources are compared in order to find the best matches for a specific request, based on a semantic similarity metric.

4   Case Study: A Privacy-Oriented Local Event Finder

In order to highlight the usage and usefulness of the proposed reasoning engine in mobile and ubiquitous Web scenarios, a case study is proposed about retrieving nearby local events and ranking them according to user preferences. Nowadays, Web platforms typically require users to expose and share their profile information in order to obtain personalized recommendations for events, products and other items. The proposed workflow, depicted in Fig. 3, represents a different general-purpose approach, where a mobile Web application (1) retrieves available information from the Web, (2) annotates it according to an OWL domain ontology, (3) exploits it to identify resources best matching user's profile and preferences, and (4) displays results in the user interface for selection and/or query refinement. Notably, all processing occurs locally on the user's mobile

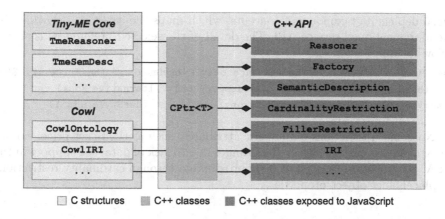

Fig. 2. Low-level architecture of Tiny-ME Wasm

Fig. 3. Framework architecture - Reference workflow

device: this enables a privacy-oriented information management and avoids the latency of interactions with a remote reasoning engine.

In order to better explain and underline the benefits of the proposed approach, let us consider the following mobile-oriented scenario. *Martina, while on vacation in San Francisco, is interested in purchasing a ticket for a musical event, spending no more than $80. She is a fan of alternative rock bands and would like to attend a tour date rather than a one-time concert.*

As shown in Fig. 3, the user can access information on local events by means of a Web application in her mobile browser. Data for the case study are provided by *Ticketmaster*[12], through a public ReSTful API[13]. In the first step (Fig. 4a), the user retrieves all events nearby according to basic parameters, such as city and date range. This represents generic information, not personalized on her preferences. However, she can select several features and preferences to define her private personal profile (Fig. 4b) and refine the initial query directly on the local device, without sending further requests to the server. The user profile is mapped to a semantic-based annotation by means of a prototypical domain ontology:

---

[12] https://www.ticketmaster.com.

[13] https://developer.ticketmaster.com/products-and-docs/apis/getting-started/.

120   G. Loseto et al.

Fig. 5 depicts its taxonomy of concepts, which maps the categories provided by the aforementioned service API. The detail of the selected preferences is shown below in *Manchester syntax*:

User_Profile: Event and (hasAudience only EveryOne) and (hasPrice max 80) and (hasStyle only Tour) and (hasCategory only Alternative_Rock) and (hasType only Group) and (hasCategory min 1) and (hasStyle min 1) and (hasAudience min 1)

Note that restrictions on numeric attributes, such as the ticket price, cannot be expressed as restrictions on data ranges due to lack of datatype support in the $\mathcal{ALN}$ DL, therefore they must be approximated through cardinality restrictions on placeholder object properties.

(a) Available events   (b) User profile   (c) Suggested events

Fig. 4. Screenshots of the Web application

After a pre-filtering step based on a maximum distance of 5 km from the mobile device location and considering only events occurring in the current week, the user profile is compared with the semantically annotated events descriptions using the matchmaking framework implemented by the Tiny-ME reasoner [10], in order to obtain the list of resources best fulfilling both user preferences and compatibility constraints. All the events, reported hereafter in alphabetical order, are tagged as individuals using the same ontology:

Crocodiles: Event and (hasAudience only EveryOne) and (hasPrice min 163) and (hasPrice max 180) and (hasStyle only Tour) and (hasType only Band) and (hasCategory only Indie_Rock)

Iggy_Pop_and_The_Losers: Event and (hasAudience only EveryOne) and
(hasPrice min 50) and (hasPrice max 100) and (hasStyle only Tour) and
(hasType only Band) and (hasCategory only Alternative_Rock)

KANKAN-The_RR_Tour: Event and (hasAudience only EveryOne) and (hasPrice
min 25) and (hasPrice max 105) and (hasStyle only Concert) and (hasType
only Performer) and (hasCategory only Hip_Hop_Rap)

Ripe-Bright_Blues_Tour: Event and (hasAudience only EveryOne) and
(hasPrice exactly 27) and (hasStyle only Tour) and (hasType only Band)
and (hasCategory only Pop_Rock)

The_Nude_Party: Event and (hasAudience only EveryOne) and (hasPrice
exactly 20) and (hasStyle only Concert) and (hasType only Band) and
(hasCategory only Alternative_Rock)

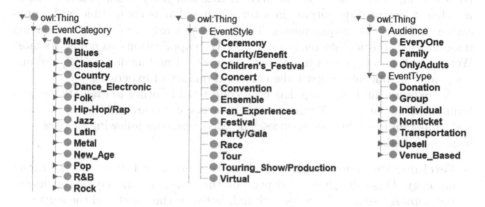

Fig. 5. Reference ontology

The returned list of events, shown in Fig. 4c, is ranked according to the
following *utility function*:

$$u(R, C) = 100[1 - \frac{s\_penalty(R, C)}{s\_penalty(R, \top)}(1 + \frac{distance(R, C)}{max\_distance})]$$ (1)

where $s\_penalty(R, C)$ is the result of the *semantic matchmaking* task [10] and
represents the semantic distance between user profile R and event annotation
C, normalized by $s\_penalty(R, \top)$; the latter is the semantic distance between
R and the *universal concept* $\top$ (a.k.a. *Top* or *Thing*) and depends only on the
ontology structure. The $distance(R, C)$ context parameter is included to exploit
the event geographical distance as weighting factor. The utility function also
converts the semantic distance value into a more intuitive percentage score, as
shown in Table 1. It can be observed that if $s\_penalty(R, C) = 0$ then the final
score is 100%, regardless of the geographic distance. Based on user preferences
and event descriptions, the most suitable event, as listed in Fig. 4c, is the individual Iggy_Pop_and_The_Losers, even if its physical distance is greater than
the other available resources.

Table 1. Musical events ranked by the utility function

Musical events	$s\_penalty(R,C)$	$distance(R,C)$	$u(R,C)$
Iggy Pop & The Losers	0.20	2.60 km	97.97%
The Nude Party	1.00	0.85 km	93.22%
Crocodiles	1.51	0.60 km	89.81%
Ripe Bright Blues Tour	4.00	1.40 km	72.59%
KANKAN - The RR Tour	6.24	0.87 km	57.68%

5   Experimental Evaluation

For any compute-intensive system, performance analysis is fundamental to assess whether it can provide outputs in a time frame that is compatible with application and use case requirements. This is particularly true when embedding reasoning capabilities into the client side of Web applications, as nowadays most Web content is consumed through battery-powered mobile devices [12] and any delay may significantly impact the perceived quality of experience [5].

An experimental campaign has been conducted in order to evaluate the performance of the proposed Wasm reasoner in terms of turnaround time of standard and non-standard inference services. For each test, the following metrics have been measured:

- **Fetching**: the time spent by the client to request and download the target ontology. This value does not depend on the reasoner, but only on the device, the ontology size, and the network link between the client and the server.
- **Parsing**: the time required by the reasoner to deserialize the ontology into its internal data structures.
- **Reasoning**: the time elapsed to carry out the requested inference service.

Tests have been executed on a 2021 MacBook Pro[14], an iPhone 12 Pro[15], and a OnePlus 7T[16], to achieve a sufficiently fair and diverse representation of Web content fruition devices, both hardware- and software-wise.

The reference dataset is inherited from [10]. Non-standard inferences have been carried out on four knowledge bases representing different SWoE case studies. For standard reasoning services, the dataset is a subset of the *ORE2014* corpus, [1] considering ontologies having at most $\mathcal{ALN}$ expressiveness, and whose

---

[14] Apple M1 Max SoC, 8 performance cores @3.2 GHz and 2 efficiency cores @2.0 GHz, 64 GB UM RAM, 1 TB SSD, macOS Ventura 13.3.1, Safari 16.4 browser.

[15] Apple A14 Bionic, 2 high-power cores @3.1 GHz and 4 low-power cores @1.8 GHz, 6 GB LPDDR4X RAM at 4266 MT/s, 128 GB NVMe SSD, iOS 15.1, Safari Mobile 15.1 browser.

[16] Qualcomm Snapdragon 855+, 1 core @2.96 GHz, 3 cores @2.42 GHz and 4 cores @1.8 GHz, 8 GB LPDDR4X RAM, 128 GB UFS 3.0 storage, Android 12, Chrome 112.0.5615.47 browser.

file size does not exceed 1 MB in OWL 2 functional-style syntax, [7] for a total of 1140 ontologies.

The experimental methods consist in visiting a Web page containing client-side JS code responsible for performing all test operations. For each ontology in the dataset, the script retrieves the ontology document, then invokes the Tiny-ME Wasm reasoner to carry out the target inference. Results are saved to a CSV file, which is then fed to the *evOWLuator* [11] framework to generate visualizations. The test Web pages and ontologies are served by an *Nginx*[17] instance hosted on a desktop computer[18], configured to serve all requests without caching. All devices are located in the same IEEE 802.11n WLAN[19].

Times are collected using the `performance.now()`[20] JS API call. By default, most browsers limit the resolution of the returned timestamp to 1–2 ms as a mitigation for timing-based attacks and fingerprinting. This is enough for fetching and parsing, but it is often too coarse for inferences. Therefore, reasoning times have been computed by running multiple consecutive iterations of each task (10 for the two mobile devices, and 50 for the laptop), subtracting the cumulative fetching and parsing times from the total execution time, and averaging over all iterations.

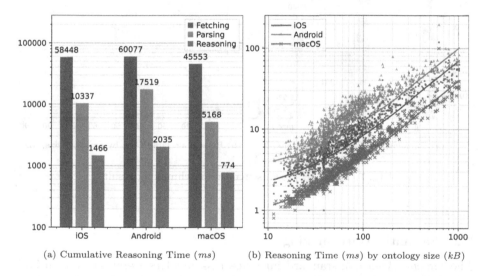

(a) Cumulative Reasoning Time (*ms*)   (b) Reasoning Time (*ms*) by ontology size (*kB*)

Fig. 6. Tiny-ME Wasm ontology classification results

---

[17] Nginx: https://www.nginx.com/.
[18] Intel Core i7-3770k CPU, 4 cores @3.5 GHz, 12 GB DDR3 RAM @1600 MT/s, 2 TB SATA SSD, Windows 10.
[19] Hosted by a TP-Link TN-WR841N router.
[20] https://developer.mozilla.org/en-US/docs/Web/API/Performance/now.

5.1   Ontology Classification

Figure 6 illustrates the results of the *ontology classification* standard inference service. The bar graph in Fig. 6a shows the total time required for fetching, parsing, and reasoning across all ontologies. The scatter plot in Fig. 6b depicts the relationship between the size of the ontology and the total time required for parsing and reasoning, with the worst case requiring about 200 ms on the least capable device. Outcomes demonstrate satisfactory performance of inference services oriented to ontology management, which is essential for supporting interactive semantic-enabled Web applications in mobile environments. Although fetching time is the most prominent component, the domain ontology can usually be fetched just once and cached to improve application responsiveness.

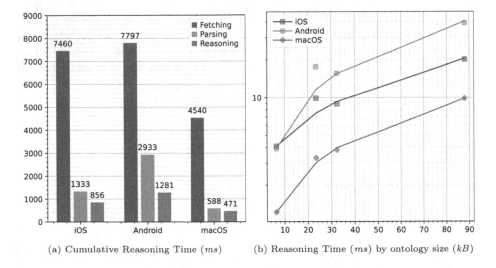

(a) Cumulative Reasoning Time (*ms*)   (b) Reasoning Time (*ms*) by ontology size (*kB*)

Fig. 7. Tiny-ME Wasm semantic matchmaking results

5.2   Semantic Matchmaking

The *matchmaking* non-standard inference task involves iterating over all individuals in each of the 4 reference ontologies in order to find the best match for an individual acting as a *request* description. As explained in [10], matchmaking starts with a *compatibility check* between a ⟨*request, resource*⟩ pair of individuals: if their conjunction is satisfiable then *concept abduction* is performed, else *concept contraction* is executed, followed by abduction on the contracted version of the request. As results in Fig. 7 show, the Wasm reasoner can carry out this inference in a few milliseconds, with 40 ms being the highest time measured for the largest ontology of the corpus.

These outcomes align with the ones in Sect. 5.1, but they are particularly relevant, as non-standard inferences are often more useful in SWoE scenarios, which Tiny-ME Wasm explicitly targets. The overall evaluation confirms that the proposed reasoner can be effectively integrated into interactive Web applications, providing both standard and non-standard inference services without negative impact on performance and user experience.

6 Conclusion

This paper has introduced Tiny-ME Wasm, a complete WebAssembly port of the Tiny-ME reasoning and matchmaking engine. The proposal represents one of the first Description Logics reasoners running on the client side of Web applications in modern browsers. It exposes all Tiny-ME's standard and non-standard inference services via a JavaScript API on top of the reasoner C core compiled to WebAssembly. Early performance tests of reasoning tasks demonstrate acceptable latency on PC and mobile platforms. A case study on a privacy-oriented Web application for location-based event discovery shows the benefits of the approach for SWoE applications leveraging well-known Web technologies, while also highlighting pitfalls of the $\mathcal{ALN}$ DL, which may be overcome through extensions to the expressiveness of the Tiny-ME core.

Future work includes full integration into the Tiny-ME codebase and build automation framework, in order to keep updates always aligned with the master development branch. Further tests on a larger set of operating system and browser combinations will refine the compatibility and performance evaluation, suggesting possible optimizations. Release to the community is planned to enable the creation of a wide range of Web apps and gather feedback from developers.

Acknowledgments. This work has been supported by project BARIUM5G (Blockchain and ARtificial Intelligence for Ubiquitous coMputing via 5G), funded by the Italian Ministry of Economic Development.

References

1. Bail, S., Glimm, B., Jimenez-Ruiz, E., Matentzoglu, N., Parsia, B., Steigmiller, A.: ORE 2014 OWL reasoner evaluation live competition. https://dl.kr.org/ore2014. Accessed 20 Mar 2023
2. Becker, C., Bizer, C.: Exploring the geospatial semantic web with DBpedia mobile. J. Web Semant. **7**(4), 278–286 (2009)
3. Bilenchi, I., Scioscia, F., Ruta, M.: Cowl: a lightweight OWL library for the semantic web of everything. In: Agapito, G., et al. (eds.) ICWE 2022, vol. 1668, pp. 100–112. Springer, Cham (2023). https://doi.org/10.1007/978-3-031-25380-5_8
4. Ermilov, T., Heino, N., Auer, S.: Ontowiki mobile: knowledge management in your pocket. In: Proceedings of the 20th International Conference Companion on World Wide Web, pp. 33–34 (2011)
5. Inan Nur, A., B. Santoso, H., O. Hadi Putra, P.: The method and metric of user experience evaluation: a systematic literature review. In: 2021 10th International Conference on Software and Computer Applications, pp. 307–317 (2021)

6. Loseto, G., Scioscia, F., Ruta, M., Gramegna, F., Bilenchi, I.: Semantic-based adaptation of quality of experience in web multimedia streams. In: 38th ACM/SIGAPP Symposium On Applied Computing (SAC 2023), pp. 1821–1830 (2023)

7. Parsia, B., Motik, B., Patel-Schneider, P.: OWL 2 Web Ontology Language Structural Specification and Functional-Style Syntax (Second Edition). W3C recommendation, W3C (2012). https://www.w3.org/TR/owl2-syntax/

8. Raggett, D.: The Web of Things: challenges and opportunities. Computer **48**(5), 26–32 (2015)

9. Rossberg, A.E.: WebAssembly Specification Release 2.0 (Draft 2023-04-08). https://webassembly.github.io/spec/core/. Accessed 14 Apr 2023

10. Ruta, M., et al.: A multiplatform reasoning engine for the semantic web of everything. J. Web Semant. **73**, 100709 (2022)

11. Scioscia, F., Bilenchi, I., Ruta, M., Gramegna, F., Loconte, D.: A multiplatform energy-aware OWL reasoner benchmarking framework. J. Web Semant. **72**, 100694 (2022)

12. StatCounter: Desktop vs Mobile vs Tablet Market Share Worldwide Jan - Dec 2022. https://gs.statcounter.com/platform-market-share/desktop-mobile-tablet/worldwide/2022. Accessed: 20 Apr 2023

13. Stepanovs, V.: BrandT: Browser Hosted OWL Reasoner. University of Mancherster May, Technical report (2011)

14. Taivalsaari, A., Mikkonen, T.: The web as a software platform: ten years later. In: 13th International Conference on Web Systems and Technologies (WEBIST 2017), pp. 41–50 (2017)

15. Terdjimi, M., Médini, L., Mrissa, M.: HyLAR+ improving hybrid location-agnostic reasoning with incremental rule-based update. In: Proceedings of the 25th International Conference Companion on World Wide Web, pp. 259–262 (2016)

16. Van Woensel, W., Abidi, S.S.R.: Benchmarking semantic reasoning on mobile platforms: towards optimization using OWL2 RL. Semant. Web **10**(4), 637–663 (2019)

17. Verborgh, R., De Roo, J.: drawing conclusions from linked data on the web: the EYE reasoner. IEEE Softw. **32**(3), 23–27 (2015)

18. Vert, S., Dragulescu, B., Vasiu, R.: LOD4AR: Exploring linked open data with a mobile augmented reality web application. In: ISWC (Posters & Demos), pp. 185–188 (2014)

19. Wielemaker, J., Schrijvers, T., Triska, M., Lager, T.: SWI-Prolog. Theory Pract. Logic Program. **12**(1–2), 67–96 (2012)

20. Yus, R., Pappachan, P.: Are apps going semantic? A systematic review of semantic mobile applications. In: 1st International Workshop on Mobile Deployment of Semantic Technologies. CEUR Workshop Proceedings, vol. 1506, pp. 2–13 (2015)

Second International Workshop on Web Applications for Life Sciences (WALS2023)

2nd International Workshop on Web Applications for Life Sciences (WALS 20223) - Preface

Anna Bernasconi[1] (iD), Alberto García S.[2] (iD), and Pietro Pinoli[1] (iD)

[1] Department of Electronics, Information, and Bioengineering, Politecnico di
Milano, Italy
{anna.bernasconi,pietro.pinoli}@polimi.it
[2] Valencian Research Institute for Artificial Intelligence (VRAIN), Universitat
Politècnica de València, Valencia, Spain
algarsi3@pros.upv.es

The recent advances in unraveling the secrets of human conditions and diseases have encouraged new paradigms for their diagnosis and treatment. In addition, the recent pandemics have brought increasing attention toward the genetic mechanisms of viruses and infected hosts. The information related to these phenomena is increasing at unprecedented rates, directly impacting the design and development of data management pipelines and their applications. New ways of processing and exposing data and knowledge on the Web in healthcare and life sciences environments are thus strongly needed.

The International Workshop on Web Applications for Life Sciences (WALS) was held in 2023 for the second time. It aimed at being an initial meeting forum for Web Engineering, Data Management, and Bioinformatics researchers working on life sciences problems, offering the opportunity to share, discuss and find new approaches to support Search, Knowledge Extraction, and Data Science on the Web, thereby achieving important results for healthcare, precision medicine, biology, genomics, and virology.

The workshop has attracted high-quality submissions; three papers (two full papers and one short paper) have been selected after a blind review process that involved two experts from the field for each submission. The full paper "Development of an end-to-end web application for visualization, evaluation, and post-processing of result data from neural network predictions for the melanoma use case." was proposed by Babak Saremi, Mohan Xu, Chiara Tappermann, and Lena Wiese. It presents a web application for semi-automated image segmentation and classification tasks, solved by means of neural networks' models. The full paper "Digital Avatars: An application to eHealth" was proposed by Rafael García Luque, Ernesto Pimentel Sánchez, and Antonio Jesús Bandera Rubio. It describes the application of the 'People as a service' paradigm to a case of telemedicine. The short paper "A DCAT Profile Approach for Citizen Science" was proposed by Reynaldo Alvarez, Jose Zubcoff, and Irene Garrigos. It introduces a Data Catalog profile for improving the interoperability of data systems used in Citizen Science.

All papers provided significant insights related to the problem under investigation; they also confirmed an interesting technical program that stimulated discussion. The program was complemented with an invited keynote by Prof. Oscar Pastor (Universitat Politecnica de Valencia), with title "Data Intensive Domains in Genomic-based Life Science: Web Engineering Implications for Personalized Health Care".

Acknowledgements. We thank the Program Committee members for their hard work in reviewing papers, the authors for submitting and presenting their works, and the ICWE 2023 organizing committee for supporting our workshop. We also thank ICWE 2023 workshop chairs Sven Casteleyn and Tommi Mikkonen for their direction and guidance.

Development of an End-to-End Web Application for Visualization, Evaluation, and Post-processing of Result Data from Neural Network Predictions for the Melanoma Use Case

Chiara Tappermann[1], Mohan Xu[1]([✉]), Lena Wiese[1,2], and Babak Saremi[1]

[1] Fraunhofer Institute for Toxicology and Experimental Medicine, Hannover, Germany
{chiara.tappermann,mohan.xu,lena.wiese,babak.saremi}@item.fraunhofer.de
[2] Institute of Computer Science, Goethe University Frankfurt, Frankfurt a. M., Germany

Abstract. Image acquisition technology advances in various fields, yet current image analysis tools limit the effective application of image analysis due to their cumbersome operation process and the requirement of professional knowledge and skills. In this paper, we develop a semi-automated web application for image segmentation and classification tasks with the support of neural networks (relieving the above-mentioned current research dilemma) using melanoma detection as a use case. The web application enables scientists to participate and improve the decision-making process of the neural network through the concept of "human-in-the-loop", while saving expensive labor costs due to its automation in image annotation and classification. In addition, our web application achieves high usability in the general user community by testing seven aspects of usability: the first impression, distinguishability and clarity of the tools, intuitive characteristics, learnability, feedback and reaction, implementation of expected functionality, and the fulfillment of usability.

1 Introduction

Web applications have become an essential part of our daily lives, enabling us to perform many tasks through a web browser. They have a lot of benefits compared to conventional desktop software. In the context of our work, web applications are software that can be accessed through a web browser and require an active internet connection. Web applications can provide the user with powerful tools without the need for a high-performance infrastructure from the user side because the backend can be deployed on external powerful servers. In addition,

---

C. Tappermann and M. Xu—Equal contribution as first authors.

© The Author(s), under exclusive license to Springer Nature Switzerland AG 2024
S. Casteleyn et al. (Eds.): ICWE 2023 Workshops, CCIS 1898, pp. 131–144, 2024.
https://doi.org/10.1007/978-3-031-50385-6_11

the increasing popularity and power of neural networks shaped many different fields of science. Neural networks are able to process numerous tasks on huge datasets to extract important features. One popular application area is the image analysis of biomedical data [4,15,17,18,24]. With the increasing amount of image data produced, scientists are in need of specific tools that can help to process these datasets. This process usually requires expert knowledge, especially in the case of biomedical image data where complex cellular structures need to be evaluated. Applications such as ImageJ [31] and Labelme [37] are able to select a region of interest in a series of images and evaluate that region. However, these evaluation processes are done entirely by hand and can therefore be a very time-consuming task. A well-trained neural network can support scientists by automatizing several processes and thus save manpower. In addition, it was shown in the past that neural networks can sometimes work more accurately than humans and thus consequently reduce human error rates [2,14,38]. However, for some complex cases, neural networks are unable to predict desired features correctly, which can often be the cause of insufficient training data availability [30]. Another important issue is the acceptance of neural networks in medical sectors, as these models are often considered a black box and misclassifications can lead to further distrust in AI-generated results [32].

For our purposes of melanoma detection, we developed a web application that facilitates access to neural networks that are provided in the backend of our application to perform image predictions. To address the above-mentioned issues, we present a fully functional prototype for image segmentation and classification tasks that use the "human-in-the-loop" concept [4]. This approach combines the power and accuracy of a neural network and the expert knowledge of a scientist who can intervene and correct the classification done by a neural network and thus help to annotate and evaluate image series more accurately and enable the scientists to perform their evaluation process using a partially automated pipeline instead of their currently completely manual process.

In this paper, we extend our prior work [36,39] for our prototype and focus on the identified users' requirements. We also elaborate on the target platform and library chosen for the implementation of the application. Another aspect we focused on is the software quality of the application. We analyzed the requirements, implemented and tested the software with a focus on usability, and also the possibility to extend the software or adjust it for further use cases.

2   Related Work

In recent years, image analysis tools have received a lot of attention from the community due to the increasing amount of image data and their versatility in different categories of images. ImageJ [31] and Labelme [37], two of the most commonly used image editing tools, can perform a series of post-processing operations such as modifying and analyzing the annotated images while completing image annotation on the dataset. These operations are done manually, which not only reduces the efficiency of scientists' work but also increases the potential human error rate. In response, several works based on machine learning algorithms designed image analysis tools to make image analysis equally efficient in large datasets. As a plugin for ImageJ, [1] implements a continuously trainable pixel classification workflow. Based on similar concept, the interactive tool proposed in [3] covers several workflows such as image segmentation, object classification, counting, and tracking. However, the operation of these two interactive tools not only requires the computing power of local devices, but also requires debugging the local environment during installation. The web application developed in [21,23] is not limited by local devices and implements the functions of region size quantification, cell counting, object classification and interest points detection. Although current commercially available image analysis tools are rich in features, the redundant features rather increase the difficulty for scientists to get started. Moreover, the machine learning models they train and the accompanying image analysis methods are not suitable for all use cases. Therefore, it is necessary to develop an end-to-end trainable web application for these use cases.

3 Fundamentals

3.1 Melanoma Use Case

According to the American Cancer Society [33], there were 97,920 new cases of melanoma in situ of the skin in the United States in 2022, including 7,650 deaths. If melanoma is detected and treated promptly in early diagnosis, the 5-year relative survival rate can reach 93%, second only to prostate cancer (98%). However, dermoscopy, an important tool for the early detection of melanoma, is highly dependent on the clinical experience of dermatologists [10]. Therefore, the development of a tool that encompasses the clinical experience of the physician and the analytical power of neural networks to segment and classify lesion areas has a positive effect on improving the early diagnosis of melanoma.

3.2 Concept of the Application

Our goal was to develop a partially automated tool for image analysis that is supported by convolutional neural networks (CNNs) which can detect the shape of a skin lesion in images and classify the lesion for the melanoma use case. To make this technology available to a variety of end-users, we focused on implementing an intuitive, web-based end-to-end-pipeline, that has high usability and offers services to segment and classify skin lesions, to post-process predictions and perform several evaluation methods on the data based on the user's needs. The main advantage of our service is, that it can improve the CNNs iteratively with an interactive "human-in-the-loop" approach; hence, our workflow provides the user with constantly improving technology while expanding our dataset to make this technology more accurate. Due to our modular architecture, our service can be run on-premise to avoid privacy implication.

3.3 Tasks and Actors

There are two types of actors or users for the software system participating in the workflow shown in Fig. 1. We have scientists or physicians as primary actors. They interact with the application directly through the user interface and process their data through it. The secondary actor is the software developer, whose job is to improve the prediction results by providing the user with updated versions of the neural networks in the background for the data prediction. Based on the different actors, we identified the tasks for the application by conducting interviews with potential end-users and by analyzing the data format. Identifying the tasks is an important aspect of the software engineering process to describe the interaction between an agent and a software system. It can be used to specify the requirements for the application [13,34]. As a result, we extracted the following tasks for the primary actor:

1. **Process files:** Upload image data or progress files
2. **Process files:** Download image data or progress files
3. **Process files:** Generate prediction for image data
4. **Process files:** Export the generated annotations for retraining
5. **Image processing:** Post-Process or correct predictions
6. **Analysis:** Apply different operations to generate additional data for analysis
7. **Analysis:** Save the processed data in a suitable format
8. **Analysis:** Edit the processed data
9. **Visualization:** Visualize the processed data for the user
10. **Visualization:** Export the results
11. **Additional features:** Tutorials on how to use the application

The tasks for the secondary actor are the following:

1. **Data generation:** Create labeled data
2. **Neural network:** (Re-)train the neural network
3. **Neural network:** Publish the network for the user

Based on these tasks, our result is an end-to-end pipeline that accesses the CNNs in the backend and a web application in the frontend. In particular, the developer is primarily responsible for training the neural networks using the provided labeled data, which can be provided either by the developer or the user depending on their domain knowledge. Labeled data can easily be created using the editor tool provided by our web service. Users can apply our application to their data to correct inaccurate predictions. The corrected data can be used to extend the dataset and improve the neural network's accuracy through iterative retraining. This process ultimately reduces the workload for users, as fewer post-processing operations are required when the neural network's performance improves. Users can then upload either a single image or image series, depending on the application, to generate a segmentation of the lesion area and a classification if the lesion area is a melanoma or not. Then they are able to correct faulty predictions for either single images or image series. For image series, users can keep previous changes without starting the correction process over again for each image. Additionally, users can perform further operations such as calculating the size of the melanoma, to detect changes in size over time for different images of the same melanoma. Users can input metadata and get an overview of all previously created data. In this step, the users can also export the image data and corresponding labels to expand the dataset. In the final step of the workflow, users can visualize the data and export the results. For the melanoma example, we visualized patient records containing images of the patient's melanoma from different examination dates. The files also provide the users with information about the count of melanoma detected for each examination and a classification for each image of the mole, classifying if it is a melanoma or not.

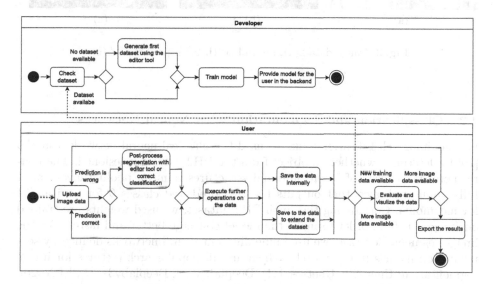

Fig. 1. Workflow of the developer and the user

4 Material and Methods

4.1 Dataset

We completed the training and testing of our neural network for image classification and segmentation on the publicly available PH2 [25] dataset, which contains 200 dermoscopic images. The dataset was partitioned for the image segmentation and the image classification task. For the image classification task, the dataset contains 160 nevis and 40 melanomas and the corresponding labels, where 0 indicates a nevus, and 1 indicates a melanoma. The dataset was partitioned into a training- and a test set in a ratio of 7:3. In contrast, the image segmentation task dataset contains 200 images with their corresponding annotations, where a pixel value of 0 represented the background and a pixel value of 1 represents the region of interest. The dataset was again partitioned into a train and a test set in the ratio of 7:3. An example for a melanoma image and the corresponding segmentation ground truth and also the prediction is provided in Fig. 2.

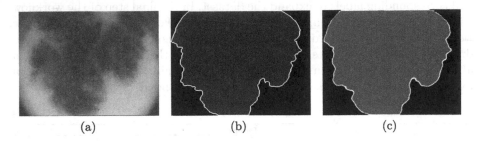

(a)   (b)   (c)

Fig. 2. Image data 2(a), ground truth 2(b), prediction 2(c)

4.2   Classification and Segmentation with Neural Networks

For the image classification task, we used the classical neural network resnet50 [16] to determine whether an object from the PH2 dataset is lesioned. The neural network consists of 5 convolutional structures, 1 mean pooling layer and 1 fully connected layer that outputs the two predicted classes 0 for nevi and 1 for melanoma. Considering the small PH2 dataset, we used weights pre-trained on Imagenet [9] in order to make the model converge better and faster. For the image segmentation task, we used nine different neural networks defined by segmentation models from Pytorch[1] which are all popular architectures for image segmentation: Unet [29], Unet++ [41], Deeplabv3 [6], Deeplabv3+ [7], FPN [20], Linknet [5], PSPNet [40], PAN [19] and MAnet [11]. The model architectures consist of an encoder, a decoder, and a segmentation head. The encoder ("backbone network") is responsible for feature extraction. The decoder is responsible for feature fusion and progressive implementation of category annotations for each pixel. The segmentation head ensures that the number of channels from decoder output is equal to the number of prediction categories, while ensuring that the size of input and output are the same by up-sampling.

4.3   Frontend Technologies

We implement the frontend and user interface as a web application using the framework *Angular*[2], an open-source JavaScript framework, based on TypeScript. An Angular application consists of modules that again are composed of components developed and published by Google. This modular architecture

---

[1] Iakubovskii, P.: https://github.com/qubvel/segmentation_models.pytorch.

[2] Angular https://angular.io/.

helps to structure large-scale software projects while keeping the application maintenance extendable at a later time [22]. A simple, well-structured and consistent design is important for a good user interface. Therefore, we used the component-based design library *Material Design*[3] that provides us with a broad range of interactive components that can be utilized across multiple different platforms. The Material Design library was developed by Google in accordance with the best practice guidelines and is therefore compatible with Angular applications. In order to develop an editor for the post-processing stage of segmenting results, we had to decide on a method for image data processing. There are different ways to display and edit image data, including raster images and vector graphics. Vector graphics are defined using objects like paths and shapes, where the information about those objects is described through mathematical formulas [12]. We analyzed different vector-based libraries for the implementation of our application and decided to use *Paper.js*[4]. Paper.js provides a wide range of basic vector-based operations and allows us to implement all required tools.

4.4   Backend Technologies

MLOps is a standard set of working procedures designed to manage all life cycles of machine learning models. It implements a set of operations for continuous integration, continuous delivery, and continuous deployment of machine learning models in a production environment. In our use case, we used *TorchServe*[5], developed specifically for the *Pytorch*[6] framework, to deploy the image classification model and image segmentation model mentioned in Sect. 4.2. After receiving a prediction task request (classification or segmentation) and data from the web application, the handler component of TorchServe will process and predict the data corresponding to the task request and return the predicted output to the web application. To ensure a consistent run time environment and to enable fast deployment of models, we install and run TorchServe within docker. Figure 3 shows the architecture of our web application and illustrates the communication between the frontend and the backend. The frontend communicates with the backend through a REST API interface. The backend consists of either *TFServing*[7] [26] or *TorchServe*[8] backend and is responsible for deploying trained image classification and segmentation models, assigning workers to the deployed models and communicating with the frontend. After processing the REST requests from the frontend, the backend generates a JSON file, with the generated prediction.

---

[3] Material Design, https://material.io/.
[4] Paper.js. http://paperjs.org/.
[5] TorchServe, https://pytorch.org/serve/.
[6] Pytorch, https://pytorch.org/.
[7] TFServing, https://www.tensorflow.org/tfx/guide/serving.
[8] Torchserve. https://pytorch.org/serve/.

Fig. 3. Communication between the web application frontend (left) and backend (right)

5 Experiment

In our work, we focused on the usability of our web application. Therefore, we performed a study testing our labeling tool to evaluate the usability of our user interface. The topic of usability covers a broad range of different aspects of user interface design and workflow design in the software engineering process. Usability describes the relationship between the user, the software, and a task to be performed and provides a measure to determine the quality of the tool to solve the task considering aspects like efficiency, understandability or intuitivity [28]. The goal of this study was to assess the intuitiveness of the application and the user's ability to use the tools in a meaningful manner for a specific use case. Our research hypotheses for the study were:

1. The application contains all the tools needed to fulfill the defined use cases
2. The application is intuitively structured to ensure that the users quickly find their way for efficient use of the required tools

The study was conducted with a senior scientist as an end user, who had to edit data for a comparable use case, without prior explanation of the application. During the study, several questionnaires were provided, which included questions for both quantitative and qualitative evaluation. Quantitative evaluation methods allow for a precise statistical evaluation and have the advantage to uncover sources of errors. Although these methods are more complicated, they can give suggestions for improvement. Accordingly, in a study where few participants are expected, it is reasonable to also use qualitative methods in order to obtain more precise findings [35]. The questionnaires are based on the questionnaire developed by Jochen Prümper and Michael Anft in 1993, which is based on the international ergonomics standard ISO 9241/10 [27,35]. Parts of the questionnaire were adjusted to the specific use case and categorized into the following sections defining seven different aspects of usability: the first impression, distinguishability and clarity of the tools, intuitive characteristics, learnability, feedback and reaction, implementation of expected functionality, and the fulfillment of usability. These categories were derived from Chlebek's usability criteria [8]. The study was separated into six different sections. At the beginning of the study, the participant was informed about the process and the objectives of the study, followed by demographic questions. In the third stage of the study, the participant was allowed to test the application briefly and ask questions. Following the familiarization period, a short questionnaire was answered to obtain the first impressions. The fourth step was to work on a suitable use case, using the labeling tool. During this familiarization period, the participant commented on the process and reported on anything that was noticed. Afterward, the remaining questionnaire was filled out, which dealt in detail with different categories of usability. In the last section of the study, a follow-up discussion of the study was conducted with the participant, who was able to discuss impressions of the study and the application. In summary, the outcome of the study was very successful. The individual aspects of the application were rated good to very good in the questionnaires. Some minor improvements were suggested that have already been implemented in the current version of the application. Therefore, the research hypothesis of the usability study can be answered positively.

6   Results

The result of our implementation process is an Angular web application, that communicates with TFServing or Torchserve in the backend to generate a classification and a segmentation mask for skin lesions for the melanoma use case. The application has a modular design and consists of a number of components and services that create the structure of the startpage the image editor page for the data labeling process, the uploader page to process and evaluate image data for the data visualization, the data visualization page, the tutorial page, and the page to export the data generated during the evaluation process to expand the training dataset. All subpages can be accessed from the startpage. The data uploader illustrated in Fig. 4 allows the user to upload images or image series and either further process the segmentation mask or adjust the classification result and also perform further calculations on the segmentation mask. The editor page is illustrated in Fig. 5 and can be used to either generate new labels for the training dataset or adjusts the segmentation mask. It was designed based on other common image-processing tools where users can select the corresponding tool in the toolbar located on the left side of the screen, and each tool corresponds to several options, which can be found in the image bar above. On the right are further options such as layer- or saving options. Figure 6 also shows an example of how the data can be visualized as patient records, showing all the patient's documented skin lesions, the corresponding classification, and how many melanomas were found over time.

7   Discussion

For the user interface of our application, we decided to use a web application. This type of software can be used on a number of different devices that supports modern web browsers, regardless of the underlying operating system. Since the service is hosted on an external server that performs all necessary computations, web apps are not restricted by the computational capability of the user's local device. Web applications offer many benefits, but they also have disadvantages. For instance, the user must be connected to the internet at all times, and delays can occur when dealing with large amounts of data if the internet connection

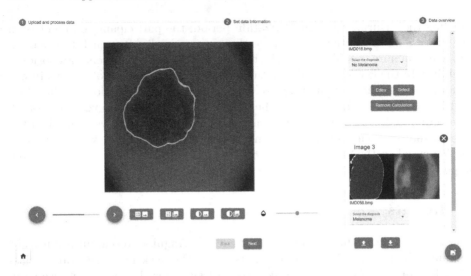

Fig. 4. Data uploader and editor

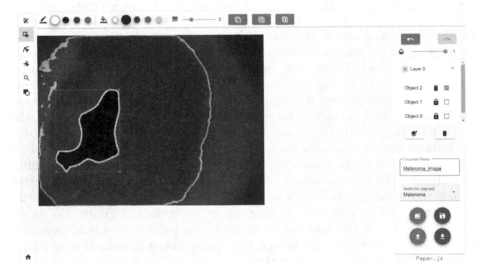

Fig. 5. Editor

is insufficient. In our case, the advantages of the web application clearly outweigh the disadvantages. Moreover, without a web application, the user would have to provide not only the editing software itself but possibly also the neural networks locally. This would require far too much computing effort. For the prototype, the range of functionalities that can be integrated into a web application is completely sufficient. Moreover, the connection to the internet is constantly

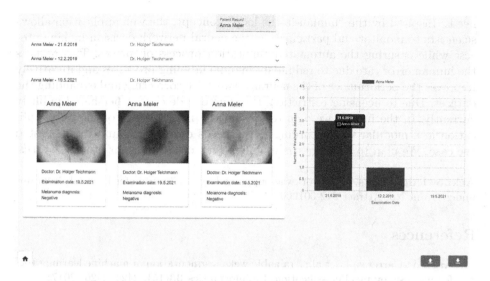

Fig. 6. Data visualization

guaranteed from all workstations at our institute, and employees could thus access the application via the intranet without having to install it.

There are different ways to display image data, including raster images and vector graphics. The first method represents the image data as a two-dimensional array of data points, or pixels, with each pixel containing information about color, brightness, and location information. Compared to raster images, vector graphics are defined using objects like paths and shapes, where the information about those objects is described through mathematical formulas. Due to this type of representation, vector graphics can be scaled almost infinitely without compromising quality, like with raster images. Therefore, we analyzed different vector-based libraries for our application and decided to use Paper.js.

8   Conclusion and Future Work

In this paper, we researched the topic of how to implement an image prediction and evaluation based on the users' requirements, an extendable software structure, and usability criteria. We found out, that a web application provides us with lots of advantages compared to common desktop applications, especially in the field of research where applications like this can be applied due to restrictions in installation rights and hardware performance. Therefore, we developed a partially-automated web application that integrates image classification, segmentation, post-processing, and evaluation based on the melanoma use case. With the support of trained neural networks, the application can perform category prediction and automatic segmentation of lesion areas on images uploaded by the user, who can also participate in the image annotation process in post-processing or apply different evaluation methods to the data according to their needs. Inspired by the "human-in-the-loop" concept, the web application allows scientists to monitor and participate in the neural network decision-making process while ensuring the automated annotation process of images. This reduces the human error rate due to redundant manual labeling processes and iteratively improves the performance of the neural network by correcting and expanding the dataset. Due to licensing restriction, the source code cannot be shared publicly currently. In the future, we plan to expand the functionality of the web application in a modular way according to the needs of our users and the requested use case. We plan to evaluate the usability with other users for other use cases.

Acknowledgements. This work was supported by the Fraunhofer Internal Programs under Grant No. Attract 042-601000.

References

1. Arganda-Carreras, I., et al.: Trainable weka segmentation: a machine learning tool for microscopy pixel classification. Bioinformatics **33**(15), 2424–2426 (2017)
2. Assael, Y.M., Shillingford, B., Whiteson, S., De Freitas, N.: LipNet: end-to-end sentence-level lipreading. arXiv preprint arXiv:1611.01599 (2016)
3. Berg, S., et al.: Ilastik: interactive machine learning for (bio) image analysis. Nat. Methods **16**(12), 1226–1232 (2019)
4. Budd, S., Robinson, E.C., Kainz, B.: A survey on active learning and human-in-the-loop deep learning for medical image analysis. Med. Image Anal. **71**, 102062 (2021)
5. Chaurasia, A., Culurciello, E.: Linknet: exploiting encoder representations for efficient semantic segmentation. In: 2017 IEEE Visual Communications and Image Processing (VCIP), pp. 1–4. IEEE (2017)
6. Chen, L.C., Papandreou, G., Schroff, F., Adam, H.: Rethinking Atrous convolution for semantic image segmentation. arXiv preprint arXiv:1706.05587 (2017)
7. Chen, L.C., Zhu, Y., Papandreou, G., Schroff, F., Adam, H.: Encoder-decoder with atrous separable convolution for semantic image segmentation. In: Proceedings of the European conference on computer vision (ECCV), pp. 801–818 (2018)
8. Chlebek, P.: Praxis der User Interface-Entwicklung: Informationsstrukturen, 1st edn. Designpatterns und Vorgehensmuster. Vieweg + Teubner Verlag, Wiesbaden (2011)
9. Deng, J., Dong, W., Socher, R., Li, L.J., Li, K., Fei-Fei, L.: Imagenet: a large-scale hierarchical image database. In: 2009 IEEE Conference on Computer Vision and Pattern Recognition, pp. 248–255. IEEE (2009)
10. Divito, S.J., Ferris, L.K.: Advances and short comings in the early diagnosis of melanoma. Melanoma Res. **20**(6), 450–458 (2010)
11. Fan, T., Wang, G., Li, Y., Wang, H.: Ma-net: a multi-scale attention network for liver and tumor segmentation. IEEE Access **8**, 179656–179665 (2020)
12. Gonzalez, R., Woods, R.: Digital Image Processing, Global Pearson, London (2017)
13. Grechenig, T., Bernhart, M., Breiteneder, R., Kappel, K.: Softwaretechnik?: mit Fallbeispielen aus realen Entwicklungsprojekten. Pearson Studium, München (2010)
14. Greenwald, N.F., et al.: Whole-cell segmentation of tissue images with human-level performance using large-scale data annotation and deep learning. Nat. Biotechnol. **40**(4), 555–565 (2022)

15. Guan, H., Liu, M.: Domain adaptation for medical image analysis: a survey. IEEE Trans. Biomed. Eng. **69**(3), 1173–1185 (2021)
16. He, K., Zhang, X., Ren, S., Sun, J.: Deep residual learning for image recognition. In: Proceedings of the IEEE Conference on Computer Vision and Pattern Recognition, pp. 770–778 (2016)
17. Iqbal, A., Sharif, M., Khan, M.A., Nisar, W., Alhaisoni, M.: FF-UNet: a u-shaped deep convolutional neural network for multimodal biomedical image segmentation. Cogn. Comput. **14**(4), 1287–1302 (2022)
18. Isensee, F., Jaeger, P.F., Kohl, S.A., Petersen, J., Maier-Hein, K.H.: nnU-Net: a self-configuring method for deep learning-based biomedical image segmentation. Nat. Methods **18**(2), 203–211 (2021)
19. Li, H., Xiong, P., An, J., Wang, L.: Pyramid attention network for semantic segmentation. arXiv preprint arXiv:1805.10180 (2018)
20. Lin, T.Y., Dollár, P., Girshick, R., He, K., Hariharan, B., Belongie, S.: Feature pyramid networks for object detection. In: Proceedings of the IEEE Conference on Computer Vision and Pattern Recognition, pp. 2117–2125 (2017)
21. Lu, A.X., Zarin, T., Hsu, I.S., Moses, A.M.: YeastSpotter: accurate and parameter-free web segmentation for microscopy images of yeast cells. Bioinformatics **35**(21), 4525–4527 (2019)
22. Malcher, F., Hoppe, J., Koppenhagen, D.: Angular: Grundlagen, fortgeschrittene Themen und Best Practices, 2 edn. dpunkt.verlag, Heidelberg (2019)
23. Marée, R., et al.: Collaborative analysis of multi-gigapixel imaging data using cytomine. Bioinformatics **32**(9), 1395–1401 (2016)
24. Meijering, E.: A bird's-eye view of deep learning in bioimage analysis. Comput. Struct. Biotechnol. J. **18**, 2312–2325 (2020)
25. Mendonça, T., Ferreira, P.M., Marques, J.S., Marcal, A.R., Rozeira, J.: Ph 2-a dermoscopic image database for research and benchmarking. In: 2013 35th Annual International Conference of the IEEE Engineering in Medicine and Biology Society (EMBC), pp. 5437–5440. IEEE (2013)
26. Olston, C., et al.: Tensorflow-serving: flexible, high-performance ml serving. arXiv preprint arXiv:1712.06139 (2017)
27. Prümper, J.: Der benutzungsfragebogen isonorm 9241/10: Ergebnisse zur reliabilität und validität. In: Software-Ergonomie 1997: Usability Engineering: Integration von Mensch-Computer-Interaktion und Software-Entwicklung, pp. 253–262 (1997)
28. Richter, M., Flückiger, M.: Usability and UX kompakt: Produkte für Menschen, 4th edn. Springer, Berlin (2016). https://doi.org/10.1007/978-3-662-49828-6
29. Ronneberger, O., Fischer, P., Brox, T.: U-Net: convolutional networks for biomedical image segmentation. In: Navab, N., Hornegger, J., Wells, W.M., Frangi, A.F. (eds.) MICCAI 2015. LNCS, vol. 9351, pp. 234–241. Springer, Cham (2015). https://doi.org/10.1007/978-3-319-24574-4_28
30. Sargent, D.J.: Comparison of artificial neural networks with other statistical approaches: results from medical data sets. Cancer: Interdisc. Int. J. Am. Cancer Soc. **91**(S8), 1636–1642 (2001)
31. Schneider, C.A., Rasband, W.S., Eliceiri, K.W.: NIH image to imagej: 25 years of image analysis. Nat. Methods **9**(7), 671–675 (2012)
32. Seifert, C., Scherzinger, S., Wiese, L.: Towards generating consumer labels for machine learning models. In: 2019 IEEE First International Conference on Cognitive Machine Intelligence (CogMI), pp. 173–179. IEEE (2019)
33. Siegel, R.L., Miller, K.D., Fuchs, H.E., Jemal, A.: Cancer statistics, 2022. CA: Cancer J. Clin. **72**(1), 7–33 (2022)

34. Sommerville, I.: Software Engineering, 9th edn. Pearson, München (2012)
35. Stapelkamp, T.: Screen und Interfacedesign, 1st edn. Springer, Berlin (2007). https://doi.org/10.1007/978-3-658-03857-1
36. Steinmeyer, C., Dehmel, S., Theidel, D., Braun, A., Wiese, L.: Automating bronchoconstriction analysis based on u-net. In: EDBT/ICDT Workshops (2021)
37. Torralba, A., Russell, B.C., Yuen, J.: LabelMe: online image annotation and applications. Proc. IEEE **98**(8), 1467–1484 (2010)
38. Werneburg, G.T., Werneburg, E.A., Goldman, H.B., Mullhaupt, A.P., Vasavada, S.P.: Neural networks outperform expert humans in predicting patient impressions of symptomatic improvement following overactive bladder treatment. Int. Urogynecol. J. **34**, 1–8 (2022)
39. Wiese, L., Höltje, D.: NNCompare: a framework for dataset selection, data augmentation and comparison of different neural networks for medical image analysis. In: Proceedings of the Fifth Workshop on Data Management for End-To-End Machine Learning, pp. 1–7 (2021)
40. Zhao, H., Shi, J., Qi, X., Wang, X., Jia, J.: Pyramid scene parsing network. In: Proceedings of the IEEE Conference on Computer Vision and Pattern Recognition, pp. 2881–2890 (2017)
41. Zhou, Z., Rahman Siddiquee, M.M., Tajbakhsh, N., Liang, J.: UNet++: a nested u-net architecture for medical image segmentation. In: Stoyanov, D., et al. (eds.) DLMIA/ML-CDS -2018. LNCS, vol. 11045, pp. 3–11. Springer, Cham (2018). https://doi.org/10.1007/978-3-030-00889-5_1

Digital Avatars: An Application
to eHealth

Rafael García-Luque[1]([✉])(iD), Ernesto Pimentel[1](iD), and Antonio Bandera[2](iD)

[1] ITIS Software, Universidad de Málaga, Málaga, Spain
{rafagarcialuque,epimentel}@uma.es
[2] ISIS Research Group, Universidad de Málaga, Málaga, Spain
ajbandera@uma.es

Abstract. The development of digital health technologies allows, among other advantages, the remote monitoring of patients' state of health. In this context, smartphones have become Telemedicine tools, as they have a high computational capacity and are equipped with sensors that make them aware of their environment and allow remote interaction. However, as in other ubiquitous computing systems, the storage, processing, and exchange of large amounts of data could put privacy at risk. In this paper, we present Digital Avatars, a software framework that allows an intensive use of the computational capabilities of smartphones following the People as a Service paradigm. This framework allows the development of evolving sociological profiles that guarantee the user's personal confidentiality without considering external servers, and minimizing the exchange of information. To demonstrate the correct functioning of Digital Avatars in the field of health, we have developed and successfully validated a use case for the monitoring of patients suffering from Parkinson's disease. The implemented system is composed of two applications (for smartphone and smartwatch, respectively), using Complex Event Processing, Fast Fourier Transform and Recurrent Neural Networks.

Keywords: Digital Avatar · People as a Service · Parkinson's Disease · Internet of Things · Complex Event Processing · Fast Fourier Transform · Recurrent Neural Networks

1 Introduction

The COVID-19 pandemic challenged current public healthcare systems and evidenced the need to adopt innovative solutions to optimize and improve patient care [4]. As a consequence, Telemedicine converged thanks to the Internet of

This work has been partly supported by project *Including people in smart city applications* (PID2021-125527NB-I00) and project *Management and Analysis of Intra- and Inter-Organizational Business Processes* (TED2021-130666B-I00), funded by the *Spanish Ministry of Science and Innovation*.

S. Casteleyn et al. (Eds.): ICWE 2023 Workshops, CCIS 1898, pp. 145–159, 2024.
https://doi.org/10.1007/978-3-031-50385-6_12

Things (IoT) by providing many intelligent devices equipped with sensors and Internet connection to make them aware of their environment and allow remote interaction [1]. In this way, smartphones have become the most popular device and can bring excellent benefits in reducing the need for hospitalization and overall medical care costs [13].

However, this evolution has also entailed more problems and risks to the security of information and privacy [8], mainly because these systems are based on centralized servers. As a result, the growing interest of some organisations and institutions worldwide is along the lines of guaranteeing and preserving the confidentiality of patient data [7].

In this scenario, this work is intended to take advantage of the capabilities offered by smartphones to develop a framework based on the People as a Service (PeaaS) paradigm [6]. The aim is to provide sociological profiles to users with personal information, enable automatic reconfiguration of their smart devices without centralization on external servers and ensure the privacy of their data. Consequently, it is perfectly suited to the main problem of modern medicine mentioned above.

The application of these virtual profiles, together with behavioural rules governing their inference, evolution and use, provided by Complex Event Processing (CEP) techniques [11], is known as Digital Avatar (DA). It is a mobile computing framework that favours dynamic programming interactions between intelligent devices. Based on this, we introduce our proposal and adaptation of the work developed in [1] to apply DA to Parkinson's disease (PD) tracking and monitoring in this paper.

The rest of the paper is organised as follows: Sect. 2 presents the concept of Digital Avatar and, describes its architecture and the benefits it brings to the healthcare field. Section 3 shows our case of using DA to treat Parkinson's disease, presents its structure, details the design and development of our prototype and demonstrates the results obtained in validating the system. The benefits and challenges of implementing this collaborative social computing model are discussed in Sect. 4. Finally, Sect. 5 summarizes the conclusions and stipulates the directions for future work.

2   Digital Avatar

The technological development associated with the IoT has led to an increase in the capabilities of smart devices and, consequently, a more significant presence of these devices and their automatic adaptation to people's demands. However, these devices are very heterogeneous, causing considerable complexity in their intercommunication and, consequently, more security threats [3].

Focusing on Telehealth, these issues are related to patient privacy as it involves using an electronic format to maintain medical records, document diagnoses, prescriptions and details of patient follow-up. Today, an electronic medical record may contain more personal information about an individual than any document [18].

To help alleviate this problem, it is necessary to improve the automation of the configuration of numerous devices to interact with them quickly and personally. To this end, the PeaaS paradigm has been adopted. The goal is to harness the potential of mobile devices to store the sociological profiles of their owners, preserve them confidentially and offer them as a service, ensuring that the person's profile is always kept exclusively on his/her device [6].

However, the interactions proposed by the PeaaS model are not just simple data exchanges but require mechanisms to configure intelligent systems and fill virtual profiles with the knowledge of the context from these interactions. The concept of Digital Avatar emerges for this purpose, representing a sociological profile that continuously evolves through interaction with the user, sensors embedded in the smartphone and other external IoT devices [15].

In this way, using Digital Avatars provides continuous communication and follow-up of doctors or caregivers with their patients. As a result, the data of each user are stored in their sociological profile in real-time. Depending on the role assigned, the other avatars can receive information and alerts for the disease in question, ensuring that the patient's personal data is preserved.

2.1 Architecture

This Digital Avatars collaborative framework has been presented in the previous work done for the care of elderly people living independently [1], based on the PeaaS model and whose level of implementation is at the application level. We propose an architecture represented as a UML model in Fig. 1.

Figure 1 represents the common structure that characterizes a DA (shaped in orange color) and, in addition, the one that refers to the proposed case study (shaped in blue color) that will be explained in Sect. 3. Therefore, focusing on the DA, applications (*Application*) run locally on the mobile device, querying and updating the information contained in the DA (its structure is detailed in Sect. 2.2).

The user's personal information (*PersonalInfo*) is stored as a DA record which inherits from class *DigitalAvatarRecord*. This establishes and updates (*lastModification*) the reading (*readPrivacy*) and writing (*writePrivacy*) levels of that information contained.

Consequently, depending on the privileges (*PrivacyLevel*) granted to each Avatar (*Contact*), that is part of a specific group (*ContactGroup*), they will only have access and control over the data they are authorized to access. This communication is done through the Digital Avatar API, which prevents unauthorized access and provides a quick and straightforward point of interaction.

Finally, in Fig. 1, it can be visualized that the application uses a CEP inference engine (*CEPEngine*) that, through *rules*, can detect and collect data to obtain new values to process. For this purpose, this engine executes scripts (*CEPScripts*) in real-time, reducing the decision-making latency and enabling its use in asynchronous systems.

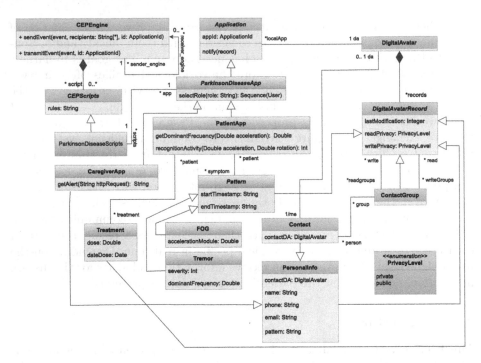

Fig. 1. Class Diagram of the Parkinson's Disease application.

2.2   Virtual Profile Structure

The DA can be represented as a language with indentation and three parameters per line YAML-based notation [1]. Consequently, each avatar represents an *Entity* composed of the following attributes: name, type (it can be the entity or a primary data type), privacy level, value (simple or a nested entity) and last update time. The levels of privacy are expressed using the reserved words, *Public* and *Private*. Moreover, the symbols *?* and *!* describe read and write permissions, respectively.

In addition to the YAML notation, the ontology defined in [1] of entities has been stipulated for the structure of the DA. As a result, this ontology allows organizing the information about the DA in entities or sections with a certain level of privacy for the data stored in each of them, which helps ensure the correct functioning and protection of the framework.

For our scenario, *Personal* and *Relations* sections have been defined. *Personal* contains the patient's personal information, contact details and the smartphone's features and, *Relations* reports the information and the permissions of virtual profiles of people who interact with the user's avatar.

According to this last entity, several groups have different privacy settings such as Family, Friends, etc. Moreover, it must be considered that if the confidentiality level is not specified, it is assumed to be inherited from the parent entity. All types of DA are stored with a certificate to validate their permissions.

```
1   -Personal: ?!private
2     -Me:
3       -Name: "Patient1": ?public
4       -Phone: 664-555: ?Family, ?Friends
5       -Birth: 29/04/1967
6       -Certificate: "FO:89:B1:QW..": ?public
7     -Health: ?!Caregiver
8       -PharmacologicalTreatment:
9         -Type: "Carbidopa-levodopa"
10        -Dose: 1
11        -Times: 2
12      -Patterns:
13        -SeverityTremor: 4
14        -FOG: 2
```

Listing 1.1. Excerpt of a Digital Avatar showing personal data.

An example of a virtual profile containing the *Personal* entity can be shown in Listing 1.1. In particular, it includes the patient's personal data and the measurements corresponding to health parameters (Parkinsonian patterns and pharmacological treatment). The personal data are private, although some entities allow for reading purposes to defined groups (through the symbol *?*). In addition, for the information associated with the patient's health, there are two sections, *Pharmacological Treatment* and *Patterns*, which only caregivers can read and write.

3   Use Case: Parkinson's Disease

Once we have presented the concept of Digital Avatar, defined its architecture and the guidelines for its application in Telemedicine, we formally define a framework to treat Parkinson's disease and, thus, demonstrate how it works and what significant benefits it can bring compared to traditional PD monitoring and tracking systems. Specifically, tremor and Freezing of Gait (FOG) patterns, two of the most distinctive features of this disease, will be addressed.

Highlighting that, for tremors, this manifestation occurs at rest, with a frequency between 3 and 7 Hz and is usually generated at the wrist. On the other hand, FOG is an inability to initiate a movement that mainly affects the legs during walking and each episode usually lasts between 2 and 3 s [17].

Our proposal appears shaded in color blue in Fig. 1. The applications that manage this neurological disorder (*ParkinsonDiseaseApp*) consult and update the data stored in the DA. In addition, depending on the user's role in the disease monitoring process they have different functionality (*PatientApp* and *CaregiverApp*).

Suppose the user is the patient (*PatientApp*). In that case, he/she has the cardinal patterns of *FOG* and *Tremor*, with their corresponding measurements of dominant frequency (*dominantFrequency*) of each localized tremor with its value on a pre-established severity scale (*severity*), detected FOG episodes (*episode*) and acceleration in the patient's gait (*accelerationModule*). These measurements are obtained by implementing the *getDominantFrequency()* method to describe the location, dominant frequency, and amplitude of a tremor using the Fast Fourier Transform (FFT). In addition, it is also necessary to use the *recognition-Activity()* function to determine different gait states and dysfunctions [10] by applying a particular type of Recurrent Neural Network (RNN), the Long Short Term Memory (LSTM) networks.

Accordingly, both the information characterizing the Parkinsonian patterns (*Pattern*) and the data associated with the pharmacological treatment (*Treatment*) are stored as a DA record (see Listing 1.1) together with the patient's data (*PersonalInfo*), all of them with a defined authorization level.

But, on the other hand, if the DA corresponds to the caregiver (*Caregiver-App*) and has privileges, the application uses the API to access and employ the information corresponding to the Parkinsonian patterns of the patient's DA. This is implemented through the *getAlert()* function, which allows visualizing and receiving notifications in the event of an urgent situation.

In addition, it can be visualized that *ParkinsonDiseaseApp* uses the CEP inference engine (*CEPEngine*), which through *rules*, detects and alerts of severe tremors (scale 5) and FOG episodes, manages the pharmacotherapy and performs an inference task from the collected data to obtain new values to process.

3.1 Implemented System

Smartwatches offer the possibility of measuring the acceleration that occurs in the wrists and, consequently, treating the Parkinsonian tremor that tends to be more predominant in that area (see Fig. 2a).

For our particular case, we have used the Galaxy Watch SM-R800NZSAPH smartwatch, equipped with the Tizen 5.5.0.2 operating system. Among the sensors it has, its 3-axis accelerometer stands out. Their primary function is to collect data from their sensors and send the measurements to the smartphone, which processes the information and hosts the DA.

Therefore, a native application in the C programming language has been coded for Tizen with a sampling rate of 20 Hz based on the Nyquist frequency, which determines that if the number of points sampled is N for a period of time T in seconds, the sampling rate is N/T and the highest frequency that equipment can measure is $N/2T$ Hz. In this way, the frequency of interest is approximately 7 Hz (maximum of a Parkinsonian tremor) and the sampling rate of the sensor responsible must be at least 14 Hz (and preferably several times more) for better signal processing.

On the other hand, to assess the FOG, the mobile phone must be placed on the right side of the pelvis [5]. Thus, the accelerometer's X, Y, and Z axes are roughly aligned with craniocaudal, anteroposterior, and midlateral movement directions. As a result, a person's gait can be measured (see Fig. 2b).

To develop the DA, we used the Xiaomi MI A3 smartphone. This device has the Android 11 operating system and the 3-axis Bosch BIMI160 accelerometer, which is in charge of measuring the acceleration associated with the patient's gait.

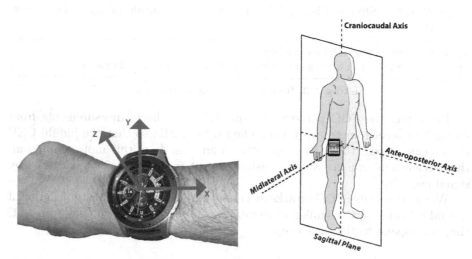

(a) Axes of the smartwatch worn on the wrist.

(b) Alignment of the mobile at the right hip.

Fig. 2. Placing the devices on the patient.

In accordance with the above, Fig. 3 shows an overview of the system where the mobile device receives the raw acceleration measurements collected by the smartwatch through Bluetooth Low Energy (BLE) communication to treat the Parkinsonian tremor. On the other hand, the *Siddhi IO* library has been chosen as the CEP inference engine. This requires that the information received be preprocessed before. Consequently, it is necessary to apply the FFT to these values and, thus, obtain the dominant frequency of the accelerometer signal, which corresponds to each tremor.

Once the tremor has been processed, a broadcast receiver is defined so that the CEP engine can collect the measurements of this pattern and generate alerts when a certain event occurs. Listing 1.2 represents a Siddhi rule to achieve this, where the source is of type *android-broadcast*, presents the identifier *Tremor-Broadcast* to receive information of any activity containing the same ID (the methods responsible for implementing the FFT), in *key-value* format and, has as attributes the scale of severity of the tremor (*severity*) and a text string (*alert*) to notify the user depending on the detected incident.

```
1  @source(type = 'android-broadcast',
2     identifier = 'TremorBroadcast',
3     @map(type ='keyvalue'))
4  define stream TremorStream(severity int, alert string);
```

Listing 1.2. Rule for collecting tremors through a broadcast receiver.

Consequently, the CEP queries these values in real-time to determine when an event (tremor) has a value of 5 (dangerous situation) and generate the corresponding alerts on the caregiver's smartphone through the broadcast receiver *outputBroadcastStream*. Listing 1.3 represents an example of how Siddhi performs that task.

```
1 from TremorStream[severity == 5]
2     select alert insert into outputBroadcastStream;
```

Listing 1.3. Rule for detecting severe tremors.

Regarding the FOG pattern, the smartphone collects measurements from its built-in accelerometer with a sampling rate of 2 Hz so that the Siddhi CEP engine can process them. Consequently, in an episode of this motor symptom, the acceleration remains almost constant except for slight variations caused by signal noise [2].

We can determine FOG attacks by employing CEP rules that establish that if several episodes have a similar acceleration value, considering the noise present, they correspond to the same event.

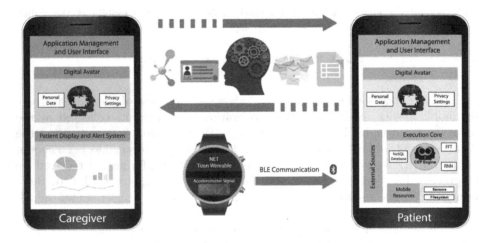

Fig. 3. Overview of the system containing the Digital Avatar.

Therefore, it has been defined that each event that makes up an episode of FOG occurs at 0.5 s (smartphone sample rate). Consequently, 4 episodes correspond to 2 s. However, for our application, a FOG consists of 5 episodes (2.5 s) to consider the sensor's latency.

Based on this, a source for CEP must be defined that collects measurements of the accelerometer integrated into the mobile phone based on this decomposition of FOG in simple events that occur every 2 Hz. Listing 1.4 represents an excerpt of how this source should be defined.

```
1  @source(type ='android-accelerometer',
2      polling.interval = '500',
3      @map(type ='keyvalue',
4          fail.on.missing.attribute='false',
5          @attributes(timestamp = 'timestamp',
6              alert = 'alert',
7              moduleAcceleration = 'moduleAcceleration',
8              marker = 'marker')))
9  define stream accelerometerStream(alert string,
   moduleAcceleration double, marker int);
```

Listing 1.4. Rule for collecting acceleration in the user's gait.

In Listing 1.4, the source is of type *android-accelerometer*, with an interval between each event of 500 ms (sample rate), in format *key-value* and whose attributes are the *timestamp*, the text string to notify the user (*alert*), the acceleration module (*moduleAcceleration*) to analyze patient gait and a *marker* to determine whether each episode corresponds to a FOG or not.

According to the marker that defines whether an event corresponds to a freezing of gait situation, to get this, it was necessary to modify the Siddhi class associated with this sensor to obtain the marker at each time interval based on the acceleration module and taking into account the signal noise.

Consequently, Listing 1.5 shows the queries the CEP engine performs based on if that marker has a value of 5 (composition of 5 events lasting a total of 2.5 s) or more and generates the corresponding alerts to the doctor through the broadcast receiver *outputBroadcastStreamFOG*.

```
1  from accelerometerStream[marker >= 5]
2      select alert insert into outputBroadcastStreamFOG;
```

Listing 1.5. Rule for detecting FOG attacks.

However, sometimes the CEP engine can detect false FOG episodes since a freezing of gait can be related to other activities (such as waiting to get on the bus, for example). For this, we have used a particular type of RNN, the LSTM networks, to characterize the gait [10]. Based on this, Siddhi only works depending on the physical activity the patient is performing at each moment.

This has been achieved through a model developed with the *Keras Deep Learning* library with a sliding window length of 100, a sliding window size of 50, 12 features, 7 classes, 32 neurons for the hidden layer, and a regularization factor L2 of 0.000001. This model has been trained and validated by choosing the batch size of 1024 and 30 epochs with the Sensors Activity Dataset by [16]. Finally, this has been exported to be used by the Android application through the *TensorFlow Lite* library.

In the same way as for tremor processing, in the pharmacotherapy, it is necessary to define a source from a broadcast receiver to obtain the processed data of the user's medication from other classes within the Android application. In

Listing 1.6, this Siddhi rule can be displayed with the attributes of the *medica-tion* name, *quantity* of each dose, *date* and *time* that the user should take each dose, how many times a day *doses* and the value *selection* that sets when the CEP engine must generate a notification (0 *no*, 1 *yes*).

```
1 @source(type = 'android-broadcast',
2     identifier = 'TreatmentBroadcast',
3     @map(type='keyvalue'))
4 define stream TreatmentStream(medication string, quantity
      double, date string, time string, doses int, selection
      int);
```

Listing 1.6. Rule for collecting medication parameters.

Based on the above, in order to generate the relevant notifications and, conse-quently, manage the patient's pharmacological treatment, a rule (see Listing 1.7) must be established to insert the medication data to the sink *outputBroadcast-Treatment* of type *android-broadcast* when the parameter *selection* has a value of 1 and, therefore, generate warning on the caregiver's smartphone about this.

```
1 from TreatmentStream[selection == 1]
2     select * insert into outputBroadcastTreatment;
```

Listing 1.7. Rule for generating notifications on pharmacological treatment.

On the other hand, the system presents a different interface depending on the function and privacy settings of the person (see Fig. 3). To achieve this, the NoSQL *Couchbase Lite* database is used, which allows the development of a simple API to access the information based on the pre-established role.

Therefore, users can access their personal information if they are assigned as patients. In contrast, if they correspond to the caregivers, they only have the patient's public data authorization.

Finally, it should be noted that such anomalies and detections are shown on the mobile device through graphs representing the variations in the acceleration of the motor symptoms presented by the patient. Although these are merely illustrative, this information could clarify the experimental results.

3.2   Experimental Results

The Digital Avatar corresponds to a sociological profile that stores its owner's data exclusively on the mobile device, which can be a common cause of problems in the performance and efficiency of the system. However, a series of tests proved and corroborated the correct functioning of the DA for PD. Below are several interesting tests that overview how the system works.

This virtual profile is responsible for monitoring the cardinal symptoms, FOG and tremor, the administration of pharmacological treatment (details of doses prescribed to the patient should be added manually) and the privacy of infor-mation depending on the established role (see Fig. 4). It is important to note that the experiments were not done with people suffering from PD, but the user involved reproduced the characteristic patterns of this disease.

Depending on the DA type, the mobile application presents a different interface. Only the symptoms associated with PD can be displayed on the caregiver's smartphone. Figure 4a represents two tremors of scale 5 (severe) whose values correspond to 6.04125 and 6.35334 Hz, respectively. These estimates are obtained by the mobile application when applying the FFT and could be visualized thanks to the Android Studio console.

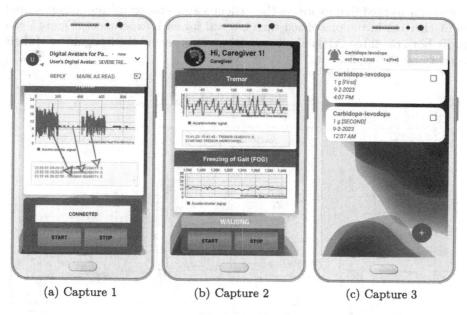

(a) Capture 1   (b) Capture 2   (c) Capture 3

Fig. 4. Results obtained from monitoring Parkinson's disease in a patient.

The second experiment combined tremor and FOG (Fig. 4b). Tremor disappears during activity or walking, as it only occurs at rest. However, it may be interesting to analyze whether it is generated during FOG attacks since he/she cannot continue the movement when the person suffers from this condition.

Figure 4b contains an instant in which the patient was walking and no tremor was detected (scale 0). The graph referring to tremors can be confusing, as it shows measurements that resemble this symptom to the naked eye but correspond to an arm movement. In addition, the system determined with an accuracy of 67 % (value obtained from the Android Studio console) that the user was moving.

Therefore, three episodes of FOG were diagnosed during the test and no tremor. As a result, the system generated an audible and textual notification for each of them on the health expert's smartphone.

Figure 4c shows the application interface managing the patient's pharmacological treatment. Two reminders correspond to the first and second daily doses in that specific case.

It should be noted that on specific occasions, the system detected that the tremor severity was 0 in a period when one was occurring. This problem may be because, in those intervals, the sample contains a smaller number of measurements. For that, the data are more homogeneous and make the functioning of the implemented algorithm difficult.

To verify that the detection performed by the application is valid, a graph has been implemented that expresses the patient's acceleration measurements stored in his/her DA in the predefined time interval for each experiment. Figure 5 can ratify both the three FOG episodes mentioned above and the recognition of their activity by the application.

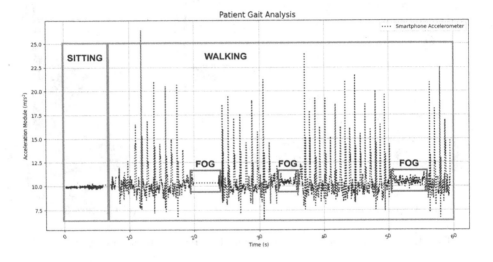

Fig. 5. Simulation of three FOG episodes.

From Fig. 5, it can be seen that the patient was initially sitting and then started walking (see Fig. 4b). Regarding the latter, the system correctly identified the three attacks of FOG (*FOG* label on the graph), which correspond to almost constant accelerations, and notified the caregiver. An example of notification appears in Fig. 4a.

4   Discussion

Smartphones and other portable devices are becoming increasingly common for remote monitoring in Telemedicine. This is due to the development and evolution of mobile phone hardware components that can serve as a tool to help patient self-management, continuous monitoring of vital signs, communication between patients and doctors and personalized medical care [13].

Consequently, the increased adoption of cloud computing in Telehealth poses many security and personal privacy issues [8]. In addition, developing these applications requires algorithms that consume many resources and, consequently, need external servers in charge of this processing [9].

However, applying the PeaaS social computing model [6], offers the possibility of reducing the large amounts of data in online communication, thereby increasing interactivity and efficiency in applications, ensuring that user data remains exclusively on smartphone. This paradigm has been employed successfully in contexts such as the IoT [12], smart cities [14] or gerontology [1].

Based on the above, our insight focuses on applying Digital Avatars to treating and remote monitoring Parkinson's disease under the PeaaS paradigm. The proposed software framework, arises as the deployment of introduced concepts in [1] for the care of independent elders and their generalization and application to other areas of Telemedicine. For our scenario, the DA offers several benefits for individuals who suffer from Parkinson's disease, their caregivers, and public health systems. Some advantages and challenges of this system are drawn.

On the one hand, we have adopted a model based on a peer-to-peer architecture for mobile devices, dispensing with the traditional client-server architecture. Based on this, each DA can decide with which other users to interact, share its data and what additional information it wants to incorporate into its avatar. As a result, it enables interoperability.

In terms of user data privacy, this framework allows personal information to be the exclusive property of the person. It prevents the exploitation of the information from being controlled by third parties that do not offer transparent management to the data owners. For our use case, each DA can monitor and detect the cardinal patterns, FOG and tremors. In addition, it offers the possibility to manage the patient's pharmacological treatment through notifications and generate alarms for their caregivers or healthcare professionals when an abnormal situation poses a risk to the patient.

On the other hand, each sociological profile stores all the values concerning the Parkinsonian patterns treated on the mobile phone, which does not infer the performance of the same. This information allows to establish patterns and trend lines and, in addition, to generate new data of extra added value based on the information collected and processed by the CEP engine.

However, this approach also presents some potential challenges and risks. First of all, smartwatches have limited storage and battery capacity. In addition, the measures cannot be processed on this device directly and must be sent to the smartphone for further treatment, and the CEP may not be entirely satisfactory on several occasions due to a high sampling rate since its execution is oriented to prepared servers.

5   Conclusions and Future Work

This paper describes the framework of Digital Avatars for monitoring and detecting Parkinson's disease. To take advantage of the computational capacity of smartphones for information processing without external servers, the principles of the PeaaS [11] paradigm have been followed. This allows us to guarantee one of the essential aspects of health systems: the privacy and transparent management of the user's data. As a result, the application of the DA to the telemedicine field drives into the considerable reduction of hospitalization prices, confidentiality, or timeouts.

Based on this, to develop the DA for our Parkinson's Disease case study, two paired applications have been designed to interact in a coordinated manner for the smartwatch and the smartphone, respectively. The results were generally conclusive for the two Parkinsonian symptoms treated, the administration of pharmacological treatment and the confidentiality of personal data. Emphasizing that the DA is exclusively hosted on the mobile phone and the large amount of data stored does not interfere with the system's performance.

According to the FOG pattern, a new method based on CEP has been developed, whereby each episode of this symptom is decomposed into events with a specific acceleration. If several events have a similar estimate (and considering the noise present), they constitute the same event. Moreover, using LSTM networks improves the system's performance for PD monitoring. While for tremor, the algorithm provides reasonable estimates. However, they are not entirely accurate on certain occasions because the measurements are more homogeneous over a smaller number of samples and do not determine whether one frequency predominates over the others.

Finally, regarding the future lines of the project, concerning application domain, we will extend the experimentation and testing of the system with people with Parkinson's disease to ensure the correct functioning of the system. In addition, it is necessary to try how the Digital Avatar can generate new data based on the information collected from Parkinsonian patterns. From an architectural perspective, we are working on the implementation of a parameterized framework which can be conveniently instantiated to develop different DA-based applications.

Data Availibility Statement. The application codes for *Android* and *Tizen* (for smartphone and smartwatch, respectively) presented in this paper are not available, as we want to increase the functionality of these for further research.

References

1. Bertoa, M.F., Moreno, N., Pérez-Vereda, A., Bandera, D., Álvarez-Palomo, J.M., Canal, C.: Digital avatars: promoting independent living for older adults. Wirel. Commun. Mob. Comput. **2020**, 8891002:1-8891002:11 (2020)
2. Cole, B.T., Roy, S.H., Nawab, S.H.: Detecting freezing-of-gait during unscripted and unconstrained activity. In: 33rd Annual International Conference of the IEEE

Engineering in Medicine and Biology Society, EMBC 2011, Boston, MA, USA, 30 August–3 Sept 2011, pp. 5649–5652. IEEE (2011)

3. Covington, M.J., Carskadden, R.: Threat implications of the internet of things. In: 5th International Conference on Cyber Conflict, CyCon 2013, Tallinn, Estonia, 4–7 June 2013, pp. 1–12. IEEE (2013)

4. Giacalone, A., Marin, L., Febbi, M., Franchi, T., Palone, M.: eHealth, telehealth, and telemedicine in the management of the COVID-19 pandemic and beyond: Lessons learned and future perspectives. World J. Clin. Cases **10**, 2363–2368 (2022)

5. Godinho, C., et al.: A systematic review of the characteristics and validity of monitoring technologies to assess Parkinson's disease. J. Neuroeng. Rehabil. **13**(1), 71 (2016)

6. Guillén, J., Miranda, J., Berrocal, J., García-Alonso, J., Murillo, J.M., Canal, C.: People as a service: a mobile-centric model for providing collective sociological profiles. IEEE Softw. **31**(2), 48–53 (2014)

7. Hernández Rodríguez, S.: El reto de la era digital: privacidad y confidencialidad de la información de pacientes. G. E. N. **72**, 00–01 (2018)

8. Jalali, M.S., Landman, A.B., Gordon, W.J.: Telemedicine, privacy, and information security in the age of COVID-19. J. Med. Inf. Assoc. **28**(3), 671–2 (2021)

9. Little, M.A.: Smartphones for remote symptom monitoring of Parkinson's disease. J. Parkinsons Dis. **11**, S49–S53 (2021)

10. López, P.F., Liu-Jimenez, J., Kiyokawa, K., Wu, Y., Sánchez-Reillo, R.: Recurrent neural network for inertial gait user recognition in smartphones. Sensors **19**(18), 4054 (2019)

11. Luckham, D.: The power of events: an introduction to complex event processing in distributed enterprise systems. In: Bassiliades, N., Governatori, G., Paschke, A. (eds.) RuleML 2008. LNCS, vol. 5321, pp. 3–3. Springer, Heidelberg (2008). https://doi.org/10.1007/978-3-540-88808-6_2

12. Miranda, J., et al.: From the internet of things to the internet of people. IEEE Internet Comput. **19**(2), 40–47 (2015)

13. Mosa, A.S.M., Yoo, I., Sheets, L.: A systematic review of healthcare applications for smartphones. BMC Med. Inf. Decis. Mak. **12**, 67 (2012)

14. Pérez-Vereda, A., Canal, C.: A people-oriented paradigm for smart cities. In: Cabot, J., De Virgilio, R., Torlone, R. (eds.) ICWE 2017. LNCS, vol. 10360, pp. 584–591. Springer, Cham (2017). https://doi.org/10.1007/978-3-319-60131-1_46

15. Pérez-Vereda, A., Flores-Martín, D., Canal, C., Murillo, J.M.: Towards dynamically programmable devices using beacons. In: Pautasso, C., Sánchez-Figueroa, F., Systä, K., Murillo Rodríguez, J.M. (eds.) ICWE 2018. LNCS, vol. 11153, pp. 49–58. Springer, Cham (2018). https://doi.org/10.1007/978-3-030-03056-8_5

16. Shoaib, M., Bosch, S., Incel, Ö.D., Scholten, H., Havinga, P.J.M.: Fusion of smartphone motion sensors for physical activity recognition. Sensors **14**(6), 10146–10176 (2014)

17. Tolosa, E., Wenning, G.K., Poewe, W.: The diagnosis of Parkinson's disease. Neurol. Sci. **24**, s157–s164 (2006)

18. Wu, Z., Xuan, S., Xie, J., Lin, C., Lu, C.: How to ensure the confidentiality of electronic medical records on the cloud: a technical perspective. Comput. Biol. Medicine **147**, 105726 (2022)

A DCAT Profile Approach for Citizen Science

Reynaldo Alvarez Luna[1]([✉]) [iD], José Zubcoff[2] [iD], and Irene Garrigós[2] [iD]

[1] University of Informatics Sciences, La Habana, Cuba
`rluna@uci.cu`
[2] University of Alicante, Alicante, Spain
`{jose.zubcoff,igarrigos}@ua.es`

Abstract. Many citizen science projects generate large amounts of data in the life sciences. In fact, the most successful and mature projects study species movements or behaviour patterns through spatio-temporal observations. However, the use of these data is difficult in some scenarios due to the heterogeneity of the sources and the lack of consensus on how to share them across different scientific communities. This work focuses on defining a DCAT profile for citizen science based on PPSR Core to promote consistency and interoperability with other DCAT-based systems, such as data repositories and search engines. This can facilitate the discovery, sharing and reuse of citizen science data across different life science projects.

Keywords: Citizen science · Data sharing · DCAT · PPSR Core

1 Introduction

Citizen science (CS) has demonstrated its ability to contribute to several areas of life sciences [3]. The impact of CS projects on the life sciences is broad, with contributions providing methods, data reports and completed research. Some of the contributions present or refer to: (i) more than 30 years of standardised bird counting [4], (ii) analysis of potential biodiversity outcomes by citizen scientists [16], (iii) review of CS in environmental and ecological sciences [12], (iv) impact of CS in biodiversity education [19], (v) monitoring of sustainable development goals [11]. Each of the cited works also shows how their volunteers' observations are consolidated into datasets that generate knowledge and patterns.

Related to data management in CS, the divergences in the methods used to construct and share the data generated in their projects are known [5,14]. These gaps limits the interoperability, reusability and access to data that could be integrated or correlated for studies with greater scope and impact. Appreciating the vital role of the data generated in CS endeavors in [6,13,17,18] the authors outline the aspirations of opening up data and discuss data management practices in projects in this area.

Supported by Wake, University of Alicante.

The major advances in consensus building for data discovery and integration have been the adoption of vocabularies for metadata definition [10,12]. It opens a way for CS projects to interact with other scientific communities even if access to the data is not open.

In this regard, it has been defined the Public Participation in Scientific Research (PPSR Core) [9] as standard to describe CS projects metadata. This model was developed for the specific domain of CS projects. However, several of the most recognised CS life science platforms (Zooniverse[1], eBird[2], Marine Board[3]) use their own metadata models and vocabularies or standards like Darwin Core[4], Schema[5] among others.

Therefore as a middle ground in the search for metadata solutions for data sharing in life sciences CS projects. This paper proposes to design a profile of Data Catalogue Vocabulary (DCAT) [21] for the definition of metadata for CS projects. DCAT is recognised by W3C as the standard vocabulary for describing metadata associated with datasets. The mix of both models helps to build consensus in the search for data sharing solutions based on Web standards. The use of Web standards for data sharing increases the FAIR (Findable, Accessible, Interoperable, Reusable) qualities of the data [22].

2   Related Work

PPSR Core is the model developed by the Citizen Science Association International Data and Metadata Working Group (CSA-DMWG) for the management of metadata for projects of this type. It is designed for the management of observations, data and project metadata. Its concept is based on the reuse of terms recognised in metadata vocabularies and standards [8]. However, its adoption or comprehension outside of CS projects or platforms is limited. One of the reasons, in our view, is the lack of a machine-readable format [9], which hinders discovery, reusability, interoperability and access to metadata.

In our previous work [1] we approached a metadata-driven solution based on DCAT as a way to reach FAIR data in the CS domain. However, this approach was limited to the dataset, but omitted attributes related to other components of the PPSR core. To the best of our knowledge, no previous work has addressed the extension of DCAT as a variant to improve data sharing practices in CS. This approach has been used in other domains, demonstrating its feasibility in improving interoperability practices and the overall FAIR qualities of data. The following section discusses some examples to illustrate this.

---

[1] https://www.zooniverse.org/.
[2] https://ebird.org/.
[3] https://www.marineboard.eu/citizen-science.
[4] https://dwc.tdwg.org/.
[5] https://schema.org/.

2.1   DCAT Profiles

A profile in the modeling context refers to a mechanism for extending or specializing an existing metamodel or model. It allows you to define additional concepts, relationships, and constraints that are specific to your domain or application, while still adhering to the structure and semantics of the base metamodel. Profiles are typically used to define domain-specific constraints, validation rules, or additional semantics on top of a base metamodel. Indeed, some DCAT profiles have been developed to cater to specific domains and use cases, showcasing the versatility and adaptability of the DCAT standard. Some notable examples include:

1. GeoDCAT-AP: This profile focuses on geographic data processing and provides a standardized vocabulary for describing geospatial datasets. It enables the discovery and interoperability of geospatial data across different systems and platforms [15].
2. Solid-Earth Sciences Data: This DCAT profile addresses the needs of the solid-earth sciences domain, offering specialized concepts and attributes for describing geological and geophysical datasets. It supports the sharing and discovery of data within the solid-earth sciences community [20].
3. DCAT-AP: As a more general example, DCAT-AP is a DCAT Application Profile that has been adopted at both national and European levels. It provides a standardized framework for describing and exchanging public sector datasets, promoting interoperability and transparency across government agencies and organizations [2].

These examples demonstrate the flexibility of DCAT as a standard vocabulary for describing metadata associated with various domains and use cases. They showcase how DCAT profiles can tailor the standard to specific requirements, enabling effective data sharing, interoperability, and discovery within specialized communities. The next section will examine the components of both models to find the extensions points and shared attributes.

3   DCAT Profile for Citizen Science

Developing a DCAT profile based on PPSR Core for citizen science projects start with the identification of domain-specific metadata, since PPSR Core defines a set of metadata elements that are specific to CS projects, such as project objectives, participation requirements, geographic area, observations and many others.

The definition of the DCAT-based profile for CS follows the activities shown in Fig. 1. Examining the characteristics of the CS domain, the definitions of the DCAT model that can be reused or extended and an exploration of vocabularies and ontologies that can be reference for the design of the profile.

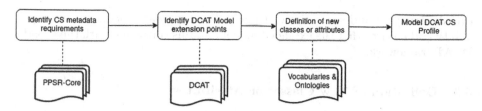

Fig. 1. Activities to define DCAT-CS Profile

3.1 Identify CS Metadata Requirements

For identifying the specific requirements of CS Projects we will examine the PPSR Core model [8], it is composed by four sub-models:

- Core Metadata Model (CMM), for general attributes.
- Project Metadata Model (PMM), for the project's own attributes, such as contact, location, objectives, among others.
- Dataset Metadata Model (DMM), for data properties.
- Observational Metadata Model (OMM), for metadata associated with observations.

In accordance with the proposed scope of this work, the three higher levels of the PPSR Core are considered (ignoring the observations model, since its management is internal to the projects), in terms of Core, Projects and Datasets. Accordingly, a mapping of the models will be carried out to identify the extension points to be implemented in DCAT.

3.2 Identify DCAT Model Extension Points

The comparative analysis of the DCAT and PPSR Core models reveals that the primary differences between the models stem from project-specific elements. When examining the information related to datasets, it becomes evident that DCAT is both very similar and more complete aggregating support for multiple distributions, data services and relationships between resources. A reduced view of DCAT classes is shown in Fig. 2.

Regarding the extension points in the DCAT model, they could be defined as related or inherited from their Resource classes. These extension points allow for the incorporation of additional domain-specific concepts and attributes into the DCAT model, enabling the customization and expansion of the standard to accommodate specific CS requirements.

In summary, the analysis demonstrates that while DCAT is already a robust and comprehensive model for describing datasets, there is still room for extending and enhancing it with CS-specific elements. By leveraging the extension points provided by DCAT, models like PPSR Core can incorporate their specific attributes and relations while maintaining compatibility and adherence to the overall structure and semantics of DCAT. This approach facilitates interoperability and ensures that the extended model remains consistent with the broader DCAT framework.

3.3 Definition of New Classes or Attributes

The extension of DCAT is based on the identification of classes and attributes that are recognisable and have semantic value. According to the previous section, the extension of the DCAT profile will focus on project-related metadata. Let us then review the main vocabularies or ontologies that describe this type of entity, some of the most recognised are:

- Funding, Research Administration and Projects Ontology (FRAPO[6]) for administrative point of view.
- Description Of A Project (DOAP[7]) for open source projects, including metadata about repositories, licenses, software.
- Project Documents Ontology (PDO[8]) for managing documents related to projects.
- Project Ontology (PROJECT [7]) is designed to describe project information, including research projects, and is not domain specific. It defines classes and properties related to planning, funding, objectives, stakeholders and activities.
- Citizen Science Ontology (CitSci[9]) is a work in progress by the CS community that has defined some of the attributes and classes defined by PPSR Core in terms that are mostly reused from other vocabularies.

By drawing upon these diverse resources and ontologies, the profile benefits from established definitions and concepts within the domain, reducing redundancy and promoting consistency. It also allows for the incorporation of specific domain knowledge and project management principles, facilitating better understanding and interoperability within the life sciences community and beyond. The analysis of the vocabularies has made it possible to establish the PROJECT ontology as the main reference, covering most of the attributes described in PPSR Core. Then, to model this first approximation of the DCAT profile, we will define the attributes mainly based on PROJECT, extending the DCAT Resource class, as discussed in the next section.

3.4 Model DCAT CS Profile

Figure 2 illustrates the proposed DCAT profile model specifically designed for CS. The diagram highlights in orange the classes that have been created within this profile to accommodate the unique requirements of CS.

---

[6] http://www.sparontologies.net/ontologies/frapo.
[7] https://github.com/ewilderj/doap.
[8] https://lov.linkeddata.es/dataset/lov/vocabs/pdo.
[9] https://ec-jrc.github.io/citsci-ontology/prj/.

It is important to note that attributes and classes from PPSR core, such as the *projectScienceType, ProjectGeographicLocation, ProjectMedia* are showed in the Fig. 2. This ensures that the profile contains the necessary elements to accurately represent the domain-specific characteristics of CS projects. DCAT also allows the establishment of relationships between resources, supporting the association of projects with their datasets in a data catalogue. By addressing these issues and extending the relevant classes within the DCAT profile model, the proposed model effectively captures the essential elements and relationships required to represent CS projects and their unique attributes within the broader DCAT framework.

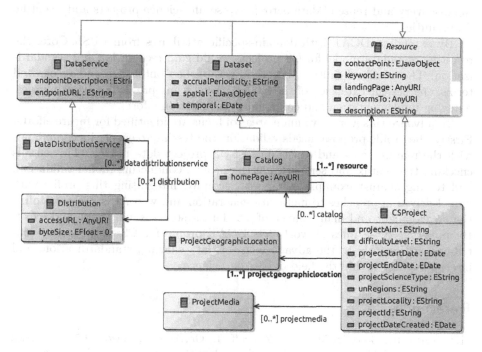

Fig. 2. Model of DCAT Profile for CS, adapted from [21]

To illustrate the feasibility of developing this approach, let us consider the scenario of studying an environmental issue. As researchers, we retrieve metadata related to this topic from Citizen Science projects on various Citizen Science platforms. Subsequently, we have to develop mechanisms for querying the metadata, as each platform implements its own variant of the PPSR core. If the transformations for the proposed DCAT profile are implemented once, there are two main advantages: (i) exposing data using DCAT enables discovery of datasets through search engines, and (ii) having a single catalogue based on DCAT provides a set of resources accessible through web standard means (projects, datasets, data services, data distributions). This allows other researcher to access and reuse the data using standard methods. The relationship in the same model of projects and datasets as resources allows to deepen issues related to data integration and communication between different communities or projects.

4   Conclusions and Future Work

In summary, the proposal to create a DCAT profile based on PPSR Core for Citizen Science (CS) projects has the potential to leverage the strengths of both standards, promoting collaboration and innovation within CS communities. This profile would enhance interoperability among DCAT-based systems, facilitating the discovery and reuse of data across diverse life science projects and scientific communities.

By extending DCAT with domain-specific attributes from PPSR Core, the resulting metadata model for CS projects would gain recognition and standardization. The profile definition, based on established ontologies and recognized terms, enables the extension of the DCAT model using pre-defined vocabularies, reducing implementation and community assimilation efforts.

To advance this work, two main areas of focus are identified for future efforts. Firstly, the profile proposal needs validation and testing to ensure its compliance with the requirements and constraints of CS project data models. This entails checking the syntax and semantics of the profile, conducting model validation, and testing against example instances. Secondly, integrating this profile with model-driven approaches to metadata generation and web APIs can streamline the development and maintenance of CS data systems, saving time and effort. By pursuing these lines of work, the DCAT profile for CS projects can contribute significantly to the advancement of data sharing, standardization, and interoperability within the field of Citizen Science.

References

1. Alvarez, R., González-Mora, C., Zubcoff, J., Garrigós, I., Mazón, J.N., González Diez, H.R.: FAIRification of citizen science data through metadata-driven web API development. In: Di Noia, T., Ko, I.Y., Schedl, M., Ardito, C. (eds.) ICWE 2022. LNCS, vol. 13362, pp. 162–176. Springer, Cham (2022). https://doi.org/10.1007/978-3-031-09917-5_11
2. Barthelemy, F., et al.: Towards a standard-based open data ecosystem: analysis of DCAT-AP use at national and European level. Electr. Gov. Int. J. **18**(2), 137–180 (2022)
3. Bonetta, L.: New citizens for the life sciences. Cell **138**(6), 1043–1045 (2009). https://doi.org/10.1016/j.cell.2009.09.007
4. Bonter, D.N., Greig, E.I.: Over 30 years of standardized bird counts at supplementary feeding stations in North America: a citizen science data report for project feederwatch. Front. Ecol. Evol. **9**, 619682 (2021). https://doi.org/10.3389/fevo.2021.619682
5. Bowser, A., et al.: Still in need of norms: the state of the data in citizen science. Citizen Science: Theory Pract. **5**(1) (2020)

6. Cooper, C.B., Rasmussen, L.M., Jones, E.D.: Perspective: the power (dynamics) of open data in citizen science. Front. Climate **3**, 57 (2021)
7. Cox, S.J.D.: Project ontology. [Ontology] (2021). https://bioportal.bioontology.org/ontologies/PROJ
8. CSA International Data and Metadata Working Group: Ppsr-core (2021). https://core.citizenscience.org/docs/#other-standards. Accessed 27 June 2023
9. CSA International Data and Metadata Working Group: Ppsr-core gitub project (2021). https://github.com/citizen-science-association/ppsr-core/. Accessed 27 June 2023
10. De Pourcq, K., Ceccaroni, L.: On the importance of data standards in citizen science— cost action ca15212. Citizen Science Cost Action (2018)
11. Fraisl, D., et al.: Demonstrating the potential of picture pile as a citizen science tool for SDG monitoring. Environ. Sci. Policy **128**, 81–93 (2022)
12. Fraisl, D., et al.: Citizen science in environmental and ecological sciences. Nat. Rev. Methods Primers **2**(1), 64 (2022)
13. Hultquist, C., de Sherbinin, A., Bowser, A., Schade, S.: Editorial: open citizen science data and methods. Front. Clim. **4** (2022). https://doi.org/10.3389/fclim.2022.943534
14. Liu, H.Y., Dörler, D., Heigl, F., Grossberndt, S.: Citizen science platforms. Sci. Citizen Sci. **22**, 439–459 (2021)
15. Perego, A., Cetl, V., Friis-Christensen, A., Lutz, M.: GeoDCAT-AP: representing geographic metadata by using the "DCAT application profile for data portals in Europe". In: Joint UNECE/UNGGIM Europe Workshop on Integrating Geospatial and Statistical Standards, Stockholm, Sweden (2017)
16. Peter, M., Diekötter, T., Höffler, T., Kremer, K.: Biodiversity citizen science: outcomes for the participating citizens. People Nat. **3**(2), 294–311 (2021)
17. Robinson, L.D., Cawthray, J.L., West, S.E., Bonn, A., Ansine, J.: Ten principles of citizen science. In: Citizen Science: Innovation in Open Science, Society and Policy, pp. 27–40 (2018)
18. de Sherbinin, A., et al.: The critical importance of citizen science data. Front. Clim. **3**, 20 (2021)
19. Torres, A.C., Bedessem, B., Deguines, N., Fontaine, C.: Online data sharing with virtual social interactions favor scientific and educational successes in a biodiversity citizen science project. J. Responsible Innov. **10**, 1–19 (2022)
20. Trani, L., Paciello, R., Sbarra, M., Ulbricht, D.: Representing core concepts for solid-earth sciences with DCAT-the EPOS-DCAT application profile. In: EGU General Assembly Conference Abstracts, p. 9797 (2018)
21. W3C: Data catalog vocabulary (DCAT) - version 2 (2020). https://www.w3.org/TR/vocab-dcat-2/. Accessed 21 May 2023
22. Wilkinson, M.D., et al.: The fair guiding principles for scientific data management and stewardship. Sci. Data **3**(1), 1–9 (2016)

Author Index

S. Casteleyn et al. (Eds.): ICWE 2023 Workshops, CCIS 1898, pp. 169–170, 2024.
https://doi.org/10.1007/978-3-031-50385-6

Printed in the United States
by Baker & Taylor Publisher Services